TEACHERS AND MENTORS

SOURCE BOOKS ON EDUCATION
VOLUME 48
GARLAND REFERENCE LIBRARY OF SOCIAL SCIENCE
VOLUME 969

TEACHERS AND MENTORS
PROFILES OF DISTINGUISHED
TWENTIETH-CENTURY
PROFESSORS OF EDUCATION

EDITED BY
CRAIG KRIDEL
ROBERT V. BULLOUGH, JR.
PAUL SHAKER

FOREWORD BY ERNEST L. BOYER

GARLAND PUBLISHING, INC.
NEW YORK AND LONDON
1996

Library of Congress Cataloging-in-Publication Data

Teachers and mentors : profiles of distinguished twentieth-century professors of
    education / edited by Craig Kridel, Robert V. Bullough, Jr., Paul Shaker.
        p.   cm. — (Garland reference library of social science ; vol. 969.
Source books on education ; vol. 48)
    Includes bibliographical references (p.) and index.
    ISBN 0-8153-1746-8 (alk. paper)
    1. Teacher educators—United States—Biography.   2. Education—Study
and teaching (Higher)—United States.   3. Education—United States—Philosophy.   4. Mentoring in education—United States.   I. Kridel, Craig
Alan.   II. Bullough, Robert V., 1949– .   III. Shaker, Paul.   IV. Series: Garland reference library of social science ; v. 969.   V. Series: Garland reference
library of social science.   Source books on education   ;   vol. 48.
LA2311.T43   1996
370'.92'2—dc20   95-47074
[B]   CIP

Printed on acid-free, 250-year-life paper
Manufactured in the United States of America

for Paul R. Klohr

in memory of

Ernest L. Boyer, 1928-1995

CONTENTS

FOREWORD

The profiles presented in this unusual and important book bring us to one essential truth. Excellence in education means excellence in teaching. In concise and moving passages, these writers tell how their lives were profoundly changed because of the influence of an inspired teacher. By word and deed, they learned about listening carefully to others before presuming to know how to solve others' problems; they learned to treat their own work and ideas with integrity because of the respect given to them by a mentor through both informal conversations and structured courses of study; they learned to take the initiative in their own education; they learned the exhilaration of having their minds stretched and challenged. And, above all else, they learned how to learn.

The stories recalled in this book also remind us that teachers, especially truly great mentors, vary greatly. We are reminded that there is a place in the classroom for teaching by lecturing, especially when the goal is the transmission of organized knowledge. There is a place for questions and answers, for structured review and drill. But we learn, too, that there comes a time when probing questions should be asked, when the teacher should challenge the student to move further from the familiar toward the unknown.

Teaching begins, of course, with what the teacher knows. Those who teach must, above all, be well informed, steeped in the knowledge of their fields. Teaching can be well regarded only if professors are widely read and intellectually engaged. One reason legislators, trustees, and the general public often fail to understand why ten or twelve hours in the classroom each week can be a heavy load is their lack of awareness of the hard work and the serious study undergirding the scholarship of teaching.

Teaching is also a dynamic endeavor involving all the analogies, metaphors, and images that build bridges between the teacher's understanding and the student's learning. Pedagogical procedures must be carefully planned, continuously examined, and must relate directly to the subject taught.

In the end, much of what the teacher must do to succeed in teaching is a matter of common sense—studying, planning, setting goals. And further, for teachers, quite simply, there remain some old-fashioned yet enduring qualities that still work—command of the material to be taught, contagious enthusiasm for the work to be done, optimism about the potential of the students, and human sensitivity, that is, integrity and warmth as a human being.

But what is it that makes the difference between a good teacher and an inspiring mentor? As the essays in this collection indicate, a mentor not only has a love of learning, but above all a love of students. A mentor directs rather than dictates, and offers guidance that inspires rather than smothers. A mentor respects students' urges to broaden their own vision of who they are and what they might become, and a mentor lives a life that embodies the beliefs that he or she espouses. And when we think of a teacher as mentor, most often we remember a person whose technical skills were matched by the qualities we associate with a good and trusted friend.

What's so disturbing is that, in recent years, the sacred act of teaching has become disturbingly undervalued at many colleges, and even in schools of education. Research and publication often form a single measure of academic progress, and all too often it is far better for a faculty member to present a paper to a professional convention then to teach undergraduates back home. Indeed, not a few of the students in this book write that their professors knowingly sacrificed publishing in favor of teaching.

The challenge is clear: When people who have contributed so much to their students can begin publicly to redefine scholarship to include teaching—both to themselves and to their students—then surely the public's esteem of teaching rises, professors who want to devote themselves to students are inspired, and ultimately the quality of education improves for all.

How, then, should we proceed?

In a recent Carnegie Foundation publication, *Scholarship Reconsidered*, we say that the time has come to move beyond the tired old "teaching versus research" debate and give to the familiar and honorable term "scholarship" a broader, more capacious meaning, one that brings legitimacy to the full scope of academic work. Scholarship surely means engaging in original research. But this, we say, is only the beginning. The work of the scholar also means stepping back from one's investigation, looking for connections. It means building bridges between theory and practice, and, ultimately, it means communicating one's knowledge effectively to others.

Specifically, we conclude that the work of the professoriate might be thought of as having four separate, yet overlapping, functions. These are: the scholarship of *discovering knowledge*; the scholarship of *integrating knowledge*; the scholarship of *applying knowledge*; and the scholarship of *sharing knowledge*.

Viewed from this perspective, teaching, for the academic, is not an awkward interruption. It is, in fact, an essential component of scholarship itself, since, when all is said and done, the work of the professor becomes consequential only as it is understood by others. Educator Parker Palmer strikes precisely the right note when he says knowing and learning are *communal* acts. With this vision, great teachers create a common ground of intellectual commitment. They stimulate active, not passive, learning and encourage students to be critical, creative thinkers, with the capacity to go on learning after their college days are over. And when defined as *scholarship*, teaching both educates and entices future scholars. Indeed, as Aristotle said, "Teaching is the highest form of understanding."

Physicist Robert Oppenheimer, in a lecture at the 200th anniversary of Columbia University in 1954, spoke elegantly of the teacher as mentor and placed teaching at the very heart of the scholarly endeavor: "The specialization of science is an inevitable accompaniment of progress; yet it is full of dangers, and it is cruelly wasteful, since so much that is beautiful and enlightening is cut off from most of the world. Thus it is proper to the role of the scientist that he not merely find new truth and communicate it to his fellows, but that he teach, that he try to bring the most honest and intelligible account of new knowledge to all who will try to learn."

What we urgently need today is a more inclusive view of what it means to be a scholar—a recognition that knowledge is acquired through research, through synthesis, through practice, and through teaching. Such a vision of scholarship, one that recognizes and rewards the scholarship of teaching, will continue to inspire each new generation.

Almost all successful academics give credit to creative teachers—those mentors who defined their work so compellingly that it became, for them, a lifetime challenge, and for their students a great inspiration. Without the teaching function, the continuity of knowledge will be broken and the store of human knowledge dangerously diminished.

In the end, inspired teaching keeps the flame of scholarship alive.

Ernest L. Boyer
The Carnegie Foundation
for the Advancement of Teaching
September 1995

PREFACE

Teachers and Mentors grew from our experiences as editors and advisory board members of *Teaching Education*. That journal was formed in 1986 to publish accounts of teaching past and present—in essence, to portray how educators conceived and organized their courses. While the contemporary portrayals of preservice and inservice teacher education classes proved quite useful, the "pedagogical vignettes" of historical figures held insight and power that we had not anticipated. Each issue of *Teaching Education* offered an opportunity for us to publish such vignettes that better situated college teaching within its historical context and, in so doing, offered a way to preserve and transmit our academic culture. As we oversaw the journal and as we re-read the published essays, we believed that such a collection solely of biographical vignettes was greatly needed.

We wish to thank Marie Ellen Larcada of Garland Publishing who displayed the foresight and courage to support a collection of biographical essays. Appreciation goes to our authors and those "subjects" who agreed to be portrayed in our collection. Special thanks goes to Lorin Anderson who continues to believe in the importance of the professoriate. Russell Long and Michael Knoll, both formerly of McKissick Museum, University of South Carolina, and Mary Bull of the South Carolina State Library provided assistance in obtaining fugitive biographical and bibliographic details. Other colleagues who have assisted in this overall project include John E. King, Janet L. Miller, Nicolae Sacalis, Alan Wieder, Susan Parker Shimp, Lyn B. Rose, and Sylvie A. Baldwin. Lastly, we express our appreciation to Drs. James T. Sears and J. Dan Marshall for accepting the editorship of *Teaching Education* and for continuing to oversee that very special journal.

TEACHERS AND MENTORS

INTRODUCTION

Teaching, Mentoring and the Professoriate

This is a book about teaching and mentoring—about the relationship between teachers and students and what it means to be a professor of education in today's academic community. This was not our original intent. Initially, we set out to prepare a collection of profiles of distinguished educators of the twentieth century.

Collections of this type exist in other fields within higher education. We thought that like others, ours would serve not only as a contribution to the historical literature but also as a useful reminder of the intellectual traditions and influential personalities that have shaped the field of education. Essays were requested and the collection began to take shape. We did not wish to romanticize nor celebrate the good old days of the 1920s and 1930s when professors wore lapel carnations and dined in the faculty club with one another and the occasional student while discussing issues of the day. Rather, knowing how short-term our memory is in education, we sought merely to preserve a bit of the past.

Biography served as the venue for this collection. "Good biographies deal with the ways people faced living—tell how they met problems, how they coped with big and little crises, how they loved, competed, did the things we all do daily—and hence these studies touch familiar chords in readers" (Vandiver, 1986, p. 61). As the essays came in, and we began to live with them, our purposes gradually changed. Individually, the essays proved interesting, but together we found that they presented a powerful statement about what it means to be a professor, about teaching as testimony, and about the fragile and somewhat sacred act of mentoring. The vignettes did touch all too familiar chords. Originally we had asked well-respected educators to write about their teachers, not realizing that the essays would point in an unanticipated direction, toward mentorship, and that mentoring would emerge as the central theme of the collection. Perhaps we should not have been surprised.

The essays forced us to compare professorial experiences. We found ourselves reexamining our own actions and professional relationships and commitments and those of our colleagues. What we saw was troubling, a weakening of traditions: generally, missing was the tradition of being well-read and thoughtful, of approaching ideas with a sense of wonder, of dedicating oneself to one's profession and institution, of displaying a sense of moral responsibility and of living a life of civility, understood not as manners or gentility but, in Clifford Orwin's sense, of living with "genuine respect for the rights and dignity of [others]" (Orwin, 1991, p. 554). While the authors and those they write about may have had moments of disillusionment and regret during their careers, they all seemed to recognize that they were part of a larger tradition, a vision of the academic life, sustained by a community and perpetuated through the lives of their teachers and their students. And this tradition manifested itself not only in the act of teaching but also in that of mentoring.

With this insight came a shift in focus, and our intentions for the collection changed. While the essays ultimately serve to give us hope as "we look back to look forward," the collection taken as a whole presents a timely and daunting challenge to recapture and reshape those reasons that brought us to the academy and to cause us to reflect upon and to re-examine our ideas and feelings about teaching and mentoring.

Conception of Mentoring

Before leaving for the Trojan Wars, Odysseus, King of Ithaca, charged his old friend Mentor to raise Telemachus, his beloved son, to be fit to ascend the throne. Mentor's influence over Telemachus was such that Athene, Zeus' daughter and goddess of Wisdom, found it useful to appear in his form to assist the boy at critical points in his development, including journeying to Pylos to obtain news of his father and assisting his mother Penelope to cleanse her household of importunate suitors. This was no ordinary relationship, as the tradition that has grown around the concept of mentoring suggests. Definitions of mentoring abound. Perhaps the simplest comes from Phillips-Jones: "mentors are influential people who significantly help you reach your major life goals" (Carruthers, 1993, p. 11). Jeruchim and Shapiro present a more comprehensive definition, one that nicely captures the focus of this book:

> In the classic definition it is, at its best, a close, intense, mutually beneficial relationship between someone who is older, wiser, more experienced, and more powerful with someone younger or less experienced. It is a complementary relationship, within an organizational or professional context, built on both the mentor's and the protégé's needs. (Jeruchim & Shapiro, 1992, p. 23)

It is a process by which the protégé is "guided, taught, and influenced" (Anderson & Ramey, 1990, p. 184). In helping a protégé, mentors serve as role models, guides, experienced advisers, trusted counselors, friends, supporters, and are characterized as knowledgeable, giving, trustworthy, interested, respecting, affectionate, and accessible (Carruthers, 1993, p. 20).

The mentor relationship is often presented as one-sided: the mentor gives, the protégé receives. But, this is not the case, as the essays well illustrate. Mentors also benefit, and the benefits take many forms including enhanced self-esteem, revitalized work interests, professional assistance on projects, friendship, and fulfillment of developmental needs among others (Murray, 1991, pp. 53-55). Without such benefits, the relationship fails (O'Leary & Mitchell, 1990).

Mentoring relationships also evolve over time, and sometimes go through phases: initiation, cultivation, separation, and redefinition (Kram, 1985, pp. 47-66). Moreover, a "mentor can be a key figure in a protégé's life for a brief and defined period of time or for a number of years" (Anderson & Ramey, 1990, p. 184). The spirit is one of embracing and of passing along: "Mentoring as one person handing another along until the moment that allows both of them together to envision possibilities hitherto out of sight" (Coles, 1993, p. 114).

Recently, given the rarity of mentoring relationships in highly competitive environments and the dramatic changes underway in work cultures (see Caldwell & Carter, 1993), increased attention has been given to designing formal mentoring programs, including those in higher education (Daloz, 1986; Lie & O'Leary, 1990). Too often such programs are more administrative—assigned—than personal and their results disappointing. Informal mentoring goes largely unseen. Yet there is a long history of extraordinarily productive mentoring relationships in higher education from which a good deal can be learned, not only about mentoring but about the often-forgotten ethical and social responsibilities of teaching and professing. It is our purpose to recall a few of these relationships, by way of reflecting on the role of professors in higher education.

Mentoring and Higher Education

The importance of mentor relationships to the academic and intellectual vitality of higher education, let alone to the quality of the professorial and student life, cannot be underestimated, an importance nicely illustrated by the distinguished jurist, Julius Getman. Underscoring the need for crossing generational lines, Getman writes:

> Although conflict among academic genera-tions is quite common, many positive personal relationships cross generational lines. The best young scholars and teachers are the ones most likely to acknowledge the influence of senior colleagues and teachers in their work. The most satisfied seniors are those who see their own influence in the work of the younger generation.
>
> In addition, most professors have been significantly influenced by mentors who personify the values that make academic life meaningful. Their achievements provide goals to strive for and standards against which the young person measures his or her progress. It is

> when academics speak about their mentors that
> expressions of caring, affection, and love are
> most clearly stated. In such conversations one
> can understand the values and dreams that have
> led people into academic life. (Getman, 1992, p.
> 269)

Despite such fond memories, something is seriously amiss in
higher education.

> The merchants have invaded the Temple
> and turned it into a market of exchange, where
> the things bought and sold are not only idols
> and consumer goods, but also human souls. All
> too often, the schools deemed to be the "good"
> ones are those which are good for the economy,
> attracting industry, grant money, and droves of
> students (Patterson, 1991, p. 12).

The money-changers are in charge; entrepreneurialism has
swept across higher education and threatens the quality of the
teaching and learning relationship that underpins educational
excellence. What is "higher" about higher education? Consider
the following:

> The critical problem today is not so much
> that many professors don't teach very well, but
> that so few of them teach at all, that a significant
> part of the crucial teaching responsibilities of
> our universities has been handed over to people
> who are unqualified. It is the shame of the
> academic intellectuals, a shabby secret they are
> loath to discuss publicly. (Anderson, 1992, p. 49)

> In 1992 there were approximately 800
> students teaching at Harvard, 600 at Columbia,
> and between 500 and 600 at Princeton.
> (Anderson, 1992, p. 55)

Common to research universities throughout America, the
practice of having students teach students severely limits access

of undergraduate students to potential mentors, and their education is impoverished as a result. Wilshire underscores the seriousness of our situation:

> The neglect of teaching in the university is an ominous symptom. I believe it signals a weakening of our will to live. For if we do not nurture our young and identify with them, we forfeit any hope in the regeneration and continuation of the species; we are walled up defensively within the confines of our egos and our momentary gratifications. But this means that we are not fully alive ourselves. (Wilshire, 1990, p. 255)

Comparing his own experience to what is common today, Getman laments that young faculty are "expected to develop sophisticated research agendas before they ever meet with a class" (Getman, 1992, p. 47). In effect, they must speak before they have anything to say, and there is an explosion in the number of journals needed to present their words in order to meet "publication quotas" for promotion and tenure, so many journals that no one can possibly keep up. Jacques Barzun (1991) once characterized this as "scholarship at gunpoint." Getman further goes on to say,

> The gap between laymen and academic specialists constantly grows. I do not think the gap is attributable to the speed with which the frontiers of knowledge are being pushed back; instead, it reflects the desire by academics to be thought part of a special, elite, intellectually rigorous world and the fear that, if what we wrote was intelligible, the claim would be more easily dismissed. (Getman, 1992, p. 47)

Under such conditions there is no possibility of achieving a "civic friendship toward our fellow citizens" (Bellah et al., 1985, p. 295), who pay the tab and who still send their children to us for educating.

When the teaching relationship is impoverished, professors, like their students, suffer. As Wilshire (1990, p. 129) remarks: "I am particularly critical of [professionalism's] academic form, for it masks out crucial educational obligations—especially to acknowledge that the most basic educational force is who the professor *is*. Are ethical qualities demanded by the educating act exemplified in the professor's life? The question is obscured." This is an important question, as McCloskey (1992, p. 245) suggests, because a "person's life is an argument." Put differently, "those of us who are teachers cannot stand before a class without standing for something . . . teaching is testimony" (Patterson, 1991, p. 16). What do we stand for, of what do we testify?

Of Teaching and Testimony

The essays included in this collection are here because we admired those who are being written about as well as those who did the writing. We did not seek a representative sample or cross-section of American professors of education. We selected our subjects because *we admire* them as teachers and mentors. In essence, we chose academics who had a profound influence on others who have become professors in the area of curriculum, foundations and, to a degree, teacher education. Our initial selections came from institutions that, during the first half of the twentieth century, emphasized the training of educational leaders at the post-secondary level. This is not surprising because these are the people whose work we studied as graduate students. Our selections were somewhat limited by the likelihood of locating well-respected educators able and willing to write about their well-respected teachers. Advanced age, health problems, and limited time proved to be serious impediments. Sadly, these conditions eliminated some educators we very much wished to include. Doggedness and determination can only accomplish so much. We realize our selection may be justly criticized, but we believe the central ideas would remain the same with or without additions and deletions. Moreover, given the embryonic stage of educational biography, there is an overabundance of educators both well and little known whose lives and careers deserve thoughtful attention. We sincerely hope our efforts will serve to encourage more biographical and autobiographical work along these lines.

We should note that most of the essays address the relationship between a graduate student and faculty mentor but not all. Included are essays that recount stories of senior professors taking more junior professors under wing, of mentoring relationships forming between professors and younger people who were not formally their advisees and one essay about a father, James Macdonald, written by his son. We mention this because only one of the essays is about undergraduates being mentored by professors. Mentoring of this kind is comparatively rare, but we believe the characteristics are the same regardless of level. Still, we look forward to future collections that capture the profound relationship of mentoring at the undergraduate level.

We wish to express appreciation to our contributors. Theirs has been an arduous task masked by the ease with which the essays are read. We sought essays by authors who would write with the richness achieved only by spending time with another. We wanted and expected the essays to take unique and individualistic forms expressive of the uniqueness of human relationships. We placed no restrictions on our authors other than the theme and the need to portray the lives and their relationship with a distinguished educator in prose that "must radiate a sense of intimacy and familiarity." The direction of each essay was entirely the author's own to determine. Our hope was that each vignette would well represent Joseph Epstein's view of the essay as "a piece of writing that is anywhere from three to fifty pages long, that can be read twice, that provides some of the pleasures of style, and that leaves the impression of a strong or at least interesting character" (Epstein, 1985, p. 400). In this we have not been disappointed.

As Getman has commented, most professors have been profoundly influenced by one or more mentors, and they become animated when they talk about them, and speak of caring, affection, and love. They also speak of intellectual challenge and adventure and of participating in a wider community of scholars, an adventure and a community of which mentors' lives testify. Despite the entrepreneurial spirit that has swept across higher education since World War II, we see within the essays reason for optimism about the professoriate. Certainly, we could sing a funeral dirge, a lament for the loss of a mythologized professorial past, but we think the essays have more to say about the future, than of the past. Professors remain among the most privileged workers. Gratitude, a feeling of being privileged, characterizes the essays. It is hard to imagine, but professors are actually paid to read and to think about whatever grabs hold of our attention and to engage bright younger people. As one of our colleagues often and laughingly remarks: "being a professor certainly beats working for a living!" He has a profound sense of gratitude for being allowed to engage in such work and to do what he loves to do. Arguments over academic freedom and complaints about too much centralization or decentralization of administrative responsibilities demonstrate that we continue to enjoy a tremendous amount of control over how we spend our time, over how we will live, together. While self-governance may be more rhetoric than reality, it is only so because we choose to disengage from community responsibilities and not because we have been denied opportunities for involvement. The quality of the communities within which we work and the value of teaching within them, of educative relationships, are determined in good measure by our personal professional commitments, by our vision of the good. If our work is unsatisfying, then we ought to look inward toward the core of commitments that characterizes our selves, out of which rises our passions, of which we testify, and toward our responsibilities, not outward for someone to blame or something to fulfill us.

Essays That Testify

The essays have been arranged in six sections. The first section contains three essays that demonstrate how protégés may present to their own students those lessons, especially about expectations, learned from their mentors. Together these essays show how powerful mentoring is as a means for building and keeping vital intellectual communities. Our example is drawn from the University of Chicago where Judd mentored Tyler; Tyler mentored Krathwohl and Bloom; Bloom mentored

Anderson. Although not organized in this way, there are other generational stories contained in the essays: at Ohio State University, Bode mentored Hullfish and Alberty; Hullfish mentored Clift and Wirth; and Alberty and Hullfish mentored Klohr, who mentored us.

Subsequent sections are organized thematically. The themes originated from multiple readings of the essays, and each touches on an important aspect of mentoring. The themes were not presented in advance to the authors; rather, they emerged. We sought to identify central ideas of each essay and then ways of clustering the essays that would bring strength and depth to the themes. Thus, while most essays present a number of ideas or concepts that potentially could have been useful for organizing the collection, we chose those that seemed to us to most eloquently capture the spirit of mentoring while simultaneously illustrating its benefits. The section titles present the themes: "Three Generations: Teaching Expectations"; "Standing for the Good: Professing and Social Responsibility"; "Modeling the Passion To Understand"; "Extending an Invitation To Share a Journey"; "Mutuality, Dignity, and Generosity of Spirit"; and "Civility, a Project Pertaining to the Public World." Each theme represents a different aspect of mentoring, which is grounded and given its particular and peculiar shape in each author's experience. There is, then, commonality in diversity.

In the Epilogue we return indirectly to these themes through the life of our mentor. We decided not to present a grandiose conception of mentoring or a culminating summary of insights from the essays. Such efforts would serve only to dishonor and trivialize the elusive phenomena that we seek to portray. Instead, one writes for us all—for experiences with our shared mentor and for our lives as professors. In this concluding statement we invite readers to reconsider their professional roles and relations with an eye toward rethinking our responsibilities as teachers—to stand for the good, and to pass along to others an enlivened and lively academic community and set of traditions.

Such is the context within which we decided to bring together this volume, a collection of vignettes whose power and thoughtfulness has affected our way of viewing ourselves and our professional lives. We see mentors living careers in different forms and manners as dictated by the definition of their work, and since "[t]he genuine scholar is impelled by a deeply ingrained curiosity, an undeniable urge to learn as well as to teach" (Altick, 1975, p. 7), we see teachers upholding the dignity of the professoriate. At the same time, each profile contains clues to assist us in redefining our professional dreams and relationships towards our students. While reading the essays we found ourselves drawn by the power of biography to, as Phyllis Rose states, "inspire comparison. Have I lived that way? Do I want to live that way? Could I make myself live that way if I wanted to?" (Rose, 1984, p. 5). The asking of questions like these has had a profound impact on each of us. We invite you to compare dreams and to think about the quality of the professional life you live as we have been compelled to think about ours. We ask: What do we stand for? Of what do we testify?

PART ONE

Three Generations: Teaching Expectations

Charles Hubbard Judd: As I Came To Know Him
by Ralph W. Tyler

Lessons Learned from Ralph W. Tyler
by David R. Krathwohl

Benjamin Bloom, Values and the Professoriate
by Lorin W. Anderson

When taken together as a whole, the three essays that follow present a vivid picture of intergenerational connection, of mentoring, of being bound by a set of relationships and professorial values that reach backward and forward in time. Charles Hubbard Judd was Wilhelm Wundt's student. Ralph Tyler was Judd's student; Ben Bloom and David Krathwohl were students of Tyler; and Lorin Anderson was a student of Bloom.

With obvious pride, Tyler speaks of his mentor, Judd, and of having met Judd's exacting standards of academic performance and hard work. Tyler went to the University of Chicago to become an educational scientist and, under Judd's tutelage, he became one—he measured up. Others, unable or unwilling to meet Judd's standards, found themselves members of the "Fired by Judd" club. Internalizing Judd's vision of the professoriate and sharing his passion for the empirical study of educational questions, for hard data, Tyler adopted his methods of instruction, including requiring students to submit weekly reports that revealed the development of their understanding of the topics under study. He also adopted Judd's commitment to professional groups as effective means for organizing and furthering the interests of education. And, like Judd, he was impatient with muddled thinking and insistent on clearly written prose.

From Krathwohl's essay on Tyler we gain additional insight into how the professoriate developed in his hands and how it was passed along. High standards remain, as does a sharp eye for talent and a ferocious independence of mind. By highlighting Tyler's departure from standardized approaches to evaluation, Krathwohl underscores his independence of mind, the kind of independence that led to Judd's attack on Thorndike's views of transfer of training. Yet, Tyler brought to the professoriate his own intellectual strengths and his positive personality. What he inherited from Judd, he invigorated, then rendered to others willing to take and cherish his offering. Sadly, what he could not pass along was his place as a senior statesperson, a repository of institutional memory now lost.

Anderson's portrayal of his mentor, Ben Bloom, echoes portions of the Tyler and Judd legacies: the value of hard work, passion for empirical research, faith in people and in their ability to learn, the insistence on clear prose—evidenced in Anderson's multiple drafts of the first chapter of his dissertation—and, once again, intellectual independence, the kind of independence that, in Bloom's case, led him to take on several of the most commonly held assumptions about teaching and learning. Anderson's link to Judd is indirect, spanning three generations but, nevertheless, quite powerful. Unknowingly, when Anderson was accepted by Bloom as a student and when he accepted Bloom as his teacher, with Bloom came Tyler and Judd. Such is the nature of mentoring, when students are worthy of their teachers, and such is the nature of a tradition that is continually passed along while constantly being reshaped.

Biographical Information

Charles Judd [born: Feb. 20, 1873, Bareilly, British India; died: July 18, 1946, Santa Barbara, CA] served as professor of educational psychology at the University of Chicago from 1909-1938. He was graduated from Wesleyan University (Connecticut) in 1894 with an A.B. and from the University of Leipzig in 1896 with the Ph.D. Other professional roles included a professorship in psychology at Wesleyan University from 1896-1898, New York University from 1898-1901, University of Cincinnati from 1901-1902, and Yale University from 1902-1909. Judd's publications include *Psychology of High-School Subjects* (1915), *Introduction to the Scientific Study of Education* (1918), *Education and Social Progress* (1934), *Education as Cultivation of the Higher Mental Processes* (1936), and *Educational Psychology* (1938). Professor Judd served in a number of leadership roles including terms as president of the American Psychological Association and chair of the American Council on Education.

Ralph W. Tyler [born: April 22, 1902; Chicago, Illinois; died: Feb. 18, 1994; San Diego, CA] served as professor of education, Dean of Social Sciences, and University Examiner at the University of Chicago from 1938-1953. He was graduated from Doane College (Nebraska) in 1921 with an A.B.; other degrees included an A.M. from the University of Nebraska in 1923 and the Ph.D. from the University of Chicago in 1927. Other professional roles included serving as a high school teacher in the Nebraska public schools in 1921 and holding professorships in education at the University of Nebraska from 1922-1927, the University of North Carolina from 1927-1929, Ohio State University from 1929-1938, and serving as Director of the Center for Advanced Study in Behavioral Sciences at Stanford University from 1953-1966. Tyler's publications include *Constructing Achievement Tests* (1934), *Basic Principles of Curriculum and Instruction* (1949), and *Appraising and Recording Student Progress* (1942) with Eugene R. Smith.

Benjamin Bloom [born: Feb. 21, 1913, Lansford, PA] served as university examiner from 1943-1959 and professor of education at the University of Chicago from 1943-1970. He was graduated from Pennsylvania State University in 1935 with a B.A.; other degrees include an M.S. from Pennsylvania State University in 1935 and the Ph.D. from the University of Chicago in 1942. Other professional roles include serving as a researcher for the Pennsylvania State Relief Organization from 1935-1936, the American Youth Commission from 1936-1938, and the Cooperative Study in General Education from 1939-1940. Bloom's publications include editing *Taxonomy of Educational Objectives* (1956) and authoring *Stability and Change in Human Characteristics* (1964), *Human Characteristics and School Learning* (1976), *All Our Children Learning* (1981), and *Developing Talent in Young People* (1985).

CHAPTER ONE

Charles Hubbard Judd: As I Came To Know Him

Ralph W. Tyler

[This essay was previously published in 1987 in *Teaching Education*, Volume 1, No. 1, pp. 19-24 and is reprinted with permission of *Teaching Education*.]

"Come in, Tyler! What can I do for you?" His clear, hearty voice and forceful handshake served as my introduction to Charles Judd, whose reputation as a scientist seeking to develop a science of education led me to the University of Chicago in September 1926 to study for the Ph.D. As he came to the door of his office to greet me, I was impressed by his tall, erect, powerful figure and his stern, yet kindly face, decorated by a goatee characteristic of European professionals at that time.

I explained that my department chairman at the University of Nebraska, where I supervised practice teachers in science, had said to me, "You are a scientist. You should study with Charles Judd, who is developing a science of education." So, I had come to study with him. Since I had taken many courses in education beyond the master's degree at the University of Nebraska and since I had very little money, I hoped to complete my doctoral program in a short time. I asked Mr. Judd, "What courses must I take?"

He replied, "Here, we do not require students to take courses. We require them to demonstrate that they have learned what the faculty believes essential for the award of the doctorate. Our courses are designed to help students learn these things and to provide opportunity for them to learn other things that they may wish to satisfy their own choice of special expertise. But you may choose other means for learning what is required of all and what is necessary for your choice of an area of expertise."

Since I arrived in Chicago the first of September and classes did not begin until the end of the month, I asked Mr. Judd what I could do during the next few weeks to make progress in my studies. He told me that I could take at once the language examinations in French and German, which were required of all Ph.D. candidates in all departments, and I could take the qualifying examination at the end of September. If I passed these examinations, I could be admitted to candidacy for the degree and could concentrate on my dissertation, as well as taking those courses which I chose in order to expand my learning and prepare for the final comprehensive examination. He then called the appropriate officials by telephone to arrange the times for my language examinations and to put me on the list to take the qualifying examination.

As I left his office, I reflected on my first meeting with Charles Judd. I was impressed by his directions, his clarity of explanation of the doctoral program, his speed of reaction in responding to my questions, and his helpfulness.

Later, in his classes, I found his lectures to be unusually clear, well-organized, and focused on general principles. He had earned his own Ph.D. under Wilhelm Wundt at the University of Leipzig, a degree in social psychology. His early research when he was Director of the Yale Psychological Laboratory was concerned with the ability of human beings to guide their behaviors by relevant generalizations. His classic experiment involved students learning to throw darts at targets. After they had developed considerable skill, he placed the targets under water. The students were initially unable to hit them. Then he explained the principle of refraction light—the light rays are bent as they pass from the water to the air and thence to the eyes of the marksman. As this general principle was understood, the students hit the underwater targets, showing the same skill they had shown with targets in the air. Edward Lee Thorndike's monumental study which refuted the long-held belief in formal discipline and in the development of general faculties of the mind through instruction in particular academic subjects had led many psychologists to the view that the transfer of what a student learned in school to the situations outside the classroom was limited to the identity of the elements in the classroom learning and those in the situations outside. From this belief came the view that learning objectives must be very specific. Thorndike's psychology of arithmetic identified more than 2,000 specific objectives for the teaching of this subject. As another example, Pendleton formulated nearly 3,000 objectives for secondary school English.

Judd was convinced that human learners could generalize their learning and the number of educational objectives could be reduced to a manageable group. He wrote in his autobiography, "I was convinced by the results of my experimental work in the Yale laboratory that the higher mental processes are not of the same pattern as lower mental processes. I had observed the growing tendency to seek the explanation of human mental life through experiments with animals, and I had become convinced that this effort to explain the complex phenomena of mental life as mere summations of the elements that appear in lower forms of behavior is fundamentally wrong." (Judd, 1932, p. 227)

In his advanced course in educational psychology, each of us carried on an experiment in generalization of student learning. My experiment was with the learning of the 100 addition combinations of two one-digit numbers. One group of children was instructed by taking every one of the 100 combinations and practicing it until it was remembered the next day. Another similar group of children was instructed by taking 21 of the combinations for practice and explaining the principle of addition, then practicing only on the 21 combinations. They were tested the next day on all 100 combinations and did as well as the children who had practiced on all 100.

This was characteristic of all of Judd's classes. Students conducted experiments to test generalizations or to derive them. Judd reminded us continually that a science of education is based on the observations and experiments with actual phenomena of learning in school and out. It is not derived by speculation or by quoting authorities who have not directly tested their conclusions in practice. He expected his students to continue their inquiries when they were practicing as teachers or administrators in schools and colleges. A group of high school principals in the Chicago area who had been students of his organized the Judd Club, which met for dinner at the University once a month. The principals selected from time to time an issue, a problem, or a topic about which they were much concerned and worked out a plan for investigation. This plan was discussed at the dinner meeting with Judd and other university faculty members who participated in the criticism and revision of the plan. Then one of Judd's graduate students was assigned as an assistant to help the principals with their inquiry.

Judd's view was that a School of Education should have not only the laboratory schools as a laboratory for studying educational problems, but also, public schools with which the university faculty and students could conduct inquiries. He sponsored the organization of the National Association of Secondary School Principals, which was housed at the University of Chicago until the outbreak of World War II led to its transfer to Washington, where cooperation with war training groups in the government could be facilitated. He worked closely with high school teachers and principals and expected Professor William S. Gray to give leadership to the faculty in working with elementary schools. Later, he appointed Floyd W. Reeves to work with colleges and universities. That valid generalizations to guide education will come from investigations of the phenomena in practice was his central belief.

In his classes, we were not only expected to carry out investigations, but also to submit a written report every week. Judd believed that through writing one developed understanding and clarity. He had no use for pedagese. If you understand something you can explain it in plain English. He read our papers and returned them with questions to be answered, and the papers were to be revised. I found this procedure so helpful to me that when I taught graduate courses later, I expected the students to submit weekly reports through which I could follow their progress in thinking and in understanding the subjects they were studying.

One other thing impressed me in Judd's classes. He was intolerant of laziness or muddled thinking. He could be sharply critical of either of these qualities. I remember one student asking when his paper was returned with a grade of "D," "Mr.

Judd, can you tell me what was wrong with my paper?" Judd replied, "Young man, does it not occur to you that if you can't write a paper that is better than a 'D,' you wouldn't understand what was wrong with it?"

This sharp reaction to student work that he considered shoddy caused some students to conclude that Judd had no sympathy with students. This notion that he was cold or unkind was reinforced by his practice of weeding out students that he thought were lazy or unwilling to attempt serious thought. They were those who memorized readings and lectures but made little effort to reflect, to observe, to seek to solve intellectual problems. As he identified such students, he advised them that they were making no progress in their graduate work and recommended that they go elsewhere to seek an advanced degree. There was a sufficient number of these persons to form a club called the "FBJ Club," standing for "Fired by Judd." They felt vindicated when some of them received the doctorate at other universities.

I do not think that Judd was generally callous in his treatment of students, or unkind. He was tireless in his efforts to instruct, to assist, and to encourage students who were industrious and thoughtful, although he was intolerant of the lazy and muddle-headed. Those who survived his initial course and were enrolled in his advanced courses were entertained monthly in his home for an evening of discussion of contemporary issues. He was active in several professional organizations—the American Council on Education, the North Central Association of Secondary Schools and Colleges, the National Association of Secondary School Principals, and the National Society for the Study of Education, to cite a few. From these activities he identified critical issues for discussion and analysis by his advanced graduate students and arranged for many of his students to participate in studies conducted by these organizations. He was co-chairman of the Cleveland Study of 1915, the first survey of a large city school system in which "scientific instruments" were used to gain comprehensive information about the structure and functioning of the system. Some of his students as well as faculty members participated in this survey. The Cleveland Conference, which is still very active, was initiated by him at that time.

A characteristic example of his kindness to those whom he respected involved Floyd W. Reeves. While Reeves was undergoing his final oral examination, his appendix burst. He was rushed to the hospital and after the operation, was told that he must rest quietly for several months. When Judd was informed of this, he went to see Mrs. Reeves and advised her to take Floyd back to their home in South Dakota to rest. When Floyd was well enough he could return to take on the job Judd had arranged for him. Then Judd pressed money into Mrs. Reeves' hand, saying that this should cover their expenses in returning home and, if not, let him know and he would send more.

Mr. Judd was always kind and helpful to me, and I knew a dozen of my fellow students who experienced his kindly encouragement and assistance. I believe that the notion of his coldness grew out of his intolerance of incompetence.

In developing the Graduate School of Education, Judd sought faculty members who viewed their subjects as fields of inquiry. In educational sociology, George Counts expected his students to make empirical studies of sociological problems relating to education. When I took his course, I investigated the educational experience of the families of immigrants from Poland who came to Chicago. Others in the class chose other immigrant groups for study. Professors Buswell, Freeman, and Gray were studying the processes children followed in learning arithmetic, handwriting, and reading.

The field of educational administration did not readily become a subject Judd considered appropriate for graduate study. He started a course in this field by bringing into a summer session a highly-regarded, successful city super-intendent. Judd told me that he was shocked when after five weeks of the course scheduled for ten weeks, the superintendent came to him saying, "I've given the students all I know about administration. What shall I do the next five weeks?" The next summer, he employed another superintendent to offer a graduate course, but he, too, simply reported on his experiences as superintendent and seemed unable to order them, to identify critical questions, to suggest testable generalizations, and the like. Finally, he persuaded Henry Morrison to come to the

University of Chicago as Superintendent of the Laboratory
Schools and to use them as the initial place to study administration empirically. From this experience, Morrison published
in 1926 *The Practice of Teaching in the Secondary School*, outlining
the concepts of mastery learning and the principles involved in
the administration of such a program. Morrison then began his
investigation of the economics of schooling.

In accounting for Judd's widespread influence on American
education, his forensic skills should be considered as well as his
phenomenal intellectual functioning. He spoke with force and
authority. His arguments were crystal-clear and persuasive.
Wherever he spoke, his audiences were large and responsive.
After receiving my Ph.D. in 1927, I became an associate professor
in the University of North Carolina. When I attended the
meeting of the North Carolina Education Association, I heard
Charles Judd speak to a large audience of teachers, administrators, and school board members. He kept them spellbound
as he interpreted the development of education in the south as it
became industrialized and explained the nature of the problems
the North Carolina schools were then facing. In February 1928, I
attended the national meetings of educators in Boston and saw
again the large audiences that came to the sessions where Judd
spoke and the loud applause that followed his speeches. He produced a powerful impression on those who heard him.

He also exercised an intellectual influence upon university
administrators. James B. Conant, then President of Harvard
University, visited Judd in 1933 to discuss the problems he
encountered with the Graduate School of Education at Harvard.
Conant wrote in his memoirs:

> What he [Judd] had to say made a deep
> impression. Apparently, until the reforms he put
> through at Chicago, the students in the School of
> Education received instruction in academic
> subjects as well as education from members of
> the faculty of education (a scheme which was in
> effect in a number of large universities as late as
> the 1960s). Such an arrangement was all wrong,
> Judd declared. The instruction in the academic

> fields should be exclusively in the hands of the
> subject matter departments. The professors of
> education should be statesmen in a profession.
> . . . I knew what Judd was talking about I
> wrote a memorandum to Dean Holmes . . . .
> "The question of following the lead of Chicago
> should be seriously considered." (Conant, 1970,
> p. 183)

Judd had a strong social conscience. When the Great
Depression followed the crash in 1929 of the stock market, he
recognized the plight of youth unable to gain employment and
without money to continue their education. He urged the
American Council on Education to establish the American Youth
Commission and persuaded Homer Raney, one of his former
students, to become director of the Commission. Later, when
Raney went to the University of Texas as president, he
persuaded Floyd Reeves, another former student, to take over
the directorship.

The Commission's first study was a comprehensive
investigation of the conditions of youth during this catastrophic
period, which was published as *How Fare American Youth?*
(Rainey, 1937). Harold Ickes, a graduate of the University of
Chicago, was Secretary of the Interior under President Roosevelt.
The Bureau of Education was in the Interior Department at that
time. Judd urged Ickes to give his support to the enactment of
two federal programs for American youth, the Civilian
Conservation Corps and the National Youth Administration.
Judd himself took a two-year leave of absence beginning in 1936
to take a major position in the N.Y.A. These were the last two
years before he reached retirement age. Later, during World War
II when a program of off-duty education was established for
members of the armed forces, Judd was appointed dean of the
teaching staff of the School of Special Service at Fort Mead. This
school's task was the training of Special Service officers for their
duties in advising and guiding the off-duty education of the
soldiers. While there, Brigadier General Osborn, Chief of the
Special Service Division, pinned a three-stripe emblem on Judd's
sleeve as a testimonial of "the unanimous praise of all the

student officers in the class for his incomparable lectures and conference sessions," and it also represented "the respect and cordial esteem of the military faculty of the school."

Robert Hutchins was President of the University of Chicago during the last nine years of Judd's tenure there. His impressions of Judd were expressed on April 15, 1948 at the naming of the University's graduate education building in honor of Charles Hubbard Judd. Among the comments Hutchins made were the following:

> Mr. Judd was a great teacher. He could teach even a university president. And he was not easily dismayed by the difficulty of a task. I was willing to learn because he made an enormous impression on me. He began to teach me about the organization of education, the relation of public and private education, and the relation of the federal government to education. When he got tired, he got George Works and Floyd Reeves to help him. He and these two assistants not only did all they could with their pupil, they also played a great part in the reorganization of the University that went on in 1930 and 1931; the creation of the College and the Divisions, the establishment of the Board of Examinations and the Dean of Students' office, and the ultimate formation of the four-year college.
> . . . [H]e [Judd] thought I did not have the courage of my convictions and to him there was no deadlier sin than that. A man who would not stand up for what he believed in or did not believe anything deeply enough to stand up for it was an object of that scorn which those flashing blue eyes could so well express. He had the courage of his convictions. For the dean of a professional school which had just won its way to recognition to recommend its abolition is, I think, unique in the history of American

education. But this is what Mr. Judd did, and he
did it because he was convinced that it was the
right thing to do. He believed that there was a
science of education. He believed that it was a
social science. He believed that the task of
preparing teachers was not the obligation of a
single school or department, it was the
responsibility of the whole university. Therefore
the School of Education should become a
department in the Division of the Social
Sciences, and the University Committee on the
Preparation of Teachers should assume the duty
of educating teachers. This action on the part of
the University of Chicago is one of the
landmarks in American education.

Mr. Judd had character; he had intelligence;
and he had knowledge. He had a tremendous
respect for facts, and he knew a great many of
them. He knew them in such a way that he
could use them. He was impatient of all
discussion which disregarded the facts. I have
often seen him sit restlessly in a meeting trying
to control himself while ill-informed persons
expressed their theories. When he thought the
time had come to put an end to all this, he
would begin with his favorite opening, "I would
like to remind you gentlemen of two or three
facts." They always were facts. They had usually
been forgotten. They were frequently decisive.
(Hutchins, 1970, pp. 10-11)

Charles Hubbard Judd was known throughout the western
world as a great educational statesman. And he was. But I
always think of him as an insightful teacher and a kindly
mentor.

CHAPTER TWO

Lessons Learned from Ralph W. Tyler

David R. Krathwohl

I first heard of Ralph Tyler in 1939, when as a senior in Hyde Park High School, I learned that he was the expert from Ohio State University who was to "improve" the University of Chicago scholarship tests I planned to take. He was converting them from essay examinations to multiple-choice format. This caused quite an uproar among the cadre of senior teachers who, for years, had voluntarily run junior and senior honors classes which were partly practice for those essay examinations. At Hyde Park, football wasn't the big rivalry, it was the competition with Evanston for University of Chicago scholarships! Hyde Park had historically won, but drawing on a racially-integrated neighborhood, these teachers were increasingly pushed to maintain that superiority. They expected Tyler to make the test one of memory for esoteric knowledge fragments. Because he was Director of Evaluation of the Eight Year Study of Secondary Schools of the Progressive Education Association, Ralph was at the forefront of developing multiple choice items to test complex thinking skills; such items composed the scholarship examinations. So the teachers' fears proved unfounded. But, at that point in time, I was aware that Dr. Tyler was not their favorite person. No doubt, they reversed that opinion when they saw the examinations or took classes from him.

The evaluation instruments for the Eight Year Study were crucial to the study's success. High schools of the time, locked into a curriculum dictated by extensive and detailed college admission requirements, feared any deviation from those requirements would jeopardize their students' applications. Members of the Progressive Education Association in particular wanted to experiment with new curricula with broader objectives. As the name implies, the study provided for experimentation over an eight-year window: three years in which students in 30 representative schools—private and public, large and small, East Coast to the West—would experience new high school curricula, then 5 years during which the cooperating colleges would admit students on the recommendation of the principal with a complete record of the students' achievements. It was in the development of the latter that Ralph and those working with him ventured into new territory to develop instruments evaluating complex thinking skills, social sensitivity, appreciation, interests and personal and social adjustment. Their work depended not only on the adequacy of each student's record but also the record of the success of the study as a whole in adequately preparing students for college. The study showed there were many ways to prepare for college education. Those schools whose curriculum departed farthest from the conventional program "excelled their controls by scores that may roughly be expressed as 27 to 7" (Aikin, 1942, p. 150). As a result, colleges and universities gradually reduced their admission requirements to a minimum, a condition which remains true to this day.

But Ralph is probably much better known for his well-thought-out process of curriculum development and a rationale for its evaluation (Tyler, 1949) which involved behavioral objectives considerably before Mager's (1962) popular book on behavioral objectives was published. First used as a course syllabus in 1934, *Basic Principles of Curriculum and Instruction* was an early forerunner of what later became the management-by-objectives movement in business and performance-based teacher education in professional education. Less recognized is the fact that he did much to further the evaluation of complex skills and abilities throughout his career. Smith and Tyler (1942), an account of the measurement in the Eight Year Study, was one of the earliest publications to show what could be accomplished, and many of the item formats developed there are still among the best for tapping those behaviors. He encouraged such development through the work of the Board of Examiners which he headed. The Board created very sophisticated examinations for the University of Chicago's

College, tapping complex skills in six-hour examinations which determined the student's grade for the entire year, regardless of class attendance or scores on interim tests (the latter were solely for the student's guidance). The examinations had to be very good for this system to work, and many were highly creative efforts.

He strongly supported Ben Bloom and his working group in creating a taxonomy or classification scheme for educational objectives. By grouping objectives evaluating the same or similar behaviors the group could demonstrate the variety of formats and multiple choice item types that were available for evaluation of complex intellectual skills and abilities as well as affective behaviors (Bloom, 1953; Krathwohl, Bloom, & Masia, 1964). Many of us in the Board of Examiners assisted in that effort as well as individuals at other institutions. With Ralph's help, Ben and I later received a grant from the Social Science Research Council to further the taxonomy work (Krathwohl, 1994).

Additional instances for the development of evaluation were provided by the Cooperative Study in General Education and the U. S. Armed Forces Institute, both of which grew out of the Board of Examiner's activities. The National Assessment of Educational Progress (NAEP) which Ralph was instrumental in developing provided still another "hothouse" for the development of evaluation instruments and techniques. NAEP is an effort to measure school achievement throughout the country by sampling various subject fields at certain grade levels on a cyclical basis. It uses a matrix sampling plan to test individuals so that though the test field is covered by the students as a whole, each student is tested only on a small part of it. Finding ways to further one's particular interests through the variety of activities in which one engages, in this case, educational evaluation, seems to characterize many, like Ralph, who have accomplished so much in their lifetimes.

That Ralph turned out so well should be an inspiration to all bright kids who have had trouble in school. He loved to recount how he trapped muskrats as a child to earn extra money and told Diana Buell Hiatt in an interview:

One day I trapped a skunk. I was interested to know how skunks made that awful smell, so I extracted the juice from its glands. As I was returning home . . . I saw a bucket of paint that was being used to redo the school radiators. I disliked attending school and thought of a way that school might be cancelled. I poured the skunk juice into the paint bucket. [Rumjahn adds that the "the Bohemian janitor . . . couldn't smell it because he ate a lot of garlic" (1984, p. 8).] When the first cold day arrived and the school's heat was turned on, the whole school learned of my deed . . . school was cancelled for the day. However, I was called on to accept responsibility. . . . I informed the principal that school was for sissies and I was getting nothing out of school. . . . After much serious discussion, the principal and my father convinced me that I should continue school. However, both thought that I had the energy and talent to work and attend school. So I went to school part time and then worked a full day at the local creamery. (Hiatt, 1994, p. 787)

Ralph's Special Capabilities

Though short and prematurely balding, Ralph had great charm, especially when he smiled; he had a twinkle in his eyes that was irresistible. But part of this appeal also resulted from some very special capabilities:

- He was incredibly organized in his speech, appearing to be talking from an outline even in extemporaneous give-and-take.
- He was unfailingly positive in outlook, rarely saying anything negative about someone else; he might indicate they were wrong but did not attack them personally.
- He sought the best in every situation and emphasized it.

- He was a superb judge of undeveloped talent and his positiveness of outlook contributed to his exceptional ability to develop it.
- He delegated responsibility widely and extraordinarily well.
- He had a prodigious memory—for people, for events, and especially for jokes.
- His combination of finding the positive, organizing his thoughts and speech, and possessing an exceptional memory, all came together in an extraordinary ability to sum up the progress in a meeting, to contribute to the solution to problems, and to build a consensus where none existed before.
- He viewed himself broadly as a social scientist, an educator who drew on the social science disciplines to solve education's problems.

Few of us have capabilities equal to his, and still fewer have his unique combination of them. I think there are lessons to be learned, however, by emulating many of his behaviors to whatever extent we are able. Toward this end, though limited by my understanding and experiences, let me look at the man and his life in more detail using the above characteristics as a framework.

Highly Organized Extemporaneous Speech

Ralph had an unusual ability to organize his extemporaneous speech. I first became aware of this in 1942-43 as an undergraduate senior doing hourly work for his Board of Examiners. I computed standard scores and other statistics for those six hour examinations as well as item analyses. Ralph was the Director, and Ben Bloom, for whom I worked, his assistant. While I had little contact with Ralph directly, I do recall that he was the first person I had ever met who, when asked a complex question, would answer, "Well, there are three aspects to that question. . . . " He would then proceed to methodically spell these out. Sometimes there were four aspects, sometimes five, though I don't recall a higher number than that. The answers always included exactly the number of parts he had indicated at the outset, and they always fit together as a unit as though perfectly preplanned, not juggled or split arbitrarily to fit! I was tremendously impressed; I still am! How could someone immediately know how they would organize their answers? I never knew whether he picked a number that was about right for how complex he thought the answer might be and then proceeded to work out one that could be so divided as he went along, or whether he really did have his answer all laid out from the outset as he indicated.   Either way, it bowled you over!

Positive Outlook

Ralph's positive outlook and his search for the good in each person meant that he always found positive statements to make about everyone. Clearly in a world where we are taught to be so analytical and critical of each other's work, Ralph was a happy anomaly. It was not just that he was unfailingly polite and smooth of temper—he had an even emotional tone about him, some might say to the point of blandness. I saw him very happy but never what I'd call ecstatic. I have seen him disappointed but never in a towering rage. But neither was his typical mood neutral; it was definitely positive.

No doubt that contributed enormously to his popularity. Everyone enjoys having positive things said about them and their work, and Ralph could carry this off without appearing to be a glad-hander.

As both an undergraduate and a graduate student, having absorbed the atmosphere of the University of Chicago which so emphasized not only critical thinking but also frankly speaking one's own mind, I used to muse over how (to my eye) such an apparently uncritical person could be so successful. Clearly this was mainly a sign of my own immaturity and lack of social understanding. I have since known others like Ralph; in my experience, they make very popular administrators who are successful even when those complimented realize that they are being put on a bit.

This characteristic carried over into his letters of recommendation which made him very popular with graduate students. Because of his national reputation, they believed a recommendation from him would carry great weight. It was not until later that I learned the word was out about Ralph's letters. When screening applications, faculty and administrators simply took his letters in stride paying special attention to any clues to negative aspects that might exist.

Overt Reinforcement of the Positive "Underside"

Ralph sought out and put the very best face on things. For instance, my dissertation was a very early study of what later came to be called "aptitude-treatment-interaction." After a three-year struggle with it while also working as Assistant Examiner to Tom Hastings at the University of Illinois and working on the *Taxonomy of Educational Objectives* as well as other test construction and research, I was very glad to get it behind me. I felt it was mainly an exercise, a learning experience of little value to the educational community. When my oral examination was over, Ralph, who was a member of my committee, asked what were my plans for publishing it? I was astounded; I was sure it was not of that quality. It was a prime example of his being encouraging and putting the best face on things. It is still unpublished and buried in the archives to this day.

I was again struck by this quality during my service with him on a federal committee he chaired. This committee was responsible for evaluating research proposals submitted to the Cooperative Research Program of the Office of Education. As judges in the first federal open competition in support of educational research, we often felt as though we were treading on eggs in making our decisions. We were certain to be carefully scrutinized, and mistakes might torpedo future funding for a badly needed program just getting underway. Peering over our shoulders were the critical eyes of those in other agencies who would have liked to have had that money, small pot that it was. This resulted in a very tough gauntlet for proposals to run, some committee members taking a very hard line, particularly on projects that were obviously those of a neophyte's or which seemed too "blue sky." By contrast, Ralph was secure enough to look for such proposals. When he felt they deserved it, he would present a very strong case for why they should be funded—often winning the day. Watching him taught me not to get caught up in the concerns of the group and to look for the positive "underside" in situations.

Recognition and Nurturing of Talent

This natural tendency of Ralph's to reinforce the good in people meant that he was a superb nurturer of talent. Add to this the fact that he was an excellent judge of a person's capability in the first place as is indicated by the quality of the individuals who staffed the Department of Education, Board of Examiners, and Eight Year Study during his administrations, individuals such as Bruno Bettelheim, Benjamin Bloom, Oscar K. Buros, Stephen Corey, Lee Cronbach, Allison Davis, Paul Diederich, Harold Dunkel, Edgar Friedenberg, Chester Harris, Maurice Hartung, Robert Havighurst, Louis Heil, William Henry, Virgil Herrick, Christine McGuire, Leo Nedelsky, Louis Raths, George Sheviakov, Joseph Schwab, Hilda Taba, and Herbert Thelen. For a number of them, it was their first position beyond the doctorate. Rubin (1994) making the same point of Ralph's special capacity of "unfettering talent in others" (p. 785) adds Ernest Boyer, Nathaniel Gage, Jacob Getzels, John Goodlad, Philip Jackson, Thomas James, and David and Frank Riesman to the list of those he helped—and this is far from a complete list. Many of these names will be familiar to current readers, but such is the nature of fame that many will not, especially to future readers. I assure you, however, each of these persons gained some kind of national recognition in his or her field. Just those named include a past president of the American Psychological Association, seven former presidents of the American Educational Research Association, and eleven members of the National Academy of Education to say nothing of other instances of recognition. Only a person who regularly worked at identifying and assisting talent could compile such a record.

Delegation of Responsibility

Ralph was a supreme delegator of responsibility. As I recall, he was Director of the Board of Examiners, Head of the Department of Education, and Dean of the Social Sciences Division, all at the same time. I couldn't imagine how he was able to handle all this until I learned how good he was at delegating. He had assistants in each of those positions on whom he relied. I experienced this in a small way. After World War II, I returned to Chicago to finish my master's degree and stayed on for my doctorate. I went back to work at the Board of Examiners for Ben Bloom, this time as a graduate assistant but with responsibility to Ralph for an examination called the Social Science Divisional Examination. Preparing it involved soliciting, selecting, and editing essay questions in specific fields from faculty across the spectrum of social sciences and then writing a broad integrative social science exam consisting of questions that usually involved analyzing and interpreting tables of data. Ralph always looked over my examinations and sometimes made a few suggestions. He was always supportive and each time would find some aspect on which he could reasonably comment positively. In addition, he sampled my grading of the responses. As a graduate assistant, I was surprised by how completely he delegated the work to me. But I think this was typical; I, as were others to whom he delegated, was pleased to be trusted enough to be given this much responsibility. It was another aspect of his ability to develop talent by giving it full rein.

An Elephant's Memory

Ralph had a fantastic memory. Perhaps that partly accounted for his ability to juggle so many administrative roles while simultaneously taking on many other consulting tasks. Louis Rubin was impressed with his memory as well. He recounts, "At a Washington dinner party I once convened in his honor, someone asked the name of the former United States commissioner of education. Tyler immediately supplied the answer and then sequentially named the entire list of previous commissioners. . . . Later . . . I realized that he used such exercises to reinforce recall—he simply would not allow himself to forget" (Rubin, 1994, p. 784).

Ralph's memory was a great help to the educational community. He had his hand in so many projects: the Eight Year Study, NAEP, the Center for Advanced Study of the Behavioral Sciences, the National Academy of Education, and the National Coalition for Equality in Learning. In each of these he was able to view the project in perspective and could helpfully give the background on how it came to be, where it was, and how that was helpful (or a problem) for where we were going. This is going to be missed! Persons such as Ralph are the institutional memory for many of the institutions and programs important to us today. They are disappearing and the historical records haven't kept up. Undoubtedly we will have a lot of lessons to learn by trial and error all over again.

Ralph's memory was so good it had one negative result. You have all known instructors who used the same notes year after year, so their lectures were standardized. Ralph never used notes; his lectures were all apparently extemporaneous. Yet students in his courses will tell you that his lectures repeated almost word for word his writing on the same subject. If you could find the particular article or document, you could almost follow him in the text as he spoke. I had been told about this and doubted that was the case until I took a course from him. I found that I could indeed follow along with only occasional asides or the elements in slightly different order. A bit unnerving but an amazing feat.

Perhaps one the most delightful aspects of his excellent memory was his love of jokes. He loved to tell stories and was an excellent storyteller in his deliberate, somewhat dry way. I can recall a cocktail party at Alex Charters' home after Ralph had been awarded an honorary degree by Syracuse University; Ralph held forth for hours with story after story. He loved to get into a competition with another storyteller and see if he could top him.

A Genius at Stripping Away Sources of Conflict to Reach
Productive Amicable Agreement[1]

Combine a superb memory, the ability to organize one's
thoughts very quickly, and keen analytical ability and you
have the ideal conference summarizer. Over time such a
person can bring a wealth of experience to solving problems. So
it was that Ralph was frequently called on to chair meetings,
to summarize conferences, and to assist in solving problems. I
understand he gave advice to six presidents. We routinely
asked him to summarize our annual Taxonomy conferences as
we were developing the framework. Ralph was superb at
cutting away the chaff and making us see the positive
contributions that, for many of us, had been covered up in the
course of working through details. I recall Ralph as the
summarizer of a particularly chaotic weekend of meetings at
which Ben Bloom whispered to me, "Let us see what Ralph
can do with this!" I think Ben considered it the ultimate challenge since we agreed the group had gone in circles. Ralph
managed to put a very positive face on it and showed there
was real progress after all.

Dr. Christine McGuire reminded me of how adept, even in
the most difficult groups, Ralph was at building a consensus. In
his unruffled, very quiet way, using his superb memory to
selectively quote a few things each person had said, he would
pull it all together quite logically and convincingly into a
coherent whole. After all, how could they reject their own
words? It was a very valuable skill.

Because the vocational educators and home economists were
able to obtain federal grants for inservice training sessions, he
was sought after by many groups and was frequently consulted
in these fields. They sought his help in developing and
reworking their curricula, becoming the earliest field to
widely adopt his curriculum development process and pre-
ceding the explosive growth of competency-based curricula.

As a very capable problem-solver, Ralph could be counted
on to tackle an issue with an open mind. It was out of his
chairing groups that the Center for Advanced Study in the

Behavioral Sciences and the National Assessment of Educational Progress came into existence. But although he was involved in large projects such as these, he always had time for small ones as well. Indeed, if the time was not already scheduled, it seemed he would always make himself available—quite remarkable for such a busy man. This was much appreciated by the many graduate students who sought his attention.

The many outside activities meant that Ralph always had a wide array of things going on. He was on the road so much of the time that many Sundays, when I went into the Board for a quiet place to catch up on my own work expecting the office to be empty, there he would be catching up with his week's mail and dictating to his long-time executive secretary and administrative assistant, Jane Keilsmeier—Jane Allison at that time. Jane was another of the capable people to whom he regularly delegated responsibility. She started working with him at age 21 after her college graduation and continued through his period at the University of Chicago, his directorship of the Center for Advanced Study, and was still working with him when at 81 he was President of the Systems Development Foundation.

A Social Science Perspective

Ralph did not think of himself narrowly as a professional educator but rather as a social scientist who used its base disciplines to attack the problems of education. Although his early career was all in professional education and he held a tenured appointment in the Department of Education, taught there, and for a long time was head of that Department, I think Ralph's self-concept during the time I knew him seemed to be that of a general social scientist. This perspective may have been deepened as a result of his term as Dean of Chicago's Social Science Division. Broadly conceived, the Division included not only the usual disciplines such as psychology, sociology, and economics but also professional schools such as the Library School and the School of Social Work and Education. This broad view of the social sciences carried over into his conception and development of the Center for Advanced Study in the Behavioral Sciences, which has a similarly wide array of scholars from the social sciences and the professions, including philosophers, theologians, and physicians. [2] It also is manifest in the conception of the National Academy of Education which he was instrumental in starting. The majority of its charter members were social scientists. Though they had worked on the problems of education, many, perhaps most, did not hold appointments on the education faculty on their own campus.

Ralph's view of professional education as a social science was reflected in the makeup of that Department at Chicago. Where relevant, many of its faculty also held appointments either in a social science department or in the Human Development Committee's program. This contrasts with the organization of most departments and colleges of education, which tend to be isolated from their liberal arts colleagues. The budgetary messiness of joint appointments when added to the problems of who and whose standards will control salary, promotion, and tenure can be so simply avoided by single appointments. Yet joint ones have important advantages. Not only do they keep education faculty more abreast of the latest and the best in their social science field, it seems one recruits stronger faculty when seeking those who both want to be related to the base discipline and who are wanted by them. Such considerations tend to offset the administrative prob- lems.

Making the Most of His Capabilities

In recounting Ralph's characteristics, it is clear that he was generously endowed with ability. But as a preacher's son who absorbed the Protestant work ethic, it is equally clear that Ralph worked hard to accomplish all that he did. Rubin notes, "As with others marked by greatness, much of his talent resulted not from inherent gifts alone but from a portfolio of meticulously honed skills. Similarly, the exceptional length of his productivity stemmed neither from good fortune nor from special blessing, but rather from a systematically choreo- graphed program to preserve his abilities. . . . " (Rubin, 1994, p. 784). Rubin visited him in a nursing home several weeks before his death and asked how the night had gone: "His response will stay with me for the remainder of my days. He said, 'Before going to sleep I always ask myself three things: one, what did I learn today; two, what did it mean; and three, how can I use it?" (Rubin, 1994, p. 789).

Ralph intentionally looked for things to admire in people, for the good in what was going on about him, for young talent to nurture, for capable people who could be stretched by delegating to them some of his responsibility, for ways to view problems in perspective as well as to organize past experiences so as to bear on current problems. The topic of metacognition is popular in psychology these days. This set of priorities to which he faithfully attended provided a kind of metacognitive framework that permitted him to accomplish more with his abilities than would otherwise have been possible. It is a lesson worth considering.

Due to failing health, Tyler gradually withdrew from active participation in policy and problem solving. Always a good listener, he would typically sit quietly during a meeting until he had something significant to say, and then lay it out magnificently in such a way as to bring the group along with him, usually putting it in the context of the background of the problem in which he had personally participated. As he realized that the days when he would be available to do this were numbered, however, he became more loquacious, often dominating discussions as he never had in the past. It was as though he was saying "Listen up, you youngsters, I won't be around much longer for you to learn the underpinnings of this enterprise. Here they are, and here is the direction that you must be sure is carried on."

Ralph died in his ninety-second year. I last heard from him as we were gathering material for the National Society for the Study of Education's Yearbook, *Bloom's Taxonomy: A Forty-year Retrospective* (Anderson & Sosniak, 1994). Since I was writing the final chapter, I had contacted Ralph and sent him a draft of the chapter to keep him informed. Much later, I received a brief letter in shaky handwriting apologizing for not having replied sooner but indicating that his illness had prevented it. He stated his interest in the project and his pleasure at seeing the progress made. Even down to the wire, he was still passing out the positives. Those of us who had contact with him were so fortunate to have known such a capable and kind individual.

The Man and His Legacy

Louis Rubin's "rich tapestry of memories" of Ralph particularly impressed me as a rounded thumbnail characterization of the man:

> . . . his bemusement over having three wives and fathering three children, each of whom married into a different religion; his ability to sleep anywhere, anytime, for seven minutes and be restored; his delight with the shiny new red Thunderbird given him by alumni of the Center for Advanced Study; his ability to ingest a 20-page proposal in 20 minutes and refer to it coherently a year later; his penchant for teaching his disciples at every opportunity, whether over egg foo young or while sprinting for a train; his pleasure when Robert Hutchins rushed across a hotel foyer to greet him; his dismay when a world-class educator insisted on carrying his bag to the cab; his tendency to turn off his hearing aid during a hopeless speech; and in Jerusalem, his joy at a pretty young teacher's delight over the nimbleness of his dancing. (Rubin, 1994, p. 785)

Many of us live on only in our students; Ralph certainly will in his. But he achieved so much more as well. I recently received a 50th reunion questionnaire form which asked "What have you done over the last 50 years?" It left exactly one inch of blank space for the answer. Ralph would have needed a book to reply, but he wouldn't have; he was so modest he apparently never responded so there is no entry in *Who's Who in America*. But, much has been written about him, for example: Antonelli, 1972; Hiatt, 1994; Keister, 1978; O'Shea,

1985; Ryan, 1977. There is a collection of his writings on evaluation (Madaus & Stufflebeam, 1989) and at least seven dissertations on his work. The latter are cited along with comments by 16 curriculum scholars and interviews with three who knew him intimately in a dissertation based on his oral history (Rumjahn, 1984). The oral history in which he cooperated is in the Regional Oral History Office, Bancroft Library, University of California at Berkeley. But it is the lasting effects of the programs he ran and institutions he built that provide the enduring monuments to his having been here.

Notes

I am most grateful for the helpful comments and suggestions of Drs. Lee J. Cronbach, Edgar Friedenberg, and Christine McGuire.

1. I am indebted to Dr. Edgar Friedenberg for this apt phrasing of Ralph's skill.

2. The Ralph W. Tyler Collection at the Center contains books donated by former fellows as works "conceived, initiated or completed" while in residence (Converse, 1994, p. 7). Currently numbering more than 1300 titles, the " . . . highly influential works in the social sciences . . . [range] from Pulitzer Prizes to honors bestowed on exceptional books by national disciplinary associations . . ." (Converse, 1994, pp. 7-8).

CHAPTER THREE

Benjamin Bloom, Values and the Professoriate

Lorin W. Anderson

It was still dark when the telephone rang. Although darkness was common during January mornings in Minneapolis, it also was early—7 o'clock. Just before the winter break, I had resigned my teaching position, effective in June. I was unsure of what I wanted to do, but I knew I did not want to teach secondary mathematics any longer—four years was enough. Although I was interested in education, I was not a particularly good teacher.

During the coursework leading to my master's degree, I had become enamored with some of the research conducted at the University of Oregon and had applied for admission to their graduate school of education. On the advice of my master's advisor, Dr. Moy F. Gum, I also had applied for admission to the University of Chicago. He thought I would enjoy the intellectual stimulation that Chicago provided. In addition, he believed I would learn a great deal from his major professor at Chicago, Benjamin Bloom.

I answered the phone, "Hello?" "Hello," said the voice on the other end. "This is Benjamin Bloom. I'm calling to see whether you would be interested in a graduate assistantship here at the University of Chicago." "Sure," I thought to myself, "which of my teaching colleagues is calling me this time?" Since I resigned so early, most of them had accused me of "burning my bridges" prematurely. Several took great pleasure in reminding me that teaching in a Minneapolis suburb was far better than being unemployed. They knew that I had applied to both universities. Deep down inside I thought that I had some chance of being accepted at the University of Oregon but very little chance of attending the University of Chicago. Neither my undergraduate nor graduate school transcripts were models of excellence. If I heard from Chicago at all, it would most certainly be via a form letter, not a personal telephone call from Benjamin Bloom.

Somehow I must have mumbled, "I'm very interested." "Good," replied the voice. "We are having an orientation session for our new students in March. Can you attend?" "I think so," I replied. "I'll send you some information, then," he said. "I'll see you in March. Good-bye." "Good-bye," I said, and hung up the telephone. Later at school, my teaching colleagues denied any foul play. When the letter from Bloom arrived, I was properly convinced and extremely pleased. But I kept wondering, why me?

In March I flew to Chicago for the orientation session. While there I discovered a partial answer to my question. I learned that Bloom had recently returned from a sabbatical in California when he telephoned me. Having no "ready-made" graduate assistants waiting for him, he was forced to seek such assistants through recruitment, hence, my early morning telephone call.

After the initial orientation session was over, I went to Bloom's office. As we talked I became aware of the photograph of a man just over Bloom's shoulder. It was only after I arrived on campus as a full-time student that I learned that the man in the picture was Ralph Tyler.

We talked about the University, the MESA program (Measurement, Evaluation, and Statistical Analysis), my career aspirations, and his current research. As he described his research, he became very animated. He rose from his seat and stood by his chalkboard. He drew picture after picture of sequential learning units and "bell-shaped" curves. As I watched and listened, it became very obvious to me that research was his life, not his livelihood.

I accepted Bloom's offer and returned to my teaching position eager to finish out the year. Mercifully, the school year ended, and I packed up and moved to the South Side of Chicago. Before classes began in the fall, I had time to read five of Bloom's major works: the cognitive taxonomy (Bloom, 1956), the affective taxonomy (Krathwohl, Bloom & Masia, 1964), *Stability and*

Change in Human Characteristics (Bloom, 1964), *Compensatory Education for Cultural Deprivation* (Bloom, Davis & Hess, 1965), and "Learning for Mastery" (Bloom, 1968). I was struck at once by the opposition in his writing: cognitive and affective, stability and change, coverage and mastery. I also was impressed with his belief, particularly evident in these final two works, that education could have a profound effect on people's lives.

It was only after I had studied with Bloom for several months that I discovered the writings that Lee Shulman much later referred to as "the forgotten Bloom." As it turned out, these writings concerning the thought processes of students (Bloom, 1953, 1954) had a more profound influence on my own research than did his more familiar or "popular" works. The central role of students in their learning became the premise on which I based my dissertation research. Specifically, my research focused on student involvement as a mediating factor between what teachers taught and what students learned. Student involvement was defined in terms of both the amount of the involvement (which later became popularized as "time-on-task") and the degree of involvement (which concerned what students were doing and thinking while they were involved in learning). To examine the degree of involvement, I relied on the stimulated recall technique that Bloom had devised in the early 1950s.

The first term I enrolled in my first course with Bloom. The course met at 8 o'clock in the morning, and few of the students were awake at that hour. To my surprise, the course was structured according to the principles of mastery learning. Objectives were clearly specified, and the course was organized into learning units. At the end of each unit we were given a formative test. The answer sheet contained not only spaces in which we could record our answers but also specific pages in the textbook and other learning resources we could consult should we answer a question incorrectly. Furthermore, we were graded according to preset standards. That is, our grades were not based on our relative standing in the class of students. Bloom actually "practiced what he preached."

All students in the MESA program enrolled in a non-credit seminar each term. Each term a different faculty member assumed responsibility for conducting the seminar; my first term at Chicago Bloom was responsible for the seminar. At the initial meeting Bloom distributed a draft of a manuscript entitled "Innocence in Education" (Bloom, 1972). To my amazement, we were asked to critique the manuscript before he submitted it for publication. I had never before been asked to think critically about a professor's writing. I had completed high school and most of college recalling verbatim what I had been taught and applying it in a rote manner to a variety of exercises. With this single assignment, the meaning of "The Taxonomy" became clear to me.

While at the University of Chicago I enrolled in three additional courses and seminars with Bloom while serving as his graduate assistant. During this time he was working on his book *Human Characteristics and School Learning* (Bloom, 1976). As a graduate assistant my primary responsibility was to locate research studies that were related to his proposed conceptual model of school learning. Much of my time was spent in the Regenstein Library searching through volume after volume of journal after journal in an attempt to find these research studies. Having spent a particularly unfruitful weekend in Regenstein, I would return empty-handed. Bloom would pause and consider my excuses. Then he would say, "I know it's there somewhere." Off I would go to once again seek the academic equivalent of the "Golden Fleece."

Bloom was a benevolent taskmaster. He fully understood and appreciated the frustration I experienced in seeking useful studies or writing drafts of my dissertation. He was always available to offer suggestions for locating "hidden studies" or improving the organization or cohesiveness of my writing. Nonetheless, it was clear from the outset that it was my responsibility to find the studies or to write in a way that communicated to him and to others. I remember writing five drafts of the initial chapter of my dissertation.

About a year after I left Chicago, *Human Characteristics and School Learning* was published. Early in this volume, he suggested that his model was "value free." That is, given the parameters included in his model, educators could help or hinder learning, increase or decrease the variation among learners. I have always disagreed with his position on this matter. Values lie at the heart of every educational decision. And, Bloom has clear values, values I endorse. He believes that virtually all children can learn well what schools are expected to teach them (mastery learning). He believes that the primary goal of schooling is to teach children to use their minds well—to think for themselves and develop informed judgment, self-reliance, and responsibility for their own learning (the *Taxonomy*). He believes that early intervention into potential problems will go a long way in preventing them from occurring (*Stability and Change*). Furthermore, more students acquiring more knowledge and skills are better than fewer students learning less knowledge and fewer skills. And although his model could be used to predict how well students could be expected to learn, Bloom clearly was more interested in understanding the ways in which students learned (or failed to learn) so that conditions could be arranged to enhance the quality of learning for the vast majority of students. Quite clearly, not everyone shares these values. In an April 1987 article in *Psychology Today* he was referred to as "the man who would ruin education."

In essence, Bloom has refused to accept the academic equivalent of religious predestination or social Darwinism . And, he has the audacity to support his beliefs with research—with empirical evidence. However, his evidence does not address what is likely to happen in the world of education; rather, it suggests what is possible (a distinction his critics often fail to understand). In his introduction to *All Our Children Learning*, for example, he writes:

> These papers can be read from the perspective of what amounts to a worldwide revolution in educational research and in our understanding of some of the factors that directly influence learning. As a result of the new ideas gained from this research, student learning can be improved greatly, and it is possible to describe the favorable learning conditions which can enable virtually all students to learn to a high standard. (Bloom, 1981, p. 1)

Bloom asked me to write an introduction to one of the sections of this book. In my initial draft I referred to him as "always optimistic." He was quick to point out that he was not always optimistic. In fact, he was not at all optimistic about the future of education; he was downright pessimistic about the extent to which his basic concepts and principles would be successfully applied in schools.

When critics asserted that if his ideas, concepts, and principles applied at all, they applied only to the learning of basic skills, he undertook a major effort to study the development of talent. He studied numerous concert pianists, sculptors, research mathematicians, research neurologists, Olympic swimmers, and tennis champions to find out what "made a difference" in their lives. Based on the findings of this study he was able to conclude that: "no matter what the initial characteristics (or gifts) of the individuals, unless there is a long and intensive process of encouragement, nurturance, education, and training, the individuals will not attain extreme levels of capability in these particular fields. This research has raised questions about earlier views of special gifts and innate aptitudes as necessary prerequisites of talent development" (Bloom, 1985, p. 3).

Bloom's contributions to education are numerous. When I first arrived at the University of South Carolina, I was expected to quote chapter and verse from "The Taxonomy." Despite the fact that the taxonomy had been written some fifteen years before my arrival at Chicago, as Bloom's student I was expected to know its every nuance. Today, some 30 years later, Bloom's taxonomy is included in numerous teacher education and staff development programs.

In 1994, I had the opportunity to co-edit a book entitled *Bloom's Taxonomy: A Forty-year Retrospective* for which Bloom wrote the initial chapter. In this chapter he reflects on the origins of the Taxonomy, the development of the handbook which describes it, and his experiences with a wide variety of applications. He also discusses its critics. In response to these critics, Bloom writes:

> The Taxonomy does not impose a set of teaching procedures, nor does it view objectives as so detailed and restrictive that a single teaching method is implied. Rather, a teacher has a wide range of choices in making instructional decisions related to objectives associated with each level of the Taxonomy.
>
> The Taxonomy does emphasize the need for teachers to help students learn to apply their knowledge to problems arising in their own experiences and to be able to deal effectively with problems that are not familiar to them. This emphasis alone should guard against the rote learning of ready-made solutions. (Anderson & Sosniak, 1994, p. 7)

And Bloom concludes:

> It is obvious, at least to me, that many of the criticisms directed toward the Taxonomy have resulted from very narrow interpretations of both the Taxonomy and its proper application. (Anderson & Sosniak, 1994, p. 7)

Programs based on the principles of "learning for mastery" are still in place today; additional programs are being developed. Not all of these programs are widely accepted philosophically. Critics have assailed such programs as "behavioristic" and "communistic." Apparently, the beliefs that all children can learn or that all children should learn are not shared by all or are frequently compromised in the day-to-day "business" of educating children. It is important to note, however, that the concept of mastery learning is being debated, discussed, and implemented some twenty years after Bloom introduced it. Few ideas survive for that length of time in today's educational marketplace.

Finally, Bloom's data suggesting that talent can be developed in all students runs contrary to those who believe that talent is inborn; that those possessing talent must be identified early and provided with unique learning experiences; that talent is a scarce commodity that must be "guarded" rather than shared. Numerous critics attempt to refute this assertion by bringing to our consciousness a single child whose talent cannot be explained within the context of Bloom's model. Bloom admits that his models are unable to explain the truly exceptional children—those who are mentally-impared, the "idiot savants," the Einsteins of the world. Nonetheless, models that allow us to predict, explain or, perhaps, manipulate the variation that exists among 90 percent of children are certainly worthwhile.

Bloom brings several perspectives to his study of education. He believes in the gathering of evidence, rather than contemplation, as the means to solve educational problems. He believes that education is a powerful source in solving both individual and societal problems. He has at least two unique capabilities: he is "timely" (that is, he is able to anticipate the critical issues facing education), and he is capable of synthesizing large amounts of information into a reasonable, justifiable conceptual framework. The two taxonomies, his model of school learning, and his model of talent development all attest to this latter capability.

Three brief anecdotes are sufficient to illustrate Bloom's commitment to his students, his institution, and his profession. Let us begin with the most personal. A few years after leaving the University of Chicago, I announced to Bloom that I was planning to be married. He inquired as to where and when the ceremony would be held. I provided the information, then told him that invitations would be sent to family members only. "Am I not family?," he asked. Needless to say, he attended the ceremony.

The second anecdote was told to me by my colleague, Tom Guskey of the University of Kentucky. Having received his master's degree from Boston College, Tom was interested in pursuing his doctoral degree. In the middle of winter he decided to visit Stanford University and the University of Chicago. Having completed a successful and "warm" visit to Stanford, he stopped at Chicago on his return trip. After a lengthy discussion with Bloom on the relative merits of Stanford and Chicago, Guskey said, "Well, then, Mr. Bloom, you would say that the University of Chicago is one of the finest universities in this country?" "In the world, Mr. Guskey, in the world!" replied Bloom.

The third anecdote is one I once again experienced directly. I had been invited to speak at a conference held at Rutgers University. In point of fact, however, I had been invited to speak simply because I had been Bloom's student. I was discouraged at that point in my academic career. Some educators at the University of South Carolina had wanted a clone of Bloom; other educators at other institutions had invited me to speak simply because I was Bloom's student. I told Bloom of my state of mind. He recounted a story of an international conference at which a famous psychologist acknowledged a hearty round of applause by saying quietly to Bloom "they are not applauding for me; they are applauding for my father (another psychologist)." Bloom turned to me and said, "They were not applauding for his father. In fact, the students attending that conference had used the textbook this psychologist had written. Of all of the American scholars attending that conference, he was the only one with whom the students had had an ongoing acquaintance because of the book he had written." The lesson was clear. Ultimately, we are judged based on what we accomplish (or fail to accomplish), not on the basis of whose child (academic or biological) we are.

But, for me, Ben is more than his accomplishments and his values. Ben believed in me. He believed in a person who had an undistinguished undergraduate career. Although I completed my undergraduate work with a grade point average around 3.0, most of my grades were A's and C's. Ben picked up on this fact. At the orientation session prior to my enrollment at the university, I asked him directly about my qualifications for the graduate program at the University of Chicago. He replied that in his opinion my undergraduate record indicated that I could achieve what I thought to be important and could get by with the rest. Rarely had anyone captured my view of my schooling as well as he did.

His insight gave me an insight into who Ben Bloom was. Ben was a teacher in the true sense of the word. He had a wonderful experiential background (after all, he had studied with Tyler), he was well read, and he was always raising questions about our possibilities as humans. Additionally, however, he sought out a few students to whom he could impart this knowledge and wisdom. And to this group of students, of which I was fortunately a member, he devoted tremendous time and effort to see that we carried on this academic tradition.

I remember distinctly my last meeting with Ben before leaving for the University of South Carolina. He wished me well. Then, he said in essence, "We've worked together closely for the past two years. I've worked equally closely with many other students over the years. Some of them did not produce what I expected them to. I didn't spend this time with you for you to become a 'run-of-the-mill' professor. I expect you to conduct research and publish the results. I expect you to develop conceptual frameworks for understanding and improving education. I expect you to teach students as well as I have taught you."

It was at this meeting that Ben implicitly shared his vision of the professorate . . . his ideals, his commitment and, above all, his expectations. I came away from this meeting with an understanding that, to use a Gestalt analogy, one's graduate education is more than the sum of the courses completed. Learning to be a professor requires learning from professors. Fortunately, I learned from one of the best.

PART TWO

Standing for the Good:

Professing and Social Responsibility

Hilda Taba: The Congruity of Professing and Doing
by Elizabeth Hall Brady

Boyd H. Bode: The Professor and Social Responsibility
by Kenneth Winetrout

H. Gordon Hullfish: Teaching From the Fire Inside
by Arthur Wirth

Apprentice to Thorndike
by Robert M. W. Travers

The clustering of essays about Hilda Taba, Boyd H. Bode and H. Gordon Hullfish is not surprising inasmuch as they each stood in a pragmatic tradition, and Taba and Hullfish were both profoundly influenced by Bode. But including E.L. Thorndike in the cluster, and under the heading of "Standing for the Good," might well surprise. In fact, both Bode and Hullfish were highly critical of the social conservatism of

Thorndike's conception of the nature of learning, and Thorndike was well aware of their criticism. Yet, running through the lives of these four educators is a profound sense of the social obligations of professors. Robert Travers observes in his essay that Thorndike was very proud of *Human Nature and the Social Order*, fully expecting it to have significant social influence. In the preface to that volume Thorndike nicely sums up his faith: "The welfare of mankind now depends upon the sciences of man." With Taba, Bode, and Hullfish, Thorndike had a profound faith in the power of ideas and in education as a tool of social reform.

Like Bode and Hullfish, much of Taba's professional life was dedicated to creating an education consistent with the demands of a developing democratic society. Brady describes aspects of this work following World War II when Taba directed the Intergroup Education project. Taba was concerned that young people learn how to live together in a world increasingly characterized by divisions of various kinds; this concern was at the center of her curriculum development work. Moreover, as Brady states, the skills associated with living democratically were not abstractions to Taba but were evidenced in how she lived and worked with others. Supporting cooperative approaches to learning, she established "democratic and equitable staff operations" where there was "no ownership of ideas." The same could be said of the others.

The theme of commitment to democratic principles continues through Winetrout's and Wirth's essays. For Bode, democracy was a "way of life," an expression of his faith in the common person's ability to make reasonable judgments when properly informed, to live intelligently, and to look beyond narrow self-interest in order to establish a wider community of interest for the good of all. His challenge was to assist others to confront the assumptions that prevented them from thinking and acting intelligently. Hullfish, Bode's student and later his colleague, shared this vision and proved himself a courageous defender of the freeing of intelligence and a tireless worker who sought to create and maintain educational methods that would "widen the area of agreement with others." Even through the McCarthy era when, on his own campus, the Board of Trustees established a gag rule on outside speakers, Hullfish remained true to his principles despite the possibility of retribution. His aim, like Bode and Taba, was to "develop a vision of the classroom that would be appropriate for the children of a free society."

The lives of Taba, Bode, Hullfish and Thorndike each illustrate nicely a point made by Wirth about Hullfish, that "our mentors offer us their deepest teaching by the stands they take in crises." Some crises are external, produced by the threat of war or persecution, while others seem to originate elsewhere as when Thorndike, prompted by deteriorating health, seemed to shift his attention more toward solving the "problems of human society." Regardless of the threat, these educators stood boldly and unflinchingly for their conceptions of the good, and in standing they invite us to reconsider our most cherished values, of what inspires us to action. They prompt consideration of the stances we take as teachers in the light of their influence on our students. What do we stand for?

Biographical Information

Hilda Taba [born: Dec. 7, 1902, Estonia; died: July 6, 1967, Burlingame, CA] served as professor of education at San Francisco State University from 1951-1967. She was graduated from University of Tartu (Estonia) in 1926 with a B.A.; other degrees include an M.A. from Bryn Mawr College in 1927 and the Ph.D. from Columbia University in 1932. Other professional roles included serving as director of curriculum in an Ohio public school from 1934-1935 and holding professorships in education at Ohio State University from 1936-1938, University of Chicago from 1939-1945 and 1948-1951, and serving as a project researcher for the American Council on Education from 1945-1948. Taba's publications include *The Dynamics of Education* (1932), *Adolescent Character and Personality* (1949) with Robert Havighurst, *Curriculum Development: Theory and Practice* (1962), and *A Teacher's Handbook for Elementary Social Studies* (1967).

Boyd H. Bode [born: Oct. 4, 1873, Ridott, IL; died: March 29, 1953, Gainesville, FL] served as professor of educational philosophy at Ohio State University from 1921-1944. He was graduated from William Penn College (Iowa) in 1896 with an A.B.; other degrees include an A.B. from the University of Michigan in 1897 and the Ph.D. from Cornell University in 1900. Other professional roles included serving as a professor of philosophy and psychology at the University of Wisconsin from 1900-1909 and professor of philosophy at the University of Illinois from 1909-1921. Bode's publications include *Modern Educational Theories* (1927), *Conflicting Psychologies of Learning* (1929), *Democracy as a Way of Life* (1937), *Progressive Education at the Crossroads* (1938), and *How We Learn* (1940).

H. Gordon Hullfish [born: Jan. 3, 1894, Washington, DC; died: June 15, 1962, Columbus, OH] served as a professor of educational philosophy at Ohio State University from 1922-1962. He was graduated from the University of Illinois in 1921 with an A.B.; other degrees include the M.A. in 1922 and Ph.D. in 1924 from Ohio State University. Hullfish's publications include coauthoring *The Educational Frontier* (1933) and *Reflective Thinking: The Method of Education* (1961) with Philip G. Smith and editing *Educational Freedom in an Age of Anxiety* (1953).

Edward L. Thorndike [born: Aug. 31, 1874, Williamsburg, MA; died: Aug. 9, 1949, Montrose, NY] served as professor of psychology at Teachers College, Columbia University, from 1899-1940. He was graduated from Wesleyan University in 1895 with a B.A.; other degrees include an A.B. from Harvard University in 1896 and the Ph.D. from Columbia University in 1898. Other professional roles included a professorship at the College for Women of Western Reserve University (Cleveland) in 1898. Thorndike's publications include *Educational Psychology* (1903), *Principles of Teaching* (1906), *The Measurement of Intelligence* (1927), and *Human Nature and the Social Order* (1940).

CHAPTER FOUR

Hilda Taba: The Congruity of
Professing and Doing

Elizabeth Hall Brady

In January 1945, Hilda Taba began the six-month exploratory phase of the Intergroup Education in Cooperating Schools project, sponsored by the American Council on Education from 1945 to September 1948. World War II had not yet ended, but there were already serious concerns in the United States about social unrest, racial conflicts and riots, and disruptions of human relations. There was uneasiness about the disparity between the avowed commitment of our nation to democracy and equality and certain events during the war then threatening urban communities.

> All of these immediate conflicts, anxieties, and misinterpretations gradually began to be considered concerns of intergroup education. As the project developed, understanding between eighth-graders and adults came to be considered as important a concern as understanding between a Negro and a white person. Essentially the dispositions, attitudes, habits of behavior, and ideas brought to both of the relationships are similar. (Taba et al., 1950, p. 2)

Thoughtful observers believed that public schools, at least in the United States, were in a strategic position to improve human relations. The school brings together under one roof representatives of a greater variety of cultural backgrounds than do the homes, churches, or social agencies. It was during this period between 1943 and 1951 that I saw Hilda regularly, initially as a participant in a workshop for secondary teachers at the University of Chicago, then as I worked on the M.A. degree and finally as a staff member of the Intergroup Project. Hilda was entering the period of her greatest professional contributions, and I was very young and very naive about education, educational theory, and educational change. Although in later years we saw each other fairly often and corresponded frequently, it was in this earlier period that she had her greatest influence upon me.

I wish I could portray for you how Hilda seemed when I first knew her. She was very energetic, enthusiastic, active, seemingly tireless. She led life at a tempo that sometimes resulted in misunderstandings and often wore out friends and staff. She was small in stature, perky in manner and in dress—she always dressed in a very individual way. There was that sense that she was always intent on the next destination and on the next task to be completed. She loved ideas. She stimulated everyone around her to talk—very satisfying and often argumentative talk about a project, or current events, or campus politics, or whatever. I can remember, for example, long discussions on whether any individual learner had enough experience of rejection in one's personal life to really comprehend what it means to be rejected as a member of a minority group. We had our own ideas and opinions, and we wrestled long and loud over this kind of issue.

The Intergroup Education project had many such issues. During the first nine months the pilot study included Cleveland, Milwaukee, Pittsburgh, and South Bend—all large industrial cities. This pilot study served to identify problems, to explore promising approaches and techniques, and to establish the basic method of cooperation. The second period—from September 1945 to September 1947—was devoted chiefly to developing a variety of programs on a fairly broad scale with eighteen school systems. More than 250 local projects in 72 schools or community groups were undertaken through the combined efforts of 2,500 classroom workers, teachers, school administrators and community people. While we faced segregated school systems among this group, by design there were no cities in the deep South in the Intergroup Project. We felt at the time that we didn't know enough to contend with the special problems that existed in those states. We were dealing mostly with northern industrial communities.

During the first two years of the project, the skeleton of the program was created. Major techniques for diagnosing needs were identified and tried out in many schools. Instructional patterns were developed for intergroup relations at all grade levels—kindergarten through twelfth grade—and in a variety of subject areas. A variety of plans and patterns for community action were also tried and studied. In those days not only teachers came to summer workshops but also ministers, pastors, police officers, and community workers. Six workshops were held: one in 1945, three in 1946, one in 1947, and one in 1948. Two hundred and sixty teachers and community workers participated. The summer workshop was an important artifact of education, one which came directly out of the Eight Year Study.

The final year of the *initial* project, September 1947-September 1948, was devoted to analyzing report findings and experiences. Three curriculum reports were prepared during this period (Taba, 1949; Taba, 1950; Taba, 1951). [The project continued as the Center for Intergroup Education and was housed at the University of Chicago until 1951.]

The home office was in New York City; during the school year the staff would go out for up to three weeks in the field and then come back for a concentrated period of describing, analyzing, and planning. We would then go out for another three weeks and repeat the process through the year. Hilda usually made the initial visit to a district to orient them to the project and to learn more about the local school system and the local community. When staff members arrived, they were taken to a school where interest had been expressed in the Intergroup Project. We came to refer among ourselves to these as "browsing" and "blowing" sessions. The first, the "browsing" sessions, would be very low key and exploratory; staff members would explain the project, describe possible areas of work, and ask about local concerns. It was typically polite and factual and often concluded with a perfunctory willingness to communicate. "Shall we come back next month?" "Yes, please do, but no more than that." The "blowing" sessions, often the second visit, were

another matter. Teachers poured out frustrations at the present
school program, at the school board, at the principal, at fellow
teachers, at anybody. They expressed their anger and fear—
there was a lot of fear—and they revealed down-to-earth
irritations and anxieties and even their own feelings of
inadequacy. Through it all the consultant would listen without
judging or advising. Eventually the consultant would help the
teachers focus on some specific concern or some specific change
they wanted to see occur. To give a very simple, brief example, I
remember one school where the teacher wanted the children to
"become more responsible" and along with this hoped that the
mothers would become more responsible, too. The teacher noted
that the children didn't do their school work and frequently
didn't have milk in their lunches or, in some other way,
demonstrated irresponsibility on the part of students and
mothers.

The teacher agreed to have the children keep a diary of
daily activity before the next visit of the consultant. When the
diaries were read she discovered to her surprise and horror
that these children whom she had seen as irresponsible were in
fact overwhelmed with duties and tasks and chores at home—
where everyone, in fact, was overworked, and where, for
example, mothers didn't have milk on hand because there was
no refrigeration to keep it cold. So from that point she began to
change entirely her view of what might be needed.

The project was experimental and was designed to explore
the development of curriculum approaches and materials. It
was intended to prepare program patterns and to equip
cooperating persons to continue exploring after the project
ended. I think this is very important—we didn't intend to close
up shop when the project was no longer funded. But that had to
be planned for. The core of the program was action in all
areas—whichever the cooperating group deemed most important for them. The project always began with the local and
immediate, and cooperative working relationships reflected an
intent to work for human relations objectives in ways consistent
with those objectives. You couldn't treat people harshly or
with prejudice and still be talking about the content of human
relations education.

Hilda loved to have people around her and she liked parties impromptu or planned. I knew well four of her homes in the United States. The one I recall best, for good reason, was the large roomy apartment on Morningside Drive in New York City. In those immediate post-World War II days housing was very difficult to find. Hilda shared her space during the early days of the Intergroup Project with whoever on staff needed a temporary place to sleep—from a single night to weeks. Her home was always open to us for parties and for holidays—my husband roasted his first Christmas goose there. She did this partly because the staff of the Intergroup Project in the early days often worked six or seven days a week. Most of us did not have families and knew no one in New York City. So the staff became something of an extended family for each other.

Later an equally large apartment in the Hyde Park section of Chicago, near the University of Chicago, became the center of our long talkative staff meetings and our wonderful parties. It was to this apartment in Hyde Park in 1949 or 1950 that Hilda's brother, Paul, and his family came upon arriving in the United States from Europe. They had suffered many of the vicissitudes of war and displacement. It was to this home also that Mrs. Kulmalik came, also from Europe. She became Mrs. K. to all of us—cook, organizer of Hilda's household and, I'm sure for Hilda, a link to Estonia and home.

When we left Chicago at the closing of the Center for Intergroup Education in 1951, Hilda became a professor at San Francisco State College, and Mrs. K. went along as housekeeper and friend. Hilda soon found a charming house in Millbrae, a suburb of San Francisco. It is there that I think of her in the last fifteen years of her life. There was a beautiful garden, a goldfish pool by the entry walk, and a beautifully furnished interior. What I remember particularly was the intriguing mix of mementos from Hilda's trips to speak all over the United States and to Europe for UNICEF. Those mementos provided a comfortable and welcoming atmosphere. There was always a wealth of books and records in all the places where she lived. I remember one of the first things that I heard about in the Morningside Drive apartment was Hilda's love of playing records and how she kept a whole stack of quilts in a closet off the living room where they could be taken out and spread on the floor so that everyone could lie down and enjoy some piece of classical music. There were always guests and parties—guests would pitch in to help in the kitchen or the garden, and exuberant conversations went on in every room.

The fourth place, although it really came third in order, was known simply as "the farm." Occupied during the Chicago years only on weekends and later for a time by Hilda's brother, his wife, and two children, the farm was in lower Michigan and was close enough to Chicago to drive to on a Friday afternoon—to stay until Sunday when we had to fight our way back through weekend traffic to the university. This was an old-fashioned, two-story farmhouse with no embellishments or fancy gadgets. Many of the staff spent the summer weekends there. I remember the farm particularly in 1946 when my husband and I had just been married. We took with us food and drink and our sleeping bags as there was little furniture. Nevertheless, we all enjoyed those weekends tremendously. It was a wonderful setting for talk of ideas on hot, lazy summer afternoons. We were constantly going over what had happened in our schools, comparing reactions of the teacher participants in the workshop, sharpening the concept of perception and the perceptions we were formulating about intergroup education, arguing about what it really was about or what it should be about, arguing about what the schools could do, learning to know each other better and also to know better the concepts that went into the theoretical framework of intergroup education.

A major point of difference in the 1940s had to do with underlying assumptions about the future of the United States. At that time, many citizens and public figures took pride in what is often called the "melting pot" theory. This point of view acknowledges with approval those immigrants who in the past became Americans by gradually giving up their own cultures in order to adopt "the American way"—certainly an assimilationist view. One national educational agency was arguing in the 1940s that intercultural education should further this point of view. At the time, I recall Hilda remarking that she would not presume to say in what direction we should go as a nation of people. This would have to develop over time. Since then, we have seen the emergence of fierce declarations of identity, separateness, and independence on the part of ethnic and racial groups. We have seen the "melting pot" superseded variously by the patchwork quilt and the tossed salad, in which each ingredient retains its integrity, and great effort and pride is directed to praise the cultural heritage of separate groups. This is not to say that the issue has been resolved. I still hear many approving references to the United States as a "melting pot" and other references to the multicultural approach which when translated means becoming "American" and discarding or giving up particular cultural aspects.

We worked long hours and very hard on the Intergroup Education project. I still value those years as the most satisfying professional experience of my life. Many people found Hilda demanding, forceful, difficult. An advantage of cooperative effort is that as a staff we could learn from each other, but also we developed skills in augmenting each other's talents, in complementing each other's deficits, and reading the feelings and reactions of the people we were working with so that we could communicate more effectively. I think I had my first opportunity during that project to really understand why a team approach to consulting or to teaching has so many advantages, because we could do just these things for each other and could therefore be more effective in schools than any one of us alone could have been.

In a staff directed by Hilda, ideas were valued for their appropriateness and meaningfulness, not for who gave voice to them. Anyone might express a good idea and that idea would be recognized for its relevance to the problem we were wrestling with no matter from whom it came. A significant incident during the first year underscored the extent to which this point of view made for a democratic and equitable staff operation. During one of our lengthy staff meetings, a senior member of the staff turned to me, the most junior, and pointing a finger for emphasis said, "Write that down for me, dear!" Of course, I did. It wasn't until long afterwards that I learned from another staff member that Hilda later called in this person and pointed out that I, though junior, was a full-fledged member of the staff and not there to provide that kind of service for others. I'm sure this was hard for people not only older than I but whose experience in education had long been in hierarchical situations where junior members did take notes for and run errands for senior members. I mention this because I think it was central to the way Hilda believed in working with people. It was a combination of respecting and valuing individuals and their ideas and the fostering of cooperative effort combined to create a congenial and productive staff experience.

Unlike other people I've known, Hilda never seemed to be seeking disciples. Perhaps that is the reason that in a sense she had many. But I have never at any time felt that Hilda was looking to have people be her disciples, to have them view her as the leader and the font of knowledge. I've known other people who did do that, sometimes by only letting out information in little bits and pieces, sometimes by insisting upon proper symbols of status and authority, but I never felt at any time that this was a necessary part of Hilda's personality or professional style.

I have digressed into these personal aspects of Hilda's life as background to why Hilda had such an influence on me and on others. I could say that she was my mentor; I think that that word used to have a different sense. Right now it seems to mean this is a person who knows the ropes and who will help me get ahead. But it used to be something else—there was a kind of element of serendipity in it. In that sense she was my mentor. There was a recognition that the ways of living and working that she had adopted made sense, that these ideas and goals were important ones, and that there could be a coherence between how one lives and the professional posture one assumes.

I wish to conclude by noting four ideas which have had great impact for me and which emerged from my time with Hilda. The first of these was our view that there was *no ownership of ideas*. This seems to go contrary to academic tradition and so it does. Hilda believed it and both preached it and practiced it. It made for freer and more open discussion of ideas in staff meetings and in working with teachers. Ideas were to be shared with others, and one did not worry about who published what first. Traditional academic life has not provided much space for the exercise of this idea—sometimes it seems we move farther and farther away because of the competitiveness and achievement orientations which have so pervaded universities.

A second idea is one of *concomitant learning*. This is a term I have not heard for some years, but when I first heard it in an early seminar with Hilda, it made a profound impression on me. Basically, concomitant ideas—good and bad—are those ideas that we learn even when something else is the primary focus. As a teacher, we may elicit an adequate performance in the skills of reading, for example. Yet, the child that is learning to read may develop a dislike of reading as a result, a determination to read only when made to read for a grade, a reward, or some external demand. If we do not consciously and deliberately plan for all dimensions of learning, the learner may acquire attitudes and feelings and ways of thinking we do not intend or want; of course, this can be a peculiarly potent problem in the area of human relations education or intergroup education.

A third important idea was certainly one of *learning inductively*. Starting with the familiar and moving gradually to new insights and new levels of understanding—this is an integral aspect of the Taba curriculum process. Often people who use this approach may still fall back on didactic methods with their adult students. Of course, one of the pervasive ideas that I learned working with Hilda was the importance of congruence of adult learning with the kind of learning we were advocating for children. This is something I find many people still don't recognize. In the groups that worked on curriculum development, and there was always one such group in the workshop, adults would be planning units for their own group of students. During the weeks of the summer they would be led gradually through the process of curriculum development as formulated by Hilda.[1] I often worked with her in that particular group and invariably at the end of the summer someone would say, " Well, why didn't you tell us all this in the beginning." This happened so often that one year I asked Hilda if we could do just that and she said, "Why not." So we did. We started the workgroup by giving them all the aspects of the curriculum framework and spelling it all out. Having explicated the curriculum design the first week, we proceeded inductively through the process. At the end of the summer someone burst out, "Well, why didn't you tell us all this in the first place." People simply don't hear what they are not ready to understand!

A fourth idea is *cooperation as a way of learning*. In recent years cooperative learning has garnered a great deal of attention as a result of research carried out at the University of California at Santa Cruz, the University of Minnesota, Johns Hopkins University, and from the efforts of a nationwide network of teachers and professors to foster cooperative learning in classrooms. Hilda not only accepted the idea that more can be learned and more can be accomplished with this approach—cooperation was also the model for staff functioning in which each person brought back descriptive case studies of work in the schools to share with the colleagues who then joined in discussing appropriate interventions. It was the mode of work which school faculties and school community groups were encouraged to try. It was also the foundation of small group learning activity in classrooms.

I found myself the other day telling an anecdote about one such experience when I visited a very bright group of tenth grade students in what was known as a very good school. Each one was working intently at their desks and I asked one of them what he was doing. He commented that each was doing a project on the importance of cooperative effort in social change. And I said, "But, you seem to be working as individuals. Why aren't you working in committees or groups?" He looked shocked and said, "But then someone else might get a better grade." How ironic this incongruence in the way of working! The staff of the Intergroup Education project had to do a lot of cajoling and persuading to get people to think that cooperation was a good way to go given the prevalence of competition.

These four ideas: *cooperation, learning inductively, concomitant learning, and no ownership of ideas* are ones that seem to me to have always pervaded the ways of working that Hilda had undertaken in her own work before I knew her, in the

Intergroup Project, and also later in her work in San Francisco. Once I was experiencing great frustration at how long change takes and how great the likelihood is that something our staff had helped create would be wiped out when we returned to the school or the district. I asked Hilda, thinking of her Eight Year Study role, if she did not become discouraged when she returned to a place where she had worked long and hard only to find no trace of her work. After some reflection she answered, "Yes, but not for long. When something you've worked long and hard for seems to just disappear, sometime later, often when you don't expect it, in some totally different place, the person you thought had forgotten shows up, or the program that had died in the other place is underway or thriving here, or something is successful that wasn't really understood in the other place—and that makes up for everything."

Notes

1. This was later developed into Hilda's curriculum text, what is considered one of the important curriculum texts of the mid-20th century. I recall in the early sixties sitting on the floor of the study at Hilda Taba's house debating a suitable title for her curriculum book, what became *Curriculum Development: Theory and Practice* (Taba, 1962). We would take a book off the shelf and try to modify and play with the title and see if it worked. Hilda remarked that she would very much like to use "The Process of Curriculum Development," a title which fit very well. However, she said, if she chose that then Jerome Bruner would think it was derivative, since his *The Process of Education* (1960), had recently been published. And she said, "Bruner is a psychologist." She implied that he lacked proper regard for education as a field of study and inquiry in its own right. This could certainly not be said of Hilda. Her doctoral dissertation, completed at Teachers College in 1932 under John Dewey, displays her high regard for the work of educators. *The Dynamics of Education* (Taba, 1932) as it was titled when published, established Hilda as an educator with deep concern for the problems and the process of education.

CHAPTER FIVE

Boyd H. Bode: The Professor and Social Responsibility

Kenneth Winetrout

Boyd H. Bode looked out over the world and saw a landscape marred by obstacles, roadblocks, varying in size, in age. Some had become huge monuments over the millennia. People brought flowers as to a shrine; at times, men with swords or guns stood guard to see that no defacements took place; poets sang songs in praise. Others were products of centuries, or decades—some but a small blip on the landscape. Each of them in its own way stood in the way of decent men and women becoming free-thinking individuals, hindered the effort, the dreams, of those who would build a more humane and a more democratic society, an educational system appropriate for solving the problems of the day.

Boyd H. Bode had a name for these roadblocks, these obstacles: he called them "Absolutes." They were the enemy, the evil empire. And Bode had a way to attack these impedimenta. It was the method of dialogue. Not quite the "I-Thou" dialogue of Martin Buber but rather the Platonic—Socratic dialogue of probes and questionings. With Bode there would be no preexistence to tap and surely no preordained truths at the end of the process. Nothing was ever quite certain once Bode got going on a dialogue. He rarely lectured the full class period. The whole period might be devoted to one long dialogue with one student, with several students, or with the whole class. Or again, he might interrupt his lecture to engage in a brief dialogue, a minute or two.

If the going got too rough for the student, Bode would break the tension with a smile followed by his loud, coughed-out guffaws. Always loud and always with this coughed-out quality, he did guffaw a lot, and this was part of the persona we students knew. He was a good man, a kindly professor, a brilliant thinker. He had a way with language; it was charming, delightful, down to earth, and incisive. One paper came back with this comment: "Interesting paper. It has one serious fault—it does not formulate the issue which is involved. This is important, since it is needed for formulating an educational program." Incisive language—to the point.

In a way, Bode was Ohio State University's William Kilpatrick and George Counts—with some John Dewey thrown in—all in one man. Bode had this aura about him. One felt it back then. Yet, in what went on in the classroom—direct impact on what took place in a measurable way in an individual teacher's classroom—the chances are that such professors as Harold Alberty, Lou LaBrant, Edgar Dale, Alan Griffin, Laura Zirbes played a more decisive role than did Bode.

Still—almost everywhere—one had this sense of the presence of Boyd H. Bode, this tall man in the rumpled blue suit (did he have another suit?) and uncombed hair. There was Bode. We felt it. He did not spread himself thin, did not hit the lecture tour to promote this or that reform. He had no blueprint like George Counts for a new social order. No blueprint for curricular reform. No new methodology to pass on. But he had a vision; he had a mission.

He did not share his private life with us. He had a son. He had a daughter, Eleanor, who followed him into the philosophy of education. We all knew how much he loved baseball. But we knew little of the private Bode.

Even after fifty years, memories remain of Bode's use of dialogue—quite vivid memories. One is with a student. The student was a young woman working on her M.A. Bode questioned her on her religion. Pushing her into this corner, then that corner. As she was on the verge of tears, Bode ended his dialogue, his probing. Bode had this gentle, grandfatherly way about him, but he could and would push students, keep them on the other end of that dialogue longer than they would wish. Bode had this mission—slay absolutes—and he would push students hard, very hard, in his war. Frederick Neff recounted a student remarking that in Bode's classes "we had to leave our souls stacked outside his door." We did. Neff writes: "He came, not as an emissary of compromise and appeasement, but with 'fire and sword,' and we soon learned both to be wary of and to delight in the barbed wit that flowed through his lectures" (Neff, 1954, p. 229).

A second dialogue—this was with an enemy, an opponent, a man on the other side of the battle line. His name was Stringfellow Barr, and he was devoted to promoting the Great Books. It was a debate sponsored by Columbus Town Meeting of the Air and the setting was Otterbein College in nearby Westerville. Barr and Bode went at it tooth and nail. Few punches were pulled. When it was over, one could hear Bode doing his guffaws surrounded by graduate students from Ohio State. It had been a rough and tough debate. Hard to say who won. This was Bode's life: He went after the issues where victories do not come easily.

A third dialogue—this with a friend, a colleague, H. Gordon Hullfish. It was in one of those large summer Bode classes. Hullfish in the last row, Bode up front by the desk. The exchanges were sharp and penetrating. The give and take as intense as that with Stringfellow Barr. But no dirty looks this time. Some of us were taken aback: How could this young man, Hullfish, so challenge this older man, Bode? What we were seeing here as in the other dialogues was the dedication Bode had for the method of dialogue and the sincerity of his quarrel with absolutes. It was a fine learning experience for those of us privileged to be present.

Somehow we students back in the 1930s got the idea that the College of Education had two representative men—in an Emersonian sense. There was W.W. Charters who represented the research and methodology aspects of education and Bode, who *Time* magazine described, ironically, as "Progressive Education's No. 1 present-day philosopher," who represented the philosophy and theory aspects. But Bode cannot be left at this distance in time in just memories, personal memories. So we must turn to his books to get perspective, insights that influenced generations of students, that influenced me. We are fortunate that he left behind a number of books, just as alive and engaging as his classroom work. He was not two persons, one in the classroom and another in his books. There was but one Bode.

First, Bode and those absolutes. *Progressive Education at the Crossroads* (Bode, 1938a) was the book that attracted the most attention and brought on the most controversy at the time of publication. Further, it could be the most relevant of his works for us as we wind up this century. It calls us to consider the peculiar place of education in a democracy and the social responsibilities of education and educators. Prompted by John Childs' review, a debate followed its publication, a debate covered in the pages of the *Social Frontier*. Sides were drawn. Bode responded.

> What troubles me is the fear that Dr. Childs, in an excess of zeal, sacrifices both the ideal and the method of democracy. . . . Under the impetus of indignation, however, he shows a disposition to identify democracy with a campaign for a specific scheme of ownership and distribution. Hand in hand with this goes a bold demand for "inculcation" and for a crusade to win adherents. . . . The . . . alternative is to center our program on the meaning or implications of democracy in a modern world. Unfortunately, this is too revolutionary a proposition to make it likely that it will be adopted very widely, but there seems to be no other choice . . . . (Bode, 1938b, pp. 39-40)

It is a small book, 122 pages, but it gives a good idea of just where Bode stood on absolutes. Absolutes had long been in the saddle and did indeed ride mankind. There was "a whole tribe of absolutes" to contend with: Plato's ideals, property rights, nationalism, racial dictatorships, and theological dicta. The concerns of the "common man" counted for but little in comparison with these "august absolutes."

For a long time these absolutes had things pretty much their own way in the academic world. They had, indeed, frequent squabbles among themselves, but there was little disposition to challenge the principles of absolutism, in spite of the fact that no one has as yet succeeded in giving a convincing account of what an absolute is really like as a "real" thing.

Since the whole weight of tradition is on the side of absolutes, which are abstractions that served to maintain an aristocratic form of society, such a system must have direct and constant reference to the conflict between the aristocratic and the democratic ways of life. "Absolutist beliefs and modes of thinking are far too deeply ingrained in our civilizations to be laid aside very easily." It is our schools which must train us to look to consequences and not to authority for guidance in our conduct.

But forces were at work. There are two sets of demands: "our traditional loyalty to the eternal verities" and "those made by a world of flux." The new demands "are growing in numbers and volumes, and it is becoming increasingly difficult to silence them in contemptuous contrast with the engaging serenity of the beautiful isle of somewhere." As Henry Adams once said: "Events would educate."

Other factors were at work. There was science. There was, in Bode's words, "this widening of the horizon." One could sense a demand for "the reconstruction of the whole mess of traditional beliefs."

And we had education. Education was moving beyond being devoted solely to skills. Now attitudes and appreciation would be part of education. Education would be seen now, "not merely as a preparation for future living but a form of present living." And once the present comes center stage in our schools, tradition and absolutes are no longer sacred. It was a new ballgame; absolutes were no longer sure winners.

What is more, we had democracy. We had it in John Dewey's *Democracy and Education* in 1916. And we got it in the teaching and writing of Boyd Bode. There would be a marriage of democracy and the schools. The "common man" would come into his own.

A few thoughts of Bode's on democracy must be mentioned. Democracy means "the continuous widening of the area of common interests and concerns"; "the maximum development of the individual"; "democracy rests on no other authority than the nature of the individual himself; it can never claim fixity or finality." It is "a challenge to absolutes of whatever kind," "to all the absolutes of history." It means "the reshaping of our entire way of life." It is "a way of life."

We have Bode's common man (as stated in *Progressive Education at the Crossroads*). Democracy "stands or falls by its faith in the common man." The good life is seen "as a continuous reconstruction of the basis of sensitiveness to all human values." Bode's message is clear. Down with absolutes; up with democracy. We pursue this dual goal by means of education. And, pray tell, what must our schools do to accomplish all of this?

Education must develop a theory. "We turn, in short, from practice to theory in order to make our practice more effective than it was before." Our schools will need to distance themselves more and more from the old philosophies and more and more incorporate science. Education "stands or falls by its faith in the common man." It will be seen as "a progressive liberation of intelligence." It is "a process of growth; it means the liberation of capacity." The specialist must be given no favors. "The specialist in education is all too often a person who cannot see the woods for the trees." Education must see to it that "no man, even though he be a teacher, has the right to appoint himself the keeper of his neighbor's soul."

If we would bring individuals, their scholarship, actions, temporal positioning into a meaningful focus, we may ask: What would Boyd Bode say, do, if he were alive today? This simple procedure should facilitate arriving at a comprehensive view of oneself as a member of a professoriate and one's own relevance to the present and perhaps to the future. A code word in these final years of the 20th century is "reinvent." In some quarters, it is the clarion call. It is no longer enough to moderate, to innovate; we must go the full route. Bode would bring this concept to the educational profession at large and in particular to the professoriate. He would want to know where we stand and what we stand for; he would want us to examine our assumptions.

Bode was an active player in the movement that comes closest to qualifying as a reinvention of education: that time when progressive education, pragmatism, and Deweyanism were center stage in the 1920s and 1930s. By comparison, today's education is in a state of doldrums. Bode would want us to get up and run today. Let's be honest. Where is the excitement, the action, the radicalism in our professoriate today?

Bode would want to stir things up. Get us moving again. And surely the need for reinvention is greater today. Writing about the decline in America has become a growth industry in the 1990s.

Bode would council the professoriate to reach out to other disciplines as education has rarely done. This could move us toward that new sense of community we hear so much about—to bring about caring, sharing, and compassion. It seems likely that Amitai Etzioni in *The Spirit of Community* would be assigned reading in his classes. Bode might very well not want to be an active advocate of the communitarianism promoted by Etzioni, but he would welcome this movement as one dimension of the reinvention process. Here, teachers might find new commitments with which to get involved. The school is a central part of communitarianism. "If the moral infrastructure of our communities is to be restored, schools will have to step in where the family, neighborhoods, and religious institutions have been failing" (Etzioni, 1993, p. 89).

> Education proceeds by tying gratification to the development of qualities that are socially useful and morally appropriate. That is, by relating satisfaction to completing a task, taking other people's feelings into account, playing by the rules, and so on, one acquires the ability to abide by moral tenets and to live up to one's social responsibilities. (Etzioni, 1993, p. 92)

Etzioni would have a year of national service as an "antidote to the ego-centered mentality," which is too prevalent today (Etzioni, 1993, p. 113).

The Bode we knew in the 1930s does not suggest one whose office would be filled with computers, word processors, fax machines. His office was simple. But yet this much seems certain: Bode would see all this technology as a part of the re-invention process. His attention would be on the entity of technology, not just one aspect of it or one tool.

Here again I see Bode placing another book on a required reading list: Richard Stivers' *The Culture of Cynicism*. Generally speaking we in education have not examined with much concern the implications of technology. Stivers states "A technological civilization greatly diminishes the opportunity for ethical action." Rather we come up with a "bureaucratic morality," an anti-morality. Technology is basically no more than "an expression of power." "Shared experience and traditions" become "irrelevant." It is a consumption-dominated world. We experience a "sterilization of time"; a "technological utopianism" exists (Stivers, 1994, pp. ix-x.). There is despair; ethics remains in the background. Bode would not likely accept all the negativism of Stivers, but this book, *The Culture of Cynicism*, could play a major part in Bode's effort to bring us to profound dialogue about our current condition.

Nothing was closer to Bode's heart and mind than the well-being of the common man. Today, turn where one may, it seems that the common man is taking some hard knocks. Polarization has become a mantra in our day; polarization into rich and poor, into dumb and bright. *The Bell Curve* (Herrnstein, 1994) is not just an intelligence score; it also tells you where someone fits on the annual income statistics. Bode would fuss over this.

Again we come upon a required book: Kevin Phillips' *Arrogant Capital* (1994). Here we encounter a conservative Republican talking revolution in the United States. Talking revolt. He even advocates a populist revolt. Not quite the message we expect from a Republican. But he does give us a dramatic platform for change; a detailed one it is. While Bode would not follow the path set forth by Phillips, he would turn to some of his ideas, his reforms.

We could go on and on. We have the rise of special interest groups and globalization. We have seen the end of communism, perhaps of socialism, perhaps of capitalism (Drucker, 1993). So much is dying; so much is being born. We suffer overloads of various sorts. Crime is on everyone's mind. However dedicated they are, our teachers, our professoriate, are not quite on the front line to solve these enormous problems. Perhaps we are unwilling; perhaps we are unable to help.

Boyd Bode as role model? Maybe. There are dangers in looking to the past for our role models. But Bode does have some promising qualities for our present professoriate. His method was in large part that of dialogue. Sincere open dialogue might help us grow, advance, inspire. Perhaps above all else, it is his faith in the common man that counts most. What have we done for the common man? Bode would agonize: Why haven't our schools become more humane institutions? Categories divide us; economics divide us. Yet, in spite of it all, Bode would not ask George Counts' question: Dare the schools build a new social order? Rather, he would ask: Dare—can—the schools bring into being the thinking individual, the democratic common man and woman?

We could use a few Boyd Bodes today. One hot summer day, and summer days can be hot and steamy in Columbus, Ohio, Bode passed several of us students on the steps of Arps Hall, on the way up to his office after having met his class. He turned to us, made a gesture to the heat and said, "I guess I'll just have to let the world save itself." Said in jest, a response to the discomfiture of the day; yet in a way he reminded me that he did have a mission. For Bode it was the war with absolutes; the cause of the common man and of the democratic society. That was his mission then; that is his message to us today. I hope he can be heard.

CHAPTER SIX

H. Gordon Hullfish:
Teaching From the Fire Inside

Arthur Wirth

H. Gordon "Hank" Hullfish came into my world at a critical moment. In July 1945, I was retraining in Texas with thousands of veterans of the European theater preparing for the assault against Japan. In early August the fury of nuclear explosions destroyed Hiroshima and Nagasaki, and by the end of that month I was back in my hometown of Columbus, Ohio—in "civvies" and completely unsure about what next. My cousin Bob Wagner, documentary film-maker at Ohio State who had completed his doctorate in education under Edgar Dale, suggested, "While you are trying to get it together, why not try a couple of courses with Hullfish and Alan Griffin? There is still time to register."

Coming to education with my A.B. and M.A. (completed in history just before the war), I found myself suddenly in new terrain. Within a few weeks I was hooked. Hullfish was introducing me to John Dewey—Dewey's concept of democracy as a form of living—a form of living that supported the search for meaning and growth in experience. "Maybe that's what all of the warring had been about," I thought. With the war behind us we had a fresh chance to create a liberating society through the education of the young and through the reconstruction of our institutions that had been near collapse in the 1930s.

Beyond the reading of Dewey and Mead, there was something about the teaching of Hullfish that introduced me to a Deweyan way of coming at life. In the years that followed his influence continued—from the way he carried himself as a person and as a professional in meeting the contentious issues of his time. I want to comment on both my experience with him as a teacher and my reflections on the way he personally brought his philosophy to bear in the "culture wars" of his era.

Hullfish as Teacher

Gordon Hullfish had an unusual capacity to make a difference in the lives of a large number of students. I was one of them. I say this not primarily to praise him but to inquire why it was so.

It seems clear to me that his power as a teacher derived from his personal vision of the job. This vision, in turn, was rooted in facts of his own life and in his philosophical view of what it meant to be a human being. In all respects it is a very American story.

As a boy he lived in Washington, D.C., in a house located on the site of the present Supreme Court building. He grew up in the shadow of the Capitol. His mother worked as a nurse to support three small children alone. Of necessity Hullfish was thrown much on his own resources, working as a newspaper boy in the region of the White House and later as a messenger at the U.S. Treasury.

He never finished high school. In fact he was continuously in trouble in school. With his bright mind and free spirit fed by the colorful, informal atmosphere in which he moved as a boy, the dull, restrictive quality of the traditional schools repelled him from the beginning. The content of studies and the sterile preoccupations of his teachers had a remoteness from live ideas and the texture of real life that made his school experience a graphic example of the waste in education that Dewey portrayed in *The Child and the Curriculum and the School and Society*:

> The great waste in school comes from [the child's] inability to utilize the experiences he gets outside the school in any complete and free way within the school itself while, on the other hand, he is unable to apply in daily life what he is learning at school. That is the isolation of the school—its isolation from life. (Dewey, 1956/ 1900, p. 75)

In an exploratory period after leaving school he held various jobs both in Washington and in New York. The chance to return to formal learning at the University of Illinois came only because a Washington lawyer saw in him a capability that needed training, and a chemist furnished the loan that made possible his entrance to the university. Since he lacked a high school diploma, the College of Agriculture was the only area of the campus with a loophole in its entrance requirements that would permit him to begin his studies. Later he switched to journalism but, in his maverick way, he elected courses that took him to the far reaches of the campus.

A new world was opening to him. He was four or five years older than most of his fellow students. While many of them were "taking" courses in the familiar credit-collecting way, the university experience, which young Hullfish never had expected to share, offered him exciting, intellectual fare. The critical point came when he encountered Boyd Bode in a philosophy course in his junior year. Here Hullfish found a teacher who made the class a place that was alive with ideas. After his youthful wanderings, a great midwestern land grant university had made it possible for him to locate the venture to which he could commit his life.

Thus one American youth, with the tenacious quality of individuality in which we take verbal pride, had two kinds of experiences in American schools. One (by far the more common) was a deadening one that nearly crippled his spirit; the other released his mind and imagination and enabled him to develop a productive, deeply satisfying life. Gradually there emerged the realization that what had happened to him might happen or fail to happen to countless others. It seems to me that this background helps to explain the second factor that gave shape to his concept of teaching: the deep and enduring hold that American pragmatism had on his mind. As he encountered the work of Boyd Bode and John Dewey, their analyses of mind, thinking, and the process of learning provided the kinds of insights that explained the differences he had encountered in the two kinds of classrooms. His own enlightening experience with a few great teachers plus the understanding of the nature of the process provided by pragmatic thought combined to give him a vision of what teaching ought to be.

While his most enduring influence may have come through his work with graduate students, his own concept of teaching might best be revealed by a consideration of his course for seniors. He loved this course, seeing it as a chance to help them assimilate ideas from previous study and to gain a perspective for their future work as teachers.

He tried to help them develop a vision of the classroom that would be appropriate for the children of a free society. In helping them arrive at such a vision, he drew on the analysis of democratic values provided by pragmatic philosophy and on his personal experience of growing to maturity in American communities. He never forgot that American society through its state-supported schools had accepted him and eventually provided him with a chance to liberate his mind and so literally to become a free man who could exercise his intellectual powers as a university professor—"the best job in the world" as he put it. While not unaware of failings of American society, he worked with a sense of gratitude for the sustenance it had, in fact, provided. In a time when cynicism is fashionable, this is a reminder that vitality can come from living with a sense of the positive virtues.

What was he telling these seniors? First, see yourself as a unique human being with the capacity to grow in understanding and character. When working from a sense of your own capacity to perceive self and world with larger significance, try to see each of your students as having such a potential. The unique self with its possibilities of developing its own design for living is a precious and exciting thing, but it is in major part a social self and requires a special kind of human community that will provide the conditions for its nurture. The classrooms of a free and democratic people should be shot through with such qualities. What are they?

First of all, teachers are needed who have a deep and genuine intellectual involvement in their field of study. They need to have thought their way personally into the subject so that they will feel that their students' lives will become significantly richer through having joined them in thought about it. The teacher needs to make the class a place where the relevant ideas of each student can get serious attention. Students have to feel free to try ideas that differ from those of the teacher, but they have to learn, too, that all ideas have to confront the test of challenge and criticism. Above all, there needs to be a climate of trust so that all can feel free to locate a position on which they can stand with dignity, even while seeking to widen the area of agreement with others. To get the students engaged with the instructor in such an examination of ideas, so that they will progressively learn to think independently and learn how to further personal learning—that is the goal, the lovely goal.

The marks of pragmatic thought are much in evidence here, and Gordon Hullfish would have been the first to acknowledge it. He felt very deeply that the pragmatic analysis gave one the power and the responsibility to make more widely available the liberalizing human experience. It provided a tool for differentiating teaching that restricted and dulled the mind from that which released it.

Viewed in this way, the subject of education became a matter of intrinsic significance, and the field of teacher education, one of strategic importance. One could help prospective teachers to see their work as containing the possibility of transforming the lives of youngsters so that they could avoid being stunted as had so nearly been the case with Hullfish himself. The philosopher of education was in a position to be an initiator of change that could move out with the energy of a reactor. All of this provided Gordon Hullfish a faith to live by, and it gave color and meaning to his total performance.

The pragmatic view permeated his teaching and writing but, as I experienced, he was never parochial or mean. In later years as I sensed problems and inadequacies within the pragmatic frame of reference and explored alternatives, I was never met with the charge of apostasy. He might have trouble really understanding how I could be attracted elsewhere, but I had the right and duty to go my own way.

There remains yet the need to give some feeling of how his view of teaching came through in practice. One would search in vain for any unusual methodology. His effectiveness derived

from the living application of his aims to the whole of his work
with his students.

He sought approaches that would give the student the
feeling that he was reaching forward into his world for meaning.
That task was the student's; but Hullfish was there as partner,
interactor, and gadfly. Many times he would initiate the tussle
with ideas. He was always on the search for a quotation or
perhaps quotations in conflict which would provide the occasion
for engaging in thought. He would try an idea, move about it
giving it further consideration, invite questions or comments,
add anecdotes (flamboyant if necessary), and move off in full
pursuit.

He admitted often that it was impossible to reach all
students, but this never freed him from making the involved, all-
out attempt, for one could never know when, even on the
darkest day, something might rouse students into thought that
would change their life.

While he had skill in initiating inquiry and had no qualms
about taking the role of leader, he knew, too, that thinking which
transformed had to derive from the personal, arduous work of
the student. This kind of thinking had to grow out of serious
reading and writing. His course outlines contained lengthy lists
of books and references, required and optional. A series of short
papers related to these readings and on topics formulated by the
student were assigned. These were read and returned with
marginal or summary commentaries in which questions were
raised and matters for further inquiry or reading suggested. He
attended to style. You could not really be honoring an idea
unless you worked to express it clearly. While graduate
assistants were employed in large sections, he himself spent
endless hours reading papers and scribbling his comments in a
tiny, vertical scrawl. It meant taking seriously the more-often-
than-not fumbling attempts of a youth to get a thought on paper.
Because Gordon Hullfish took the time and effort to treat your
idea in earnest, you were forced to act with integrity toward
yourself and your work. I remember how impatiently I would
await the return of my papers so that I could begin to decipher
the comments which might encourage or irritate but that always
acted as a spur to the next effort. When one of his colleagues

from an eastern university asked him how he could put so much time and energy into these efforts, his reply was simply, "I am a teacher." This meant that he was somewhat deficient in the finer niceties of grant seeking, and it meant a shorter personal bibliography. Each of us, of course, has to make our own decisions where items of such magnitude are involved!

With all of the pressures of an active campus and community life, he kept himself remarkably available to students. I remember once an invitation to follow up one of my papers with him while he cultivated a patch of sweet corn that he was growing on a remote corner of the university golf course. Along the way I found myself working and sweating as we used hands and hoe against the weeds, and we talked until the moon was in the sky.

One might fairly ask, I suppose, if this style of teaching is not hopelessly dated—if it is not rooted in a simpler stage of our past where real person-to-person relations were possible. Perhaps the pressures of mass numbers and the complexities of a highly technical culture require approaches that follow a different model. It is possible. It remains to be shown, however, what consequences follow from the alternatives.

With all of us it is the interplay of the many facets of our character that gives clear definition to the person. Gordon Hullfish had distinctive mannerisms, some of which were consciously cultivated. He loved to pull out the bag of Bull Durham at the dinner table and demonstrate his prowess in "rolling his own" or to have stories center about his idiosyncrasies and exploits. In his office he would fall into his familiar slouch and pace the floor as he pursued an idea. This, often as not, would culminate in a raucous laugh that would bound out the door of his office and fill the corridors of Arps Hall. I shall never return there without half-expecting to hear that sound.

With it all there was the unfailing commitment to the life of the mind and a capacity to have a genuine personal relation with students. I once heard Max Lerner recount Carlyle's definition of the essence of real teaching. "It is a matter of getting little fires started," he said. "And how to do that? What is required, sir, is to have a fire in the belly." Gordon Hullfish had that fire.

Hullfish and the Culture Wars of His Time

As I have indicated, Hullfish's teaching supported the quest for meaning of all of his students—regardless of where they were on the ability scales. It was his way of inducting them into a democratic community of inquiry. One might describe his style as "dialogical," I suppose, although I never heard him use the term.

In his way of coming at teaching, there was no compulsion "to keep book" on right or wrong responses no grading on the curve. The evaluation, frankly, was a matter of Hullfish's assessment of the *quality* of the student's intellectual performance and involvement in the process. To hell with pretensions of quantitative objectivity. Students in that era accepted the process. I never heard of a lawsuit filed against H.G.H.

Behind this approach to teaching there was, of course, a commitment to the philosophy of critical inquiry of John Dewey. That tradition inspired not only the style of his teaching but also his conduct in the culture of the profession and the larger society in the 1920s, 1930s, 1940s, and 1950s.

He lost no time getting into the controversy at the very beginning of his professional career. A major faultline in twentieth-century education was the division between the educational theory of Edward Thorndike and that of John Dewey. The division was widening by 1924 when Hullfish completed his dissertation, *Aspects of Thorndike's Psychology in Their Relation to Education Theory and Practice.* He was put in the thick of the debate when the O.S.U. Press published the dissertation as a book (Hullfish, 1926). Hullfish's critique of Thorndike clarified concepts and values that set the direction of his future work.

"The educator of today," Hullfish said, "is standing at the crossroads. He is faced with the necessity of making a choice, of deciding upon the direction in which he plans to move" (Hullfish, 1926, p. 101). Teachers, he said, can either take the line of least resistance and unthinkingly let their work be set by conflicting psychological doctrines that support the discordant status quo of the moment. Or they can choose to think their way clearly into positions with internal consistency that they can make their own.

A primary choice Hullfish made clear was between the theory and practice of either Thorndike or Dewey. Thorndike, Hullfish argued, was an inappropriate model to follow for democratic education. The basic problem was Thorndike's insistence that all learning was analytic and ultimately is determined by elements in the environment; it leads teachers and students to the mechanistic assumption that the only learning that counts is learning that can be counted.

Thorndike's psychology, Hullfish said, is an orientation that ignores the role of *meaning-seeking* which is the distinctive mark of being human. Meaning-seeking, on the other hand, was at the very heart of Dewey's famous technical definition of education as "that reconstruction of experience which adds to the *meaning* of experience, and which increases the ability to direct the course of subsequent experience" (Dewey, 1916, pp. 89-90). In contrast to Thorndike's tendency to see learners as passive recipients of environmental conditioning, Dewey conceived the task of learners was to be active constructors of meaning that led them to see themselves and their world with new understanding.

In elaborating on the inadequacies of Thorndike's theory, Hullfish said that a fatal flaw was the isolation of the individual as a passive accumulator of information. This ignores, said Hullfish, the fundamental fact that humans are social beings with selves and minds that grow out of social interaction. Fruitful learning that supports growth in experience and self-expression requires a particular kind of community—democratic community that both respects individuality and also brings ideas of individuals under testing in conjoint reflective criticism.

The best way to help students with the turbulent change of the twentieth century is to have them learn reflective thinking skills in schools that are communities of free inquirers. Thus, Hullfish, as early as the drafting of his dissertation, was taking his stand with democratic inquiry as the central value to support in education. That conviction guided him in taking a public stand in the years to come when the values of free inquiry were under threat.

In the 1930s sharp controversy arose within the progressive education movement itself. In the depth of the Depression when families and children were devastated by unemployment, the impression grew among many progressives that capitalism was failing and ought to be replaced by some form of socialism.

The Progressive Education Society, The John Dewey Society for the Study of Education and Culture, and the journal *The Social Frontier* were engaged in vigorous social critique. When George Counts wrote *Dare the School Build a New Social Order?* (1932), the book became the rallying point for many progressives on the political left, including those attracted to Marxist analysis.

In the protracted debate Hullfish and most of his O.S.U. colleagues took a stand against what they saw as an abandonment of inquiry for an indoctrination platform for schools. They themselves were critical of capitalism that deeply wounded the society by its excessive greed, but they rejected the idea of forming teachers into a vanguard for a new economy. Teachers, they argued, should focus on their central responsibility to teach the skills and values of critical inquiry and to demonstrate those values in the way they functioned in schools. As the evils of Stalinism were exposed, the pull to the Left among progressives receded. The progressive education movement, however, was seriously weakened by the internal divisions as well as by strident attacks from the political Right as the hysteria of McCarthyism gained momentum.

The stance of Hullfish and colleagues on the side of free inquiry in the 1930s and 1940s put them in a position of strength as the College of Education came under fire in 1951. Partly in response to McCarthy-type attacks, Harold Rugg was invited to give The Boyd Bode Lecture. The conservative Board of Trustees of the university, panicked by the audacity of the faculty of education, condemned the college for bringing a speaker who was "espousing un-American propaganda." The O.S.U. Board empowered the President to screen all outside speakers before invitations were extended. The college, under the leadership of Dean Donald Cottrell, openly criticized the board as "engaging in unwarranted interference with our obligations and responsibility as professional men and women" (Tanner, 1991, pp. 28-29). The Executive Board of the John Dewey Society, of which Hullfish was a member, asked Benjamin Fine of the *New York Times* to investigate the matter. This resulted in articles by Fine which featured the events at O.S.U., and a nationwide discussion on academic freedom followed. Under the pressure of public debate, the board retreated and acknowledged that university faculties properly had the responsibility for inviting speakers—although in cases of "doubt" the president should be "consulted." Hullfish and progressive colleagues gave public support to Dean Cottrell during the bitter confrontation and continued to resist even the recommendation "to consult." They held firm and taught us that our mentors offer us their deepest teaching by the stands they take in crises.

In spite of the "win" at the university, attacks on the freedom and dignity of teachers in the country at large mounted in the ugly climate of the 1950s. (A Truman Loyalty Oath held that employment could be denied to prospective federal employees who were members of an organization designated by the attorney general as "subversive" or who had *"sympathetic association"* with such organizations (Tanner, 1991, pp. 95-96).

In view of these attacks the board of The John Dewey Society commissioned H. Gordon Hullfish to be editor of a yearbook *Educational Freedom in an Age of Anxiety* (1953) to address the attacks on academic freedom.

In the foreword, Hullfish with William Van Til and Vivian T. Thayer underscored the need to sound the alarm:

> We have moved swiftly from a time when the main task was to hasten the further achievement of educational conditions consistent with the democratic aspiration to one in which the survival of the democratic spirit itself is our major concern. (Hullfish, 1953, p. xi)

In the book Hullfish with colleagues like John Childs, Horace Kallen, M. F. Ashley Montague, and Alan Griffin explained the fallacy and delusion of using authoritarian means in the name of democratic ends. The message was badly needed, but the climate for progressive causes remained bleak. Hullfish in 1955, then President of the Progressive Education Association, was forced to announce the disbanding of the association in view of the decline in membership.

Hullfish had one more sad duty to perform. In 1957, after a valiant effort to save the journal *Progressive Education*, Hullfish, who had succeeded W. H. Kilpatrick as President of The John Dewey Society in 1957, had to announce the discontinuance of the journal.

Discouragement and depression would be understandable in one who had to preside over the dissolution of so much of what he had championed for decades. Hullfish, however, while retaining his role as president of The John Dewey Society, was soon back at work with a colleague and former doctoral student, Philip G. Smith of the University of Tennessee, writing a book, *Reflective Thinking: The Method of Education* (1961).

The book's preface stated its intention: first, to help teachers to recognize that the method of thinking, of reflective activity *is* the method of *learning*; second, to elaborate with sample techniques to create situations that challenge individuals to think; and third, to get teachers to value the act of inquiry as the most precious possession of those who attain freedom (Hullfish, 1961, p. vii).

The book is written clearly, unpretentiously, with empathy for teachers and the limitations and strains they work under. Toward the end of the book, I found a recommendation on the subject of "student writing" presented as one of those techniques that "create situations that challenge people to think." It was his description of the technique of "student writing" that had turned my life around in the first months after "returning to the world" after World War II.

Since it gets "to the heart" of what he was about as a teacher, I have chosen to quote at length. After acknowledging the many stresses and responsibilities that drain the energies of teachers and that provide understandable excuses for why it is impossible to read a lot of student writing, Hullfish says:

> It does seem fair to ask, however, what could be more important for a teacher in his capacity as a teacher, than to engage in the direct and intimate exchange of ideas with

individual students? And this is exactly what he may do when he reads seriously what students seriously write. Moreover, what is more important for the student, as a student, than to engage in the intellectual struggle to gain control of his ideas as, through writing *and rewriting*, he endeavors to communicate with others? Some teachers have stolen time in order to make thoughtful and sensitive comments on student papers and have been gratified to be told, "This is the first time anyone ever read my papers seriously.... "

What should be the concern of the teacher as he reads the written work of students? There is no simple answer to this question. The student should be helped to get control of a sentence. He should learn the value of a crisp sentence or, indeed, of a complex one.... He should develop a respect for words as tools of thinking; hence he should treat them with the same care that a tool deserves....

A sensitive teacher . . . will read each paper, therefore, in relation to the student who wrote it. If the student has a tough hide, the marginal notations can be sharp. . . . If the student has been timid about writing because of an insecurity bred of inexperience, a gentle marginal touch, rather than the use of a spur will be indicated. If deceit is indicated, his hand should be called. But the wise teacher will want to be sure of his ground before issuing his call .... One conclusion is beyond dispute—namely, the way in which teachers who ask for writing treat it has a direct relationship to the classroom atmosphere which their actions establish. (Hullfish, 1961, pp. 226-227)

After underscoring that the teacher's proper concern is with the substance of writing, Hullfish offered suggestions for kinds of

"comments which may involve the student and teacher in a
further, and an improved sharing of thought":

> "Have you read what X has to say on this
>   point?"
> "I like this, can you expand?"
> "Opinion or fact?"
> "Would it help to break this sentence?"
> "An illustration would help here."
> "Let's talk about this point."
> "Is this consistent with what you say at the
>   bottom of page 2?"
> "Good point. I hadn't thought of it; hang on to
>   it; develop it further."
> "Would your father agree?"
> "Careless writing here; try your hand again."
> "You have this in control; how about applying it
>   to . . . ?"
> "Do you really think so?" (Hullfish, 1961, pp.
>   227-228)

As I read these "comments," an image comes to mind of the
papers I wrote in the fall term of 1945 with Hank's tiny scrawls
in the margins. They led to my getting hooked on the field he
loved. I am grateful.

The Bull Durham, which he enjoyed so much, turned out to
be his final enemy as he died in 1962, the year after the publication of the book.

Notes

I have drawn upon comments about his teaching that I felt
the need to write in 1962—the year in which his death was
approaching. See "H. Gordon Hullfish and a Vision of
Teaching," *Educational Theory, 13*(3) July 1963, pp. 207-211.

CHAPTER SEVEN

Apprentice to Thorndike

Robert M.W. Travers

[This essay was previously published in 1987 in *Teaching Education*, Volume 1, No. 1, pp. 46-49 and is reprinted with permission of *Teaching Education*.]

My first contact with Edward L. Thorndike was through a letter I received from him in May 1938, when I was still a student at the University of London. The letter virtually invited me to spend a year in his Institute at Teachers College as a research assistant. I was quite unknown to him except for the fact that I had a friend who had put my name in the hopper for the assistantship. That friend was Raymond B. Cattell, who had spent the 1937-1938 academic year working with Thorndike in a similar assistantship and with whom I had earlier edited a volume on the application of behavioral sciences to social problems.

I was ready to pack my bags and leave for America even before the final arrangements were completed. After enduring the deep anxiety of waiting for the final details to be worked out, I sailed for America on a freighter in late August and landed in New York on September 11, 1938. I had held a typical European's view of America as a place belonging either to a daydream world or as a place out of a storybook, and at first, America hardly seemed real: I wondered whether it was all just a dream. America still retains for me something of that dream-like quality.

I arrived at Columbia University with a romantic view of what Thorndike's Institute of Educational Research would be like. In physical appearance it was much the same as any other professor's untidy establishment, and yet one sensed immediately the profound respect and warmth that everyone felt for the great man. Each seemed to have the feeling of being at least some small particle in the history of educational progress. The intellectual and personal presence of Thorndike dominated the Institute but in a very subtle way. He had a profound and deep influence on each of us but was not in any way directive in the manner in which he ran things. In fact, he never seemed to run the Institute at all. It seemed to just run on its own steam.

I was a novice, provided with marvelous opportunities to learn from one of the world's great professors, and professors impart their wisdom in many ways. The common way is through lecturing and discussion. The rare way is through example and precept. Thorndike had spent his early days at Teachers College instructing students in traditional ways, but by the time I worked with him, his instruction was entirely by example. The model from which one learned was not that of an organization, administered effectively for doing research, but rather that of a single, incredibly productive individual who produced study after study without much help from anybody. He had an office manager who coped with such problems as the sale and distribution of his intelligence tests and who occasionally ran independent studies of her own. Irving Lorge, whom Thorndike had brought to the Institute as a young student, did most of the spade work related to word counts and semantic differential counts, but Lorge was largely an independent agent at that stage of his career, building a reputation for himself at Teachers College. The Institute, despite its size and relative affluence, was a one-man enterprise. Young students in the Institute were exposed to the overwhelming presence of one successful man whose entire life was a model of how the newly emerging social and behavioral scientist could influence the course of education and perhaps even the course of history.

Yet the contacts between the research assistants in the Institute and Thorndike were quite minimal, even though his presence was overwhelming. We gathered in his office on Monday mornings to discuss some topic and sometimes to discuss our work. Often he would use these meetings as occasions to make trial presentations of his own ideas. He gave us almost no direction, though sometimes he handed out assignments such as gathering information from the library or completing some statistical work. Often the meetings were no more than discussions of whatever problem any participant might have on his mind.

It has taken me a lifetime to understand the full significance of the model Thorndike presented. At the time I worked with him I viewed him as a scientist who managed to apply his scientific knowledge to the improvement of education. Such was the myth that surrounded Thorndike at Teachers College, a myth that historical accounts of Thorndike and his work have perpetuated. The myth has done much to hide the full significance of Thorndike and his work and has resulted in a failure of those who followed to benefit fully from the model that he provided.

As I grow older and reflect upon my personal knowledge of Thorndike, I see two separate and quite distinct individuals at work, both of whom influenced me. One was Thorndike the scientist, a role he assumed during most of the working day. From breakfast to dinner, Thorndike was a scientist concerned with the expansion and integration of knowledge. The second Thorndike came to life toward evening—Thorndike the inventor. Most of the materials he developed for schools were designed and constructed during the evening hours. That is what he did for relaxation, if one can call it that.

Thorndike the scientist had gone through many stages during the forty or more years of his productive life. His doctoral dissertation was of such significance that it became the foundation for his entire life, an achievement that few can match. His later work had shown a steady development and an integration of new ideas. His intellectual development was on a grand scale, ever expanding his system of psychological ideas to include new aspects of behavior. He was confident that he had discovered great truths about behavior and that he had a total overall picture of the way in which human behavior functioned. Unfortunately, no good study has yet been made of the development of Thorndike's conception of human behavior and the way in which he attempted to produce an ever more complete picture. Such a study would require a thorough examination of his work over a lifetime. When I worked for

Thorndike as a research assistant, he was in the final stages of his life's work.

Thorndike's main interest during the final stages of his work was in using his ideas about learning to solve some of the problems of human society. The culmination of this work was his book *Human Nature and the Social Order* (1940).He was immensely proud of this work at the time of its publication and did not live long enough to see it evaluated as one of his less significant works.

The year in which I worked for Thorndike was his last at Teachers College. His health was failing, and he did much of his work at home. Yet he came into the office on most days and checked the clerical work related to his ongoing enterprises. Those who worked in the Institute had fleeting glimpses of the aging Thorndike, seeing him as a man of still-untiring energy, determined to use every moment he still had for furthering knowledge. Aware he did not have much time left, he was still determined to use every available moment for professional ends.

Yet, for the young insecure research assistant like myself, Thorndike, too, at times, demonstrated an insecurity that was comforting. On one occasion he seemed so happy that some minor educational institution offered him an honorary degree. He hardly needed the degree, for major institutions had already bestowed upon him greater honors, but he still needed the occasional pat on the back. Such incidents gave the assistants in the Institute the feeling that the great Thorndike still shared with us many common feelings. He still needed what we needed most—an occasional word of encouragement.

The second Thorndike we knew much about but never saw directly. That was Thorndike the inventor, the Edison of the educational world. When I worked for Thorndike, my view of him was overwhelmed by the myth that Thorndike's practical contributions to education were direct outgrowths of this scientific work, but they were only remotely related to it. The nearest that his practical applications came to his research was in his development and use of intelligence tests. Most of his applications and inventions were far removed from his particular scientific work.

We never saw much of Thorndike the inventor of educational devices. We knew that he was proud of his contributions to science, but how he felt about his evening work inventing new tools for the teacher and administrator remained largely a mystery. We saw him strictly as a scientist and assumed that his contributions to the classroom were outgrowths of his scientific work. They bore some relationship to the techniques involved but were remote conceptually from the laws of behavior derived from his work. His educational inventions were tied to data collection that involved counting the frequency of events, as when he counted how often a word occurred in widely read American printed materials, but the frequency variable as such was not crucial in his scientific work. His process of invention began typically with finding out how often something happened, or just judging how often something happened, as when he decided in *The New Methods in Arithmetic* and *The Psychology of Arithmetic* (Thorndike, 1921; Thorndike, 1922) that certain problems were either commonly encountered or rarely encountered in daily life. But that is where the contact between Thorndike the inventor and Thorndike the scientist ended. Thorndike the scientist followed in the great scientific tradition of Newton and Darwin. Thorndike the inventor was more in the tradition of Edison and Ford, a very different tradition from the scientific.

The model of Thorndike the scientist was the model that had impact on the younger members of his staff, so much so that his model as an inventor never had impact either on those who worked with him or those who wrote about him in later years. It is only quite recently that I have come to realize that there were two models that could have had impact on me. Unfortunately, the inventor model has simply faded into oblivion. Yet most of the great developments in education have been inventions rather than applications of scientific discovery. Consider just a few. The workbook is perhaps the invention that has had the longest and deepest impact over at least 2,300 years. Plato's proposal to rewrite mythology to include values appropriate for children represents a form of invention that is still pursued. Later, the invention of special literary materials for children was an idea that dominated education. The slate and later, the steel pen were inventions that had enormous impact on the classroom. The idea that education should begin with objects, as Comenius proposed, was an important invention. The workbook for children led to the later development of the textbook, to which Thorndike added his own inventions. The daily events in the school today are more a result of a long history of educational invention than they are the outcome of research, though some modern research workers have invented things that have resulted in some change in the school curriculum. Thorndike has a special place in the impressive history of educational invention.

Most of those who worked with Thorndike at the height of his prestige and influence disappeared into obscurity. A few were deeply influenced by him, but it was not the kind of influence that led to the establishment of a Thorndike school of psychology along connectionist lines. His influence came more in the message that in order to be a productive thinker, one had to be totally immersed in one's work. Thorndike wrote in a memorandum in 1938 that he expected only four of those who had worked as his young assistants to become known in their fields, naming Abraham H. Maslow, Raymond B. Cattell, Irving Lorge, and myself. We all shared the common attribute of being compulsive workers and were totally absorbed in our work. None was a standard bearer of the psychology of learning that Thorndike had envisaged. Perhaps the novices in the Institute found the scientific stature of Thorndike too overwhelming to even try and follow. Yet the presence of Thorndike during my year in the Institute had a lifetime influence on me, and the longer I live, the more I recognize the ways in which Thorndike has had impact on the ways I think and behave.

PART THREE

Modeling the Passion To Understand

From the Classrooms of Stanford to the Alleys of Amsterdam: Elliot Eisner as Pedagogue

by Thomas E. Barone

Doing Philosophy: Maxine Greene and the Pedagogy of Possibility

by William Ayers

In Class with Philip W. Jackson

by David T. Hansen

Laura Zirbes: A Teacher of Teachers

by Paul R. Klohr

Cutting across four institutions and six decades, Elliot W. Eisner, Maxine Greene, Philip W. Jackson, and Laura Zirbes embrace a rare conception of teaching. For them, to speak of living, of life, is to speak of teaching; teaching is a way of encountering experience with others and of extracting meaning from it, of seeking understanding by learning to see from different and multiple perspectives. To teach is to journey, to travel without a map, using Barone's image of Eisner, to adventure into the unknown.

Radically differing in style, the four essays that follow present a glimpse of the passion to understand that each professor modeled—that was or is each professor. Intellectually aflame, each professor confronted the conventions of the academic fields, the well-worn pathways, and rejected them. Eisner challenged the behavioral objectives movement and nudged along qualitative approaches to studying education; Greene confronted a disengaged philosophy, a philosophy of the head but not of the heart, and began "doing philosophy"; Jackson turned his back on a psychology of control and moved toward one of mind and experience; and Zirbes, seeing cognition and creativity as cut of the same cloth, rejected the science of education of her era, a male-dominated, high-status science, and developed means for supporting and enriching the creativity of young children. Pioneers all.

In their quests, each turned to the arts for insight—not because they represent a higher moral ground, as is sometimes claimed, but for their potential to enrich life, to educate perception, to enable seeing broadly and feeling deeply and differently. For the same reason, each showed little respect for disciplinary boundaries and instead studied and read widely, passion serving as guide. In the shops they visited in Holland, Eisner surprised Barone with the ease in which he spoke knowledgeably of a particular Buddha and of African masks. Expecting nothing from graduate education, Ayers was awestruck by Greene "gleefully blurring genres—philosophy, anthropology, literature, psychology, science, the arts." Hansen describes the same tendency in Jackson. Zirbes, Klohr reports, read new publications in psychology, sociology, and anthropology long before the library had them.

Though each was willing to "sting" students, as Hansen reports of Jackson, when such comments were necessary to overcome complacency, more than anything these teachers nourished student potential by the lives they lived with them. Using Ayers' words, these teachers gave their students "access to an active mind, inquiring openly and in full view." To so openly share themselves with others requires being centered, secure in self. Mentoring of this kind cannot be practiced. It is not role-playing; rather it is an expression of who and what one is as a person.

Biographical Information

Elliot Eisner [born: March 10, 1933, Chicago, IL] has served as professor of education and art at Stanford University since 1965. He was graduated from Roosevelt College of Chicago in 1954 with a B.A.; other degrees include an M.S. from Illinois Institute of Technology in 1955 and an M.A. in 1958 and the Ph.D. in 1962 from the University of Chicago. Other professional roles include teaching high school art in Chicago from 1956-1958, serving as an instructor of art at Ohio State University during 1960-1961, and holding a professorship in education at the University of Chicago from 1961-1965. Eisner's publications include *The Educational Imagination* (1979), *Cognition and Curriculum* (1982), and *The Enlightened Eye* (1991). Professor Eisner has served in a number of leadership roles including terms as president of the American Educational Research Association, National Art Education Association, and the International Society for Education through Art.

Maxine Greene [born: Dec. 22, 1917, New York, NY] serves as the William F. Russell Professor Emeritus at Teachers College, Columbia University, where she has held a position since 1965. She was graduated from Barnard College in 1938 with a B.A.; other degrees include an M.A. in 1949 and the Ph.D. in 1955 from New York University. Other professional roles include serving as a professor of English at Montclair State College from 1956-1957 and a professor of education at New York University from 1957-1965. Greene's publications include *Teacher as Stranger* (1973), *Landscapes of Learning* (1978), *The Dialectic of Freedom* (1988), and *Releasing the Imagination* (1995). Professor Greene has served in a number of leadership roles including terms as president of the American Educational Research Association and the American Educational Studies Association and, presently, director of The Center for Social Imagination, the Arts, and Education, Teachers College.

Philip W. Jackson [born: Dec. 2, 1928, Vineland, NJ] currently holds the David Lee Shillinglaw Distinguished Service Professorship of Education and Psychology at the University of Chicago. He was graduated from Glassboro State College in 1951 with a B.S.; other degrees include an M.Ed. from Temple University in 1952 and the Ph.D. from Columbia University in 1954. Other professional roles include serving as professor of educational psychology at Wayne State University from 1954-1955. In 1955, Jackson accepted a professorship of education at the University of Chicago and served as principal of its laboratory nursery school from 1966-1970 and as principal of the laboratory school from 1970-1975. His publications include *Life in Classrooms* (1968), *The Practice of Teaching* (1986), *Untaught Lessons* (1992) and the editorship of the *Handbook of Research on Curriculum* (1992). Professor Jackson has served in a number of leadership roles including terms as president of the American Educational Research Association and the John Dewey Society.

Laura Zirbes [born: April 26, 1884, Buffalo, NY; died: June 9, 1967, Columbus, OH] served as professor of education at Ohio State University from 1928-1954. She was graduated from Columbia University in 1925 with a B.S., in 1926 with an A.M., and the Ph.D. in 1928. Other professional roles included serving as an elementary teacher in the Cleveland public schools from 1903-1919 and as a researcher and lecturer at the Lincoln School, Teachers College. Zirbes' publications include *Spurs to Creative Teaching* (1959), *Focus on Values in Elementary Education* (1960), and *Guidelines to Developmental Teaching* (1961). Professor Zirbes served in a number of leadership roles including terms as chair of the National Education Commission of the American Association of University Women, secretary-treasurer of the American Educational Research Association, and as a member of the executive committee of the Educational Policies Commission.

CHAPTER EIGHT

From the Classrooms of Stanford to the Alleys of Amsterdam: Elliot Eisner as Pedagogue

Thomas E. Barone

On that first morning in Holland we awoke, Margaret and I, to a delightful surprise. Peering out of our third-floor window we could hardly believe our eyes. Overnight, the rooftops of Utrecht had, against the odds, been powdered with snow. Late March serendipity! —for native New Orleanians even January snowfalls remain minor miracles. We dressed hurriedly and crawled down the steep and narrow stairway to share our discovery with our hosts. Along the way Margaret suggested that the Eisners, having endured the Dutch weather since January, would not be as impressed. But I guessed correctly that they would be pleased for us. "And it won't interfere with our sightseeing," said Elliot, as if he had expected the unexpected.

Ellie Eisner had accompanied her husband to the Netherlands, where he was spending the spring semester of 1985 as Visiting Professor at the University of Utrecht. My wife and I had decided to "spring break" in Europe and had accepted the Eisners' generous invitation to stay in their typically narrow, vertical Dutch townhouse. Upon our arrival from Paris the previous evening, the Eisners helped us sketch the outline of our itinerary for the next three days. On this, our first day, we were to "do" Amsterdam. And as Elliot guided the two of us (Ellie would run daytime errands and join us for dinner) toward the train station, I did not yet understand the snowfall as a harbinger. I could not have foreseen how this singular day would be studded with serendipitous occurrences, or how later it would come to encapsulate for me the essence of the Elliot Eisner—the mentor, the friend, the teacher/critic, the connoisseur of life—that I, before and since, have grown to admire and appreciate.

****

Eleven years earlier, no snow had greeted Margaret and me as we arrived in Palo Alto on Labor Day. The warm weather was not unexpected. Indeed, anticipating my Stanford experience, I had researched many facets of my graduate student setting—the Bay Area, the campus, the doctoral program, and the writings of the man who would be my advisor. No big surprises, thank you. Even as I attempted to decide a year earlier on the doctoral programs in curriculum to which I would apply, I had sequestered myself in the Tulane University library to pore over publications of potential mentors. I was keenly aware that my own non-technicist educational philosophy—not to mention my preferred "literary" style—was not currently in fashion. Understanding (somewhat, even then) the potential threats to the intellectual integrity of disempowered doctoral students, I was searching for an established scholar with similar inclinations who might provide a safe place for honest, but apparently somewhat dangerous, work. After reading a few articles by Eisner [I best recall "Educational Objectives: Help or Hindrance?" (Eisner, 1968) on the limitations of the then-sacrosanct objectives movement], I decided to apply to Stanford in hopes of studying with him.

By that late summer of 1974 when I first met Eisner in person his career was impressive, even, to a starry-eyed doctoral student, intimidating. Most of his early articles contain evidence of two primary passions, the arts and education. Elliot had already begun to explore in his writing intersections of the two, including the relationships among the arts and curriculum, teaching, and evaluation. For Elliot, embarking upon an educational project is much like beginning a painting, play, sculpture, or story. One must use intelligent and informed judgment throughout both artistic and educational projects in order to maximize meaning. But neither in education nor in making art can ultimate outcomes be foreseen: final visions arise only well into the process of give and take between artist and material, teacher and student, student and curricular content. The artist travels with aspirations in hand but *sans* detailed blueprints. Along the way, the artist welcomes chance intrusion, entering into negotiations with emergent qualities of experience, incorporating them into the construction of an ultimate vision.

So does the good teacher. So does the active student. Indeed, as Elliot would ask, isn't this always the way we negotiate with the world when we are fully alive?

****

It certainly was the way we lived that day in Amsterdam. Heavy, wet flakes were falling as we disembarked from the express train. Our plans for the day promised varied emotional tones, from a visit to Anne Frank's House to time in the renowned Ryksmuseum. The first was a solemn and moving experience. Much respectful silence all around. Later, as we entered the museum, I expected Elliot Eisner, Stanford Professor of Education and Art, to hold forth as teacher/critic/docent to the quite tutorable. Instead, no lessons, more silence, and for Margaret and me the pressure was on. Left alone to ferret out Meaning, we strained under the intensity of the occasion, attempting to focus all our intellectual and emotional energies, all that we had ever learned and experienced, on hundreds of dark and weighty masterworks. After a couple of hours, weary of the burden of teaching myself, I finally (but still rather bravely, I thought) mumbled something about art museums and cognitive overload. To which Elliot, looking relieved, responded, "Me, too; let's go."

Go where? Outside the snow had stopped but we were soon to find its equivalent nestled in between the lines of the day's formal itinerary. The real serendipity, it turned out, lurked in the narrow moments between our planned stops. The day's biggest surprises, its teachable moments, were awaiting us in, of all places, boutiques and antique shops.

****

Ultimately, in any worthwhile doctoral program, a student will experience a similar silence, one accompanied by an inevitable loneliness as he or she struggles with shaping the contours of a personal contribution to the future of a chosen field of study. The only alternative, after all, is the fraudulent one wherein a dissertation advisor talks explicitly and narrowly: we know of lesser figures in academia who dispense to underlings prepackaged, paint-by-number dissertation topics designed to be colored in as pieces of a larger study. But mentors worth their salt know the importance of absenting themselves from the private site of intense dissertation generation, emerging only occasionally as critic and respondent to the work-in-progress. Of course, much conversation, a lot of teaching and learning, precedes the loneliness of the long-distance thesis author. And some of it occurs, of course, in formal classroom settings.

My first course with Elliot at Stanford was entitled "Curriculum Theory and Curriculum Change." Designed as an introduction to the field, the course included discussions of readings from each of the major curriculum orientations identified in the book he had co-edited with another of his students, Elizabeth (Beau) Vallance (Eisner & Vallance, 1974). The second course, taken a year later, was devoted to exploring issues surrounding arts-based forms of qualitative research, a relatively new passion of Elliot's. For each of the courses Elliot taught, prearrangements were minimal. Never producing anything resembling a detailed itinerary, map, or script, he would, alone or in consultation with a few doctoral students, sketch out a syllabus by identifying relevant topics and issues and selecting relevant readings. The ensuing journey consisted then of conversation, occasionally (in the form of a monologue crafted for and rehearsed on other occasions) one sided, but nearly always intellectually provocative and characterized by unexpected (for both professor and students) side-trips down interesting ideational alleyways.

But the highlights of my experiences with Elliot at Stanford were to be found not in catalogued courses but in less formal gatherings where all participants *really* traveled without a map. The Qualitative Research Study Group consisted of Elliot Eisner and five or six interested doctoral students who met weekly to discuss important issues related to arts-based forms of qualitative inquiry, especially art criticism and educational criticism. Alfred Schutz, Clifford Geertz, Susanne Langer—the scholars whose works we examined were a varied lot, most selected by Elliot, some by students. But there were rarely any "close readings" of their texts, and any attempts to discover "correct" interpretations were interspersed with movements toward establishing intertextual connections with our own ongoing projects. Indeed, some sessions were set aside solely to break the silence on our own work, to secure critical feedback from peers and professor. Elliot presided over, moderated, or better, facilitated the discussions of the Study Group, but the twists and turns of an unfettered exchange of ideas were omnipresent in these sessions.

****

Working without a map in Amsterdam can be as challenging, but also as rewarding, as a freewheeling study group. Traveling with a map means moving more expeditiously toward your predetermined destination. Without it you are more observant, more likely to find yourself in a richer conversation with your surroundings. You are more tempted to turn down intriguing alleyways. Elliot had walked through Amsterdam before and was convinced that he didn't need a map to guide us smoothly from Site A to Site B. Soon, however, it appeared that we were lost.

But "lost" is, of course, a relative term. One might say that the three of us were "lost" only in relation to our original destinations of the Anne Frank House and Ryksmuseum, just as one can be "lost" in a scholarly reading or discussion only when one aims toward a correct, predetermined, final understanding. One is never lost, however, if the experience of reading, discussing, traveling is an inherently vital and educational one. And we three tourists were certainly not lost in terms of the myriad of interesting sights on all sides of us. Especially the antique shops.

It began almost immediately on the first crooked leg of our trip, as we moved from the train station to the Anne Frank House. But it continued between there and the cafe where we paused for lunch, between lunch and the museum, and after the museum on the way to dinner. Elliot would glance down a narrow street and, like a hawk who spots the slightest movement in the distant underbrush, spy a shop with potential for providing a certain form of nourishment. "Let's see what they have in here," he would say, and in we would go. And lo and behold, inside were delights that Margaret and I could not have anticipated. What we found were things of excellence from cultures around the globe. We also found a lover of beautiful artifacts, a collector with seemingly encyclopaedic knowledge of art from every inhabited continent, who was willing and eager to talk.

****

One of the books we confronted most intensely in our
Qualitative Research Study Group, a favorite of Elliot's then and
of mine ever since, was John Dewey's *Art as Experience* (1934).
Among the insights in this major work on aesthetics are those
about art criticism. Since "criticism," wrote Dewey, "is
judgment," to understand the nature of criticism one must first
understand judgment. Bad judgment is, said Dewey, "judgment
that is final, that settles a matter, [and] is . . . congenial to
unregenerate human nature," while good judgment is

> development in thought of a deeply realized
> perception. The original adequate experience is
> not easy to attain; its achievement is a test of
> native sensitiveness and of experience matured
> through wide contacts. A judgment as an act of
> controlled inquiry demands a rich background
> and a disciplined insight. It is much easier to tell
> people what they should believe than to
> discriminate and unify. (Dewey, 1934, p. 300)

Especially on those occasions when we explored Elliot's
favorite texts [Langer's *Problems of Art* (1957), for example] did
he model for us the kind of criticism—judgment—of which
Dewey wrote. His method was a mixture of a loose version of
Socratic maieutics (disciplined questioning designed more to
provoke controlled inquiry than to reach foregone conclusions)
and insights drawn from a native sensitivity toward and wide
contacts with the subject matter. As we, his students, strained to
acquire an "original adequate experience" with these masterworks, Elliot would bring his judgment to bear, rarely telling us
what to think about a text but more often providing the kind of
criticism that first calls attention to particular ideas in and
qualities of a text and then places them into wider contexts.

But here is the most intriguing fact about those sessions: Of
all the activities in which Elliot could have engaged on a
Tuesday night, this was what he chose to do. Participation in the
Study Group was voluntary for all, certainly for the instigator.
Elliot must have initiated the sessions out of love. But a love for
what? The ideas in the readings? Us, his intellectual prodigy?
Without, I hope, sounding overly ponderous or pretentious, I

want to say that Elliot, like the rest of us, participated in those Tuesday evening sessions out of a love for life. Because the experiences there made him feel alive. Dewey, after all, insisted that heightened vitality was the hallmark of true experience:

> Instead of being shut up within one's own private feelings and sensations, [experience] signifies active and alert commerce with the world; at its height it signifies complete interpenetration of self and the world of objects and events. . . . Because experience is the fulfillment of an organism in its struggles and achievements in a world of things, it is art in germ. (Dewey, 1934, p. 19)

I certainly recall experiencing such fulfillment as we wrestled with the brawny ideas in those readings and discussions. But an additional dimension of those sessions which contributed to fulfillment for Elliot was, I think, the opportunity to play the role of critic/teacher. One final excerpt from *Art as Experience* helps to explain:

> [A good critic is already] keenly sensitive to the unnumbered interactions that are the material of experience. . . . [But] critical judgment not only grows out of the experiences of objective matter, and not only depends upon that for validity, but has for its office the deepening of just such experiences in others. (Dewey, 1934, p. 324)

I think the Study Group was born out of a desire for an opportunity to arrange and chaperone a *rendezvous* between us and some of Elliot's favorite subject matter, to be (actively) present with us as our own intellectual awarenesses were expanded and our judgments honed through contact with those materials. I think it was born out of a need to travel with others who had not yet seen the sights that he had seen, to subtly steer them toward the kind of significant experiences, the "deeply realized perceptions," that made his own professional life worth living. For Elliot the connoisseur of excellent "subject matter," being alert to qualities in the world, being able to perceive them deeply, appreciate them broadly, experience them fully, makes life worth living. But Elliot the critic/teacher lives to give others those greater reasons to live.

****

The most enduring image that I retain of our jaunt into that Amsterdam winter-spring is of Elliot against a window inside a shop, backgrounded by the lightly falling snow, focusing joyfully and intently, through touch and sight, on a Japanese Buddha. His precise words are gone now, only vague recollections of certain qualities in his utterances remain. These were the familiar ones of delight and earnestness, a seemingly contradictory mix of emotional tones I had come to associate with the Elliot of our Study Group. Elliot was once again in his connoisseur-and-critic mode, deeply absorbed now not in scholarly treatises but in beautiful artifacts from everywhere and eager to share his perceptions and judgments within this different field of subject matter.

Having experienced the art collection at his home, I knew that Elliot's interests in well-crafted objects were wide ranging. But until Holland I had not realized the breadth and depth of his knowledge and appreciation. For example, with that particular Buddha and many others, Elliot would pinpoint era and location of origination and have the information confirmed momentarily by the shop owner. And on we moved to other shops filled with African masks, and then with Chinese vases, stunning artifacts, many familiar to Elliot, that he was enabling us to see for the first time. ("Why is this piece so appealing to you, Elliot?" "Look at this quality here or that one there.") To Persian rugs. Dragging one toward the window light, he said "You've just been to some cathedrals in France. Do you see the colors of stained glass windows here and here?" I was instantaneously returned to Sainte Chapelle. Associations made, appreciations acquired, I saw anew both rug and vibrant chapel light.

And one last burst of guided delight. Elliot saw Margaret and me admiring a watercolor of some Dutch women at the shore, and he pointed to particular areas of impressive technique. Hardly a masterpiece, but glimmers of quality here and there: the artist worked well with a good choice of materials. The painting embodied many of the soft, brooding qualities we had observed in the Dutch landscape.

And, unlike other pieces we had craved, it was within our budget. The 1985 watercolor by the Dutch painter Horrix now adorns the wall in our living room, serving dual roles as object d'art and souvenir of a special place and moment in time.

****

"Hardly a masterpiece." "Glimmers of quality." Of course, that (or any) painting cares nothing about the judgments of the critic. But what of a student and the judgments of his mentor? The metaphors of mentor-as-artist and mentee-as-artwork are hardly precise: Although he chose to work with us for the glimmers of potential he observed, we should not be considered Elliot's raw materials. We could never be molded. Human beings can never be as malleable as clay, never as predictable as stone. Although his influences upon their content and style were/are unmistakable, the signatures of his students would always remain their own.

But there were times at Stanford when it did not seem that way. Part of the struggle of the doctoral candidate involves making a unique contribution to a field even as one is being initiated into that field. But at the outset one's own professional identity awaits formation. The good notions all seem to be taken. The ideas in one's essays seem, only a day or week later, to be stale and trite and obvious or already written, better, by someone else. Even worse, that someone else may be one's mentor.

The sense of intellectual identification with an academic father figure can indeed be overwhelming, so that even the phrasing and tempo of one's writings seem to be a pale copy of a vivid original. This sense of dependency can be deepened when one is at the edge of the field, tilling soil that lies outside traditional boundaries. One is intellectually exposed, one is nervous, one's future is at stake, one is new at this, one needs to be covered from attacks by marauding traditionalists until one learns to fend for oneself. A commanding figure in the field can provide that cover. Elliot has done so for many of his doctoral students.

My dissertation defense in 1979 was not the most pleasant of experiences. A few of the examiners were, I daresay, in league with the marauding traditionalists. Much of the interrogation focused on methodological issues (for example, the meaning of validity and objectivity and subjectivity in relation to arts-based inquiry) that are still being explored today. Back then, however, the traditionalists were much more incredulous. Elliot told me afterwards that I had held my own ground, but to say that his presence there was important is to win a prize for understatement. The whole exercise unfolded within the shared understanding that Eisner gave credence to this radical notion of dissertation-as-arts-based-endeavor. His stature afforded me the necessary cover while I reloaded during that very early skirmish in what have since come to be known as the paradigm wars.

I am certain that I would have been unable to muster the courage necessary for fighting alone. But it was only years later that I fully appreciated the degree of intellectual courage demonstrated by Elliot Eisner throughout his career. Only now can I comprehend how professionally risky it is for any academic—even a tenured Stanford professor—to advance notions as avant garde as some of Elliot's. But a sense of intellectual integrity and a responsibility to his chosen field demanded that courage.

Moreover, "fighting the good fight" can be exhilarating as well as challenging. Indeed, at the party following the defense I felt simultaneously elated and fatigued.

"Whew! It's exhausting when you swim upstream," I said.

"It's how you know you are alive," he answered.

****

In ancient Greece the pedagogue was a wise servant who would walk with a student from the privacy of the student's home to the public place of the school. At the school the student was expected to engage in the learning of various technical matters. But along the way the "slave companion" would seek out opportunities to instruct about the larger affairs of life, helping the boy to place the merely technical into the contexts of the wide world outside the school. This activity embodied a kind of moral education, instruction about character, teaching about how to live. If we confine ourselves to this sense of the term, then pedagogy was what was occurring in those alleys of Amsterdam. This was, to be sure an artful, indirect form of teaching, as pedagogue and students together abandoned reliance on the rote, the mundane, the routinized, the expected, for the more complex human capacities for imagination and judgment. Pedagogue and students together practiced living more fully.

****

Of course, the centrality of these capacities of imagination and judgment in the educational process has been the focus of Elliot Eisner's pedagogical efforts throughout his life and career, with his "students" in Holland, with his students at Stanford, with his professional colleagues who have been led (some reluctantly) to understand the need to subjugate the technical elements of the activities of educational program design, teaching, research, and evaluation, to the larger dimensions of artistry and criticism.

I have pointed to courage as a hallmark of Elliot's intellectual leadership, a courage born out of a deep sense of professional responsibility. But a second hallmark of that leadership was civility. Indeed, there must reside within the soul of any true educator a respect for those whom he would educate. So while his views on educational research might have seemed contentious and revolutionary to some of his colleagues, Elliot's outlook remained consistently generous and expansive. Consider that he never attempted to advance the cause of arts-based educational research at the expense of social science. Instead, he would merely insist upon space for additional settings at the research table. Elliot knew that one does not persuade one's peers in the professoriate of the value of your own ideas by repudiating their work. The good pedagogue leads gently by the hand, accepting the experiences of the student while guiding toward new possibilities.

With courage, civility, and earnest delight, Elliot Eisner guided the field of education in this fashion. Thanks to him, members of that field who had been moving along rather predictably were presented with a delightful surprise.

Through the pedagogical efforts of Elliot Eisner—embodied in his writings, in his service activities, in his presentations at zillions of podia, in untold numbers of teachable moments—members of the educational profession were persuaded to see subject matter that they never expected to see, to experience chance intrusions about which they would soon begin to exercise judgment. Thanks to the pedagogy of Elliot Eisner, the field of education has acquired greater character. So many of its members, I mean, are now more fully alive.

Notes

When my wife and I travel abroad, she keeps a detailed journal that we delight in reading and rereading years later. Many of the details in this account are extracted from that journal.

CHAPTER NINE

Doing Philosophy: Maxine Greene and the Pedagogy of Possibility

William Ayers

The venerable hall where John Dewey had lectured years before was filled to overflowing on that first fall evening, awaiting the start of Maxine Greene's introduction to philosophy class. The air was expectant, crackling with an edge of loss and possibility as only autumn air can; the antique room reeked of tradition and nostalgia. I was a new graduate student, and several people had told me to take this class, but I had never met Maxine Greene and had no idea what to expect. The room was musty, the topic quaint, perhaps even decrepit—my expectations were decidedly low. And yet in the often familiar, sometimes odd collision of chance and choice, I found myself that first night only a couple of rows from the front—eye to eye with the podium—when Professor Greene arrived. I didn't know it then, of course, but it would become a seat I would seek out at every opportunity during my years at Teachers College and beyond.

Maxine Greene entered the room slowly, surrounded by animated students, weighted down with two shoulder bags brimming with papers and an overload of notes and books. I saw an already diminutive woman made tiny by the cargo accompanying her and yet luminous somehow at the center of a crowd, the sudden, surprising eye of the storm. She moved steadily toward the podium, stopping often, speaking in turn to each student who sought advice for this, permission or a signature for that, and unloaded the chaos of paper and books, shuffling through it, sorting, arranging, re-arranging, speaking all the while. By the time the last student had retreated to her seat—and without announcement or formal notice—class was underway. Like an intimate conversation with an old friend which is picked up, carried on, and then interrupted to be continued in the future, Maxine Greene's lecture was filled with spontaneity, intimacy, incompleteness, and forward motion.

"We were talking earlier—some of us—about what it might mean to *do* philosophy," she was saying, "as opposed to analyzing positions or searching exclusively for clarifying language. What might it mean to pose distinctive kinds of questions with respect to our own practice and our own lived situations, the kinds of questions that might make us more than 'accidental tourists,' more than clerks or bureaucrats or functionaries?"

Her way of speaking had lost nothing from a Brooklyn upbringing, and it was infused, moreover, with a lifetime encountering literature, existentialism, politics; her voice, husky from the ubiquitous cigarettes she then smoked, was filled, as well, with purpose and passion. Philosophy, she explained, had been understood in the classical mode to be a "love of wisdom" or the "queen of the sciences." Once philosophers broke with the notion that reason was tied inexorably to the "eyes of the mind"—and that Truth, Beauty, Goodness, and so on, could be apprehended by those wise enough or privileged enough to see through those eyes—philosophy began to be variously conceived. If it was any longer a "queen" at all, it was a queen whose crown had slipped considerably—it became a second-order discipline, one that did not possess its own ascertainable knowledge, one that was obligated to criticize, to question, to examine, to think about. William James had said that philosophy begins in wonder; Ludwig Wittgenstein associated it with resisting the "bewitchment of intelligence by means of language"; John Dewey with thinking about "what the known demands" in terms of attitude and action. Others thought about "doctrines ignorantly entertained," about "thinking about our own thinking," about the "identification of options and alternatives." Isaiah Berlin had spoken of philosophers "asking queer questions," not to be confused with ordinary factual questions or questions to be settled by logical argument or mathematical inquiry.

"Where is the nearest school?" Maxine Greene asked. " And how do state regulations affect that school? Does the curriculum include both physics and chemistry? Such questions, obviously, are variously answerable—like questions in the social sciences and even the natural sciences. But they are not the queer questions Berlin had in mind. Contrast them, then, with these: How are we to understand freedom? How are we to understand fairness, and how can it be reconciled with individual rights? How can we justify a commitment to critical reflection, aesthetic awareness, open-ended growth, or intercultural understanding to a public preoccupied with the need to focus on skills and proficiencies alone? Or more specifically, is it fair that my child be bussed to another neighborhood to go to school? Is it possible for the child of fundamentalists, say, to study Darwinian evolution in school and still accede to the creationist position? These are the types of questions that arouse the philosopher."

No philosopher myself, I was nonetheless aroused, as if startled from a dream by a flash of lightning. Professor Greene was challenging the popular notions of philosophy as a credo ("my philosophy is") or a high-sounding irrelevance ("that's just philosophy") or a condition of resignation ("I was philosophical about it"). She recalled that when she had begun graduate school and had told her mother that she was studying philosophy, her mother had given her a long, cold look, full of disdain, and responded, "All right, Maxine, *say* something in philosophy."

But much more than discussing philosophy, she was challenging her students (and, I felt, me, personally) to join her in "doing philosophy": becoming more intentional and aware, confronting issues as they emerged in our own consciousness and our lives, interrogating our situations carefully and responding thoughtfully to what we uncovered and discovered. I thought of Amilcar Cabral's admonition to African revolutionaries: "Tell no lies; claim no easy victories." And I remembered Paul Potter's advice to young radicals in the early sixties: "Live your life so as not to make a mockery of your values." And Bernardine Dohrn's challenge to herself and her comrades later in that same decade: "We must—each of us—shed our privilege, reject our false consciousness, reinvent ourselves in complete opposition to war and racism and oppression. We must, if we are to live at all, live our lives as self-determined, rebellious and free." I was captivated.

"Doing philosophy" with Maxine Greene could be—had to be—both exhausting and exhilarating. Keeping up was the first challenge: she is a person on whom nothing is lost, an intensely observant person, vigorous as well as open in pursuing what is there to be seen. She sees largely what narrower minds miss, and sees particularity in vivid, nuanced detail. She is a voracious and acquisitive reader—and she reads, beyond philosophy, literature, science, the arts, politics, poetry, educational research, essays on feminism, and more—and the sources of her thinking include all of that as well as films and music and paintings and conversations and chance encounters and dance and political rallies. She somehow maintains the capacity to access a huge amount of what she has encountered, and she seems to draw infinitely upon it, inventing new connections, surprising ways of seeing, remarkable ways of being and acting. In one class session we talked of the role of the arts in human consciousness and the ways in which "only beings who can think about the ways they are determined can free themselves." References were made that evening to Alice Walker, *Billy Budd*, Sartre and Dewey, Hannah Arendt, Isaac Asimov, Nat Hentoff, the murders of Leon Klinghoffer (who has a name) and the countless Palestinians in the bombed-out refugee camps (who remain nameless), *Breaker Morant*, *A Room of One's Own*, and the cab driver who had told Maxine earlier that day that he hated the Cloisters because "it's up on that hill."

The explosion of the rocket ship carrying the teacher into space focused class another evening on the American infatuation with technology—"technicism" Maxine called it—and the degradation of science in the twentieth century through its marriage to technology, and on *Shoah* and *Hiroshima* and Lao Tse and Marguerite Duras and Albert Camus. "The problems we face," she said, "are not really technical—they are moral, they are ethical. A reliance on technical solutions leaves us still gasping, still empty."

At the very least students were given access to an active mind, inquiring openly and in full view. Because she harvested her teaching from her own lived experience, it always had an improvisational feel to it—fresh and vital and inventive, yes, but also firmly rooted in a coherent ground of core beliefs and large purposes. We could see imagination at work and questioning that knew no limits and dialectics. And students were invited, if they chose, to join in, to open themselves in dialogue and pursuit. "The purpose of this course is to shock ourselves into new awarenesses of what we take for granted and often do not see," she announced in her course outline. "It is to try to empower individuals to clarify and ground their own beliefs about the projects they have chosen for themselves to the end of creating themselves as thoughtful, articulate, critical, and humane practitioners in a profoundly uncertain world." When I hear people today talking about "high expectations for learners," and watch that, too, degenerate into a slogan, I think of Maxine Greene's expectations of us as a standard to strive toward, and of "shocking ourselves into new awarenesses" as a goal.

"My field of study is lived situations," she said one night, and that notion hit like a thunderbolt. She was gleefully blurring genres—philosophy, anthropology, literature, psychology, science, the arts—knocking down barriers, insisting on her right (and ours) to use everything—any discipline, any curriculum, any encounter—as nourishment, as a source to pose our own questions, confront our own problems, challenge our own fates. "I was proposing an arts project to a local school council last week," she said one night. "The council voted to spend their money on metal detectors instead. I was inadequate to explain the importance of the arts. On the other hand, what do I know of guns and knives and the importance of metal detectors? Maybe they're right."

"We are free and fated, fated and free," she often said, quoting Hannah Arendt, one of her teachers years before. "We are conditioned, entangled, thrust into a world not of our choosing, but also free to understand what is happening to us, to interpret, to envision possibilities, to act against all the 'determinisms,' to repair the deficiencies we find. We cannot choose to live in a non-nuclear world, for example, but we can, indeed, we must choose who to be in light of the threat of nuclear annihilation. Like Dewey, we can look at the world as if it could be otherwise, and then act on our own freedom." She told us, for example, about her feelings of horror as homelessness overwhelmed the city. One cold night, taking pity on a man she often saw sleeping across from her apartment, she steeled herself and invited him in for dinner. "What do you want from me, lady?" he snapped. "I ain't going nowhere with you." She admitted a sense of relief.

These were some of the riveting themes of her teaching (and her life). There are others:

• People are "condemned to meaning"—sentenced to create lives as meaningful in the face of disorder and inhumanity, to read our lived worlds and to name ourselves in "our dreadful freedom."

• We can, with John Dewey, conceive of "mind as a verb rather than a noun," and can thereby open to the possibility of attentiveness, engagement, and action.

• Freedom is neither an endowment nor a commodity nor an icon; freedom is not the Statue of Liberty, the flag, or any little fetish. Freedom can be thought of as a refusal of the fixed, a reaching for possibility, an engagement with obstacles and barriers and a resistant world, an achievement to be sought in a web of relationships, an intersubjective reality.

• To be human is to be involved in quest, a fundamental life project that is situated and undertaken as a refusal to accede to the given.

• Teaching, too, involves a sense of the possible, of seeing alternatives, of opening new landscapes.

• The opposite of "moral" in our lives is not "immoral," but is, more typically, "indifferent," "thoughtless," and "careless."

None of this, for her, was put forth in class as simple, self-evident, or settled. She was not easily satisfied with principles or commandments or laws, even (or especially) her own. She demonstrated again and again a resistance to fad, to convention, to dogma of any kind. She chastised and prodded herself for our benefit, insisting on our right, indeed our responsibility to choose: "But still, I can't help myself, I wish you would choose Mozart and not rap." Pausing she added, "But maybe rap is better than Kohlberg in raising sharp moral issues."

Criticized by a student for assigning Marx, whose ignorance and insensitivity to issues of race and gender were righteously exposed, she replied, "I think you're quite right, but, then, I don't go to Marx to learn about racism or sexism." Challenged by a group of students to cancel class for the Jewish holidays, she steadfastly refused: "I don't celebrate religious holidays, but, of course, I recognize the importance of this to you." She typed her notes from class that evening and scheduled another class for any who wanted.

And on another evening, when some students pushed the chairs and desks into a large circle as an emblem of equality and open discussion, she entered with a look of mild disdain, took her assigned seat, and said, "I don't think any of you signed up for this class to hear from each person equally. I certainly want access to your needs and desires, but I am not enslaved by them. I want to welcome your responsiveness, too, but let's not make a fetish of chairs in a circle."

"Some of us look with optimism at America becoming great again," she said one night. "We feel pious, patriotic, competent, and taken with the possibility of upward mobility. Others look with dread at a militaristic resurgence, at American power tied to indifference and decreasing public participation, at American wealth amidst vast poverty." She challenged students to think of how their consciousness of the world plays on the way each of us looks at our own roles and responsibilities. "I must challenge mostly the muffled view, the way routines and methodical systems allow a life of habit and not choice."

And questioning the "given," interrogating the "taken-for-granted," choosing a life is not all somber—seriousness—Maxine Greene is witty and fun-loving and full of humor, and her classes often rocked with laughter. One night she talked of the "facticity" of our lives: "I didn't choose my parents, my femaleness, my Jewishness, my being a New Yorker." Against these "facts" one makes a life, "but even what is given, you want to find a way to choose or reject." She described her early days at Teachers College, the tea-drinking gentility and delicate conversation of the faculty club, the precious, some would say repressed, culture of the WASPs who dominated the place, and one afternoon, a door flung open and a loud voice shouting, "HELLO MAXINE!" A new colleague, vulgar, loud, disheveled, "smelling of the delicatessen." "I was never so proud to be a Jew," she purred with a sly laugh.

The challenge, as always, was to choose in the muddy complexity of living a life without benefit of any entirely adequate road maps or any perfectly satisfactory court of last resort. Maxine Greene is a person of strong opinion and point of view and action, who can simultaneously question almost everything, and use almost anything as a source of her questioning. She can act on behalf of her values, and still hold even her own beliefs as, if not entirely contingent, at least worth another look. She can work hard and speak eloquently on behalf of women's rights, for example, or peace, or the environment— calling her an "anti-imperialist," an "environmentalist," or even a "feminist" feels somewhat false, a superficial reduction in her case. She is somehow beyond the labels, even the "good" ones, and perhaps in that there is an abiding lesson for all of us: "My field of study is lived situations"; "My goal is to challenge the taken for granted, the frozen and the bound and the restricted." When a group of curriculum "reconceptualists" attempted, she feared, to make her a kind of guru, she stopped going to meetings—I was reminded of Bob Moses, a civil rights leader in the South, changing his name when people insisted on him becoming a modern-day savior. When the "critical pedagogy" people embraced her, she continued interrogating and challenging all the pedantic posturing, all the certainty and settledness of the new dogmas. Running into an old friend at Paulo Freire conference years ago—someone making a name for himself as a neo-Marxist educator—I was asked, "You study with Maxine Greene—she's somewhat quaint, soft in her thinking, isn't she?" That he has moved from Marxism to "cultural liberation" is somehow not surprising. As for Maxine Greene, she embodies relationship, connectedness, attentiveness, aliveness to possibility, engagement with complexities—her own life project of citizen philosopher, activist, teacher. "Teacher can be posited as a goal, something to reach for," she said. "If ever I've arrived, I'm dead." This is what she seeks, imagines, holds as a possibility.

I was fortunate—I began teaching at the age of twenty in 1965 in a project linked closely with the civil rights movement. Our models then were citizenship schools and freedom schools springing up all over the South, teach-ins just beginning in the large universities, Myles Horton's Highlander Folk School. I absorbed the idea early that the hope for freedom and the practice of education could be linked, that teaching could be a powerful and natural key to social change. Because I first discovered and invented my teaching in upheaval it has remained, for me, an adventure full of struggle and quest, part of something larger, something far beyond itself. Teaching as pacification, teaching as the transmission of some certified, sanctified stuff, teaching as classification or invasion—this is what we were working against. What we sought was teaching as dialogue, teaching as resistance, teaching as action toward freedom.

And so when I was swept away from the classroom to a direct and dangerous confrontation with war and the state during those turbulent times, I experienced an unexpected coherence. Returning to a more formal teaching situation years later, I stepped into something close and familiar. No doubt, in teaching as in politics I could accede to an easy certainty, but for me teaching is (or can be) in important ways like fighting for justice, for peace, for freedom.

I expected no affirmation for any of this when I returned to graduate school at Teachers College, Columbia University, at the age of forty. Frankly, I was going for a credential alone; I would take only the minimum requirements; I would learn the language of the anointed, and I would move on, untouched. I expected no particular challenge, no substantial nurturance, no serious demand. But here I was wrong, for something dazzling—burning, bright, nourishing, and insistent—stood in my way.

I was by no means Maxine Greene's best student. I was no star in her universe. At one point I angled for a job as her teaching assistant, offering to read papers or exams for her. She was a little aghast: "Students want my reactions to their writing, not yours." Another time, she responded to a paper I had submitted: "The first paper is . . . illuminating as an instance of existential choice. . . . The second is, well, O.K. It uses a metaphor I think is questionable . . . and, it is a romanticized view. I have to think of teachers and learners as situated, entangled, determined, engaged. . . . " This second part was soon published to wide critical praise. For me, Maxine Greene's luke-warm response and serious challenge remains the truest reading.

Maxine Greene has a boundless generosity—a willingness to share her time, her energy, her mind (especially her mind) with thousands of current and former students. Her table is always set for visitors, and whenever one arrives, she is welcomed and embraced. Maxine knows people as well as events and can see to the heart of a friend as well as an issue. Her constant humility, sometimes glaring when set against her accomplishment, is a living example of inner security, wisdom, and maturity. She declines calling attention to herself, celebrating instead the accomplishments and possibilities she sees in others. She knows herself and knows her mission.

Every encounter with Maxine—her latest article, a book re-read, a lecture recalled, a card in the mail, a phone call or a conversation over coffee—remains for me, a sweet and perfect moment of support and challenge, of surprise and reunion. It is an opportunity to notice more of what there is to notice, to see more, to think more deeply, to *do* philosophy. I leave wanting to read more, to stay wide awake more, to resist the numbing effects of habit and convention, to consider the possibilities. Recently we talked on the phone, and she asked, "What do you make of the world?" We talked a long time. "I find in Europe cause for real despair. . . . But maybe at least in the children I can still see some hope." Now I want to do more, to care for children more, to embrace people more, to dance more, to fight the power more, to move beyond where I am now. I feel spaces opening up before me; I feel called upon to pay closer attention; and I feel challenged to act on what I now see and understand. What more could any student ask of his teacher than that?

CHAPTER TEN

In Class with Philip W. Jackson

David T. Hansen

I enrolled in a half-dozen of Professor Jackson's courses during my graduate career at the University of Chicago. I also had the opportunity to work closely with him as a research assistant in a three-year-long endeavor that he directed called The Moral Life of Schools Project. Professor Jackson also chaired my dissertation committee. I have written what follows from the point of view of those student days, which is why I will write in the past tense even though Jackson is as active a scholar today as he has ever been. I will take the liberty of saying some things on behalf of classmates, although neither they nor Jackson's students before or since that time should be held accountable for anything I shall have to say. Finally, while I do not know a soul alive with a better sense of humor than Jackson nor anyone with a warmer feeling of joie de vivre, I focus here on the teacher who, over the course of forty years, has shaped the role of professor in a most distinctive and uncompromising way.

Readers of Plato's *Dialogues* will remember the metaphors employed to capture Socrates' conversational practice. Socrates is a "stingray" whose skillful questioning "numbs" people as they become aware of how little they know. He is a "gadfly" who jolts others out of their complacent beliefs. He is a "midwife" who helps others develop their ideas and judge whether those ideas are vivid or stillborn. Socrates' passion for intellectual conversation is so unbounded that he even describes himself as suffering from a "malady."

Jackson's deep love for inquiry and for talking about inquiry is not so extreme that it would qualify as a malady, although I believe he would resonate with Dewey's self-reflection that "while I am quite regular at my meals I think that I may say that I had rather work—and perhaps even more play—with ideas and thinking than eat." This caveat aside, it seems to me that the other metaphors I have recalled illuminate both Jackson's style and his impact as a teacher.

Jackson began his university career in the 1950s strictly as a lecturer in the classroom. At that time, he was a card-carrying educational psychologist, an intellectual affiliation that began to wane, however, well before his pioneering *Life in Classrooms* appeared in 1968. That book takes a detailed, extended look at what goes on inside elementary school classrooms. Over the years, the book has released many an educational researcher from the spell of experimental methods and encouraged them to pursue inquiry in natural settings. It has had an enormous influence on the emergence of what is today called qualitative research. As Jackson's philosophical interests in education took center stage in his scholarly life, he abandoned lecturing and emphasized whole-group discussion of individual texts and ideas. In so doing he became something of a stingray with students, albeit not in the single-minded way in which we see Socrates conducting himself.

Jackson typically started class by asking a question like "What kind of a text is this?" That question stumped many students. Many had never been asked to think about such a thing. One could almost feel in the ethos of the classroom the response, "What do you mean, What kind of a text is this? This is an 'assigned reading,' that's what it is, and we're dutifully here to listen to you explain it to us!" But if we expected Jackson to explain things to us we were headed for disappointment. Gradually, students would begin to speak up, and in fact would begin speaking up quite eagerly once they realized that doing so was precisely the point. As we did so, Jackson would sometimes rephrase our comments, also in ways that impressed us since his ability to make plain our often inarticulate gropings was amazing. We would begin to wonder: Is Aristotle's *Ethics* a blueprint for the ethical life, a set of propositions about how to live, a challenge to our political beliefs? Is Wordsworth's "Ode on Immortality" a commentary on art, on religion, on the life of the mind, or is it all of the above or none of the above? Is Dewey's *Art as Experience* (1934) a book about art or is it a work of art itself? Is it aesthetic criticism, a philosophical critique, or a work of educational counsel on how to improve our moral sensibilities?

As far as I recall, Jackson never explained his "method" of leading a discussion of such questions. But it became evident in time. The conversation was always open: any member of the class had the license to pose further questions or to suggest a direction the talk might take. There was no lesson plan detectable in Jackson's approach, no set of passages or ideas in the reading we had to cover. Much of what we read would remain untouched in class, which meant we simply passed by (at least as a group) innumerable ideas and claims authors were making. We simply had no idea what passages would become the center of our talk, nor what ideas and issues would emerge as the most important to us. In time, it became apparent that each class was destined to be an adventure into the unknown. This approach helped people to stop reading for the "answer" and to think carefully about their *own* reactions to the reading. It became clear that the purpose of the conversation was not to master what Plato, Rousseau, Dewey, or anyone else had to say about education. The purpose was to think as well as we could about the reading and the issues it raised for us. The purpose was to explore new possibilities. Sometimes, Jackson would make this aim explicit by asking questions like "What would it mean if we took so-and-so seriously, and we reformed education in light of it?" and, more dramatically, "What would it mean to live our lives according to what this person has written?" The utter seriousness with which Jackson took these questions was contagious for many. His classroom became a kind of laboratory: what will we talk about today? what new ways of being will we sound out? what would our lives really be like if we lived by these ideas rather than by our self-satisfied, comfortable assumptions? Many in Jackson's classroom were truly "stung" by these questions and came to cherish the intellectual liberation they promoted.

However, some students reacted to the sting by distancing themselves from the whole premise of Jackson's approach. Some lacked intellectual discipline and generosity, reading into the texts and into the conversation their prior convictions and opinions—as if what everyone else in class had to say was irrelevant to them. Jackson would routinely call into question viewpoints on the authors we read that were not supportable from the texts themselves. This frustrated some people, who appeared to perceive graduate education as an occasion to display what they already knew rather than as an occasion to learn something new. Some students took it upon themselves to "inform" us about the career of a particular author and what previous scholarship had to say about the person's work—as i f they were thereby bringing us "the word" and we could abandon all this classroom chatter.

Jackson's reactions to such people were frank and unsparing although never unkind. He never said directly, in my memory at least, that they did not understand that the purpose was not to haul in a host of critics (which Jackson himself could easily have done) or that their wise summaries of an author's work were full of holes. He would either let silence reign—in effect, waiting for the class itself to decide how to respond—or h e would sputter "So what?" or "What do you want us to make of all that?" His annoyance got the better of him only when someone proffered an opinion in a casual, off-the-cuff, or self-satisfied tone. Jackson would sometimes snap back impatiently and almost angrily as if outraged that anyone would waste this precious moment of their life—and his—by acting so complacently.

This is what most endures from my memories of Jackson's classroom: that the project of learning to think for oneself is not a sideshow to life, it *is* life itself, in fact how we treat this text and one another's ideas for the next hour is *decisive* for the kinds of people we will become. Jackson's approach promoted the moral obligation of respect: respect for authors, in the sense of trying to understand what they were saying, and respect for what other participants in class were trying to say—even if we ended up disagreeing with all of it. His approach prodded us to think about who and what we might become if we took these ideas to heart—if they were to become our creed, the guide to how we might live. It asked us to accept the premise that we will never understand new ideas or their potential if we do not take them seriously on their own terms rather than insisting—

hard habit to break!—on reading our own viewpoints and prejudices into them. The approach beckoned us to consider critically what is different from or even alien to our own ways of thinking. It steered us away from the narrow-minded path of pigeon-holing ideas and the pedantic path of relying on the experts. The approach was confounding to those who wanted "straight answers," particularly straight answers from the professor. It was an adventure to those who realized, in one (usually inchoate) way or another, that we were drawing nearer to the meaning of education.

I recall moments of wonderful tension in class as we scoured the text and our minds for how to respond to a question or as we sought to put into words the question that most needed asking at the time. Jackson cultivated this environment by keeping us focussed on ideas rather than entertaining a lot of personal anecdotes. He referred to us by our last names, not even adding a "Ms." or "Mrs." or "Mr." He would respond in discussion by saying: "Okay, Jones"; "Mustoe has the floor, then Amburn"; "So are you saying, Arcilla, in response to DePencier, that ... "; "Go ahead, Alston, and then Pillsbury." I am still not quite sure why Jackson addressed us this way, save that it promoted distance which I think he found productive for pushing us intellectually. It was also clear that he was not concerned about being liked personally and that he was not there to "like" us. His comments on our often garbled arguments in class were always fair-minded, but he avoided words of personal approval or disapproval. He was never paternalistic nor was he a friend, at least in class. It was not until I began work as a research assistant that Jackson said to me one day, "As long as we're going to be working together closely, let's use first names." After several years of knowing him as "Professor Jackson," I actually found it difficult to get used to calling him "Phil."

In brief, Jackson acted as if our being there in the doctoral program reflected an intellectual commitment on our part and that we had enough independence of mind and spirit to want to take the initiative ourselves in our own education. He presumed an interest on our part in thinking. For some students this was spectacularly true, and I remember learning a great deal from them. For others, Jackson's assumptions about intellectual seriousness gradually became their own, too. For still others things did not come together and they left, perhaps wishing they had received something more than high expectations and demanding standards.

None of this is to say that Jackson was aloof in class or in the hallways and offices of Judd Hall. I think he avoided terms of personal approval or disapproval—e.g., "I like your idea"—because he wanted to suggest that he was not the final arbiter of ideas. In time, it became clear that the authority in Jackson's classroom resided in the conversation itself, in the shape that ideas began to take, in how we resonated to them or found them wanting or misleading or objectionable—regardless of from whom the ideas came. In time, many of my peers and I could hardly wait for the next class. We were spurred by curiosity about what others would say about the readings, and we were drawn—drawn powerfully—by the experience of having our views and interests taken so seriously.

Jackson's classes were fun, even entertaining, even when he went into "gadfly" mode. A student might describe teaching in glowing, almost spiritual terms, to which Jackson would reply: "What do you mean, 'teaching is a sacred act'? What about driver's education or auto mechanics school? These folks are teachers, too, aren't they?" The effect of Jackson's questions was often to jar the entire class into a whole new line of thinking. When current issues in education came up, he could hardly resist stinging his own research community with barbs such as, "All these studies, and yet I sometimes wonder whether we know less today about the meaning of education than we did before they all began." He would briefly recount a visit to another city's school system or his attendance at some important conference. With reddening face and rising voice, he would share his dismay at what people were doing in the face of all commonsense. This is not to say that Jackson belittled others or their plans and hopes. Quite the contrary. We were taken by his stories precisely because they reflected such genuine concern with how awry things so often go in the public realm. Although he never spelled it out, I think the moral of Jackson's reports from the front was how helpful it would be if educators stopped reforming everything in sight and instead examined their own values and assumptions. To reform things often means reforming other people, which is a remarkable assignment to grant oneself if one recalls that reforming people does not necessarily mean the same thing as educating them. Jackson seemed to imply that if educators modeled reflection and self-criticism, they might promote such qualities in the larger society, which would surely be a change with more far-reaching consequences than those that have issued from many reform efforts.

As a rule, we did not spend much time in class examining current educational research—including Jackson's own. Not once in my six years as a student with him did he ever assign any of his many books or articles. I am sure that many students who took their required philosophy of education course with him never realized how prolific and influential a scholar he has been. I think Jackson assumed, rightly or wrongly, that we could explore current research either on our own or in other courses. He did have an intimate knowledge of what was happening in the research community. Sometimes, one or another line of inquiry would arise in discussion—e.g., does current research on classroom discourse support or refute Wittgenstein's view of language games. We would take up such issues and go as far as was appropriate with them. But the titles of Jackson's courses are telling: Dewey as educator, Wittgenstein as educator, Wordsworth and Coleridge as educators. He did teach standard departmental offerings with titles like principles of curriculum and the aforementioned philosophy of education. However, his syllabi always included a liberal dose of Aristotle, Plato, Dewey, as well as contemporary philosophers.

In my view Jackson taught this curriculum not because of any disinterest in educational scholarship, to which he has been such a major contributor. Rather, he has long been taken with the broad, complex question of how we should perceive and describe our everyday human experience. He has been absorbed with thinking about the consequences for human conduct, including for educational practice, that flow from our answers to the question. Jackson's quest has led him to Dewey,

Wittgenstein, Wordsworth, and others who made this same inquiry part of their life projects. His quest has fueled his long-term love affair with poetry and painting, arts which are so deeply engaged with the question of how we see our lives and our place in the world.

I believe Jackson also taught this curriculum because he has long been repelled by the notion of joining a particular academic camp or of becoming labelled as a certain kind of scholar with a certain fixed line of thinking. He has resisted attempts to fit his writings into some preconceived academic territory. I recall his stance being downright exasperating to some (as was his habitual reluctance to spell out his own views on the readings assigned for class discussion). It was almost as if Jackson refused to play by the rules, refused to settle down and stay at home in one or another intellectual camp. That posture flies in the face of the university system. A great deal of the scholarship that takes place in that system is predicated upon the construction of "houses," each centered upon a theme, an idea, a problem. Groups of scholars form and assemble the bricks that go into their construction. Additions go up, sometimes parts are pulled down or redone in the light of new work. These enterprises are reflected in the curricular offerings and even in the physical layout of universities, with history in one building, biology in another, and so forth. While Jackson would hail the social benefits that have accrued from such an arrangement—without minimizing its costs—he taught as if he had too much intellectual curiosity and restlessness to remain comfortable in any particular house. I think this is why he taught writers who were themselves explorers, who sought to think honestly, tenaciously, and with intellectual and moral passion about human experience.

In time, it began to dawn on my peers and me that our teacher was indeed something of an enigma. He was as well-versed in educational scholarship as any professor we knew, and yet his teaching was centered neither upon ongoing research nor upon building a knowledge of the field. His teaching was based on exploring the new rather than the known, on trying to grasp the thread of curiosity that gives rise to meaningful inquiry. Looking back from the distance of a few years, I think Jackson's courses invited us to reconsider what it means to call education an "applied field." Without ever doing so explicitly, his courses drew out the unexplored question of what "application" means. The term usually calls to mind cliches such as "relevance" and "is it practical?" However, its substantive meaning seems closer to the enactment of what we can see. That is, to apply what we know asks about the constitution of knowledge itself. It asks about the makeup of our minds—our ways of seeing the world. Application, then, is dependent on the quality of thinking and seeing that precedes it—and that accompanies it, because as Dewey among others has shown perception and practice are interdependent. To make use of a familiar adage, seeing the cup as half full or as half empty has profound consequences both for what we do and for the spirit in which we do it. I think that for Jackson there is nothing more practical than caring about and thinking about what forms our perception. There is nothing more decisive for practice than what frames our seeing. At least that was one message emitted by his entire approach to teaching.

In talking with Jackson in class and out, it became apparent that he viewed scholarship as a conversation among a community of inquirers, regardless of their formal disciplines, training, or affiliations. My peers and I participated in several inter-disciplinary discussion groups and seminars in his company, and it was obvious that he was at home as much with philos-ophers, literary critics, and anthropologists as he was among his fellow scholars of teaching and curriculum. Yet that "home," to return to my earlier metaphor, was not a building but more a state of mind. It had more to do with the spirit of inquiry than its current law, the latter embodied in various scholarly sub-groups. There really was no way to pin Jackson down. The academic and institutional structures with which all professors deal did not define him or his oeuvre. As far as I can tell, neither at that time nor since has Jackson had any interest whatsoever in being a spokesperson for a particular intellectual viewpoint or for a particular set of questions or concerns. Many have tried to convert him into that or to treat him as if he were indeed representative of a particular method or set of beliefs. As I suggested previously, some students left his classes irritated if not angry that he refused to show his true colors, not realizing that Jackson's palette seems always to be evolving as is what he is endeavoring to see.

The philosopher Gilbert Ryle sheds light here in the way he distinguishes genuine inquiry from its many counterfeits and alternatives. Ryle argues that genuine inquiry requires journeying into the new regardless of outcome. "I do not mean," he says about controversies in his field,

> that all philosophers really see eye to eye. It would, I am glad to say, be nearer the truth to say that they seldom see eye to eye if they are any good and if they are discussing live issues and not dead ones. A live issue is a piece of country in which no one knows which way to go. As there are no paths, there are no paths to share. Where there are paths to share, there are paths; and paths are the memorials of undergrowth already cleared.
>
> Nonetheless, though philosophers are and ought to be highly critical persons, their wrangles are not the by-products of loyalty to a party or a school of thought. There do, of course, exist in our midst and inside our skins plenty of disciples, heresy-hunters and electioneers; only these are not philosophers but something else that goes by the same long-suffering name. Karl Marx was sapient enough to deny the impeachment that he was a Marxist. So too Plato was, in my view, a very unreliable Platonist. He was too much of a philosopher to think that anything that he had said was the last word. It was left to his disciples to identify his footmarks with his destination. (Ryle, 1966, pp. 13-14)

My peers and I never did take on the role of disciple or follower. This was partly due to Jackson's approach to teaching, which was almost designed to prohibit this kind of relationship. That approach implied not only that he had no interest in being a "leader" but that the sheer idea of intellectual "followers" was stultifying, perhaps even an oxymoron. At one time or another, I suspect each of us came near that point. I recall moments of intense intellectual confusion when I would have been happy to settle for being a follower. But we were students, not disciples. We called ourselves the "C & I Dogs," because we were enrolled in the Curriculum and Instruction program, and because we were like a pack, roaming together through classes and endless conversations. It is true that we yapped at Jackson's heels and surrounded him with our barking enthusiasm. But he was no trainer or feeder, rather he was the most interesting teacher around. If we "followed" him, we followed his example by endeavoring to pursue the questions and concerns that most animated our own spirits and minds. Jackson's questions were not ours, nor did he seek to make them so. But his conviction in the value of asking live questions, and of pursuing them with courage and fortitude, became something to which we all aspired.

A visit to Jackson's office was as much an adventure as taking one of his classes. Like many others, I ventured there for talks with him about texts, papers assigned for class, the state of educational affairs, and more. Jackson was welcoming, respectful, attentive, as if always mindful of the delicate role a teacher can play in a student's development. Yet he was not sacramental about such matters. His natural delight in humor won the day and he could not help but tease and cajole students along their journey although even the teasing seemed artful and purposive. I recall writing a 70-page paper on Plato's *Theaetetus* to fulfill one of our doctoral requirements. My paper was twice as long as it needed to be. I was very proud of it. I went to Jackson's office to hear what he thought. I saw a gleam in his eye when I sat down and immediately became worried. Sure enough, he took up my mini-tome in hand, as if weighing it, and said "This calls to mind those announcers who cover golf games on TV. You know how they always speak in quiet, reverential tones: 'Now the green is about 30 yards off, he'll have to wedge this with care to center it. But everyone on the circuit knows this is his forte, so let's see how he handles it'." Jackson continued in the same whispering tone of voice.

Without ever stating it in so many words, he informed me that my paper was written in a pretentious, preachy, and overly-somber tone, as if it were truly the wisest thing ever written about the *Theaetetus* not to mention the human condition. I was staggered by this discovery—"at first I was like a man who has been hit by a good boxer, things went dark and I felt giddy"—and yet I was not devastated because I immediately realized that Jackson was right. I also realized that he was endeavoring to help me, like a midwife who assists in bringing to life something new. He laid my mini-tome back on his desk. Without looking at me, he asked: "What are you trying to say here?" He was suddenly so serious. I remember taking a deep breath before I replied, as if I were about to enter unknown territory. And so I was, for this had become a fine time not to worry about all the scholarship I had pored over on Plato and the *Theaetetus* but rather to say as clearly as possible *why* I was devoting part of my life to studying this dialogue. Jackson was asking: what is the significance of what you are doing, both in terms of what is going on in this dialogue—what is its significance—and what is going on in your own developing understanding of the meaning of education?

I was able to say some things that afternoon and we talked for quite awhile. The upshot became my first published article, a much revised version of my initial paper that I called "Was Socrates a 'Socratic Teacher'?" I have been trying to convey here that as far as my classmates and I were concerned, Philip W. Jackson certainly was.

CHAPTER ELEVEN

Laura Zirbes: A Teacher of Teachers

Paul R. Klohr

No reflection on Laura Zirbes turns out right without first casting her professional life into the lived context at Ohio State University during those years of her long tenure there. Her career is especially significant in the history of elementary education, for it documents the continuing struggle of that field of study to achieve recognition and professional status.

Reid (1993) ably describes Zirbes in his biography, *Towards Creative Teaching: The Life and Career of Laura Zirbes*. He refers to her as one of the "Dauntless Women": a second generation of women leaders in education following several such greats as Patty Smith Hill, the prime mover of kindergarten. No epitaph more readily fits Zirbes. And as Reid asserts, "The ultimate reason for studying any person is to learn how he or she was important in her own times." I want to extend that to say, "And also, now."

My memory of Zirbes as a significant influence in my own professional life fully supports both Reid's thesis and my own conviction of her contemporary value as a theoretical-historical bridge between then and now. I sense that such relationships between historically significant work and what we see as currently promising ideas tend not to be recognized.

My first encounter with Laura Zirbes (I use "encounter," for that is the way one typically came to know her) was on a cold January morning in 1946. A large woman with her arms loaded with several big mailing tubes and other packaged materials, she was fumbling to open the heavy doors of Arps Hall, the College of Education building at Ohio State University. Here I digress to point out that this building was named after a former dean, George Arps, who had studied in Germany with Wundt, the father of scientific measurement of behavior. Some of us graduate students were almost certain that his ghost still lingered on the top floor, which then housed one of the nation's largest psychology departments, yearly turning out many of the professors of psychology who were staffing departments throughout the country in post-World War II America. Moreover, the building also housed a major research bureau headed by W.W. Charters with his activity analysis approach to curriculum development. On hand, too, were Edgar Dale and his associates with lists of words that children at different grade levels were able to recognize. This "word list" was the "scientific" basis eagerly sought by publishers of graded basic reading materials. Much of this Arps Hall aura was anathema to Zirbes.

When I knew her, she had learned to live with the tensions of two worlds—the so-called "scientific" world where she was officed and her own world which was, at that time, an alternative one which she was convinced was more fully scientific in the Deweyian sense of that term. Despite the tensions of these polarized views within the college, there was during the years of Zirbes' tenure a "civility" about the discourse among her colleagues. This contributed to a collegiality often rare in higher education in the 1990s.

My offer to help Laura that January day was quickly taken in a transfer of part of her load to my arms as we moved into the Elementary Education Center, a ground-level space she had wrangled from the male-dominated administration in a time of a great shortage of classrooms on campus. "You are Klohr, aren't you?" she said, peering through the steamed-up, heavy lenses of her glasses. "[Harold] Alberty said you might come by."

My hesitancy in meeting up with Zirbes and my initial awkward response to this chance encounter had roots in the myth, then widespread among the local graduate students, that there was a deep chasm between the two strong departments of elementary and secondary education. In pursuing doctoral work one must, if he or she were wise, pursue one or the other. To the contrary, my experience as a classroom teacher had suggested a doctoral program in curriculum should be *both* elementary and secondary. This proposed direction was strengthened by my observations in the experimental University School on campus which had a K-12 curriculum with planned continuity between what were traditionally viewed as elementary and secondary levels.

A beginning graduate student with only a bachelor's degree, I responded rather awkwardly: "When can I schedule an appointment?" She gave a quick, "Why not now?" Shedding her coat and indicating a seat at one of the tables that were a part of the informal setting she had created for the Center, she began. "I understand from Alberty that you have got hold of a tough problem—one that also worries me. What ought to be the relationship between elementary and secondary curriculum? Now, let's face what we can do about it." This, I discovered, proved to be a typical Zirbes response to most professional issues—both theoretical and practical.

Before I could respond, she continued : "I have a class here in a few minutes. Why don't you sit in on it and see if you think I can bring anything useful to your graduate work. Now, help me put up some of these pictures I got in New York over the Christmas break."

Zirbes often brought back from her trips carefully selected reproductions of artwork. These she shared with the University School elementary grades, sitting with groups of children to get them to understand why they liked one picture over another.

With the teacher education class that followed our initial conversation, she developed that day the concept of how the visual arts might be integrated into the curriculum. At that time, art in most schools was largely a matter of coloring or filling in mimeographed outlines on small sheets of paper. I came to know that, for Zirbes, the arts should be a major core running throughout the curriculum. She developed a sound rationale for such a curriculum design. Her arts involved a wide range of activities with all kinds of visual experiences as well as activities in dance, music, and drama. On campus, the University School, which had been established in 1932 and had become one of the most experimental schools in the Eight Year Study, included a four-to-five-year-old kindergarten as well as elementary, middle school, and secondary school levels.

The curriculum design of those early years in the K-12 sequence had evolved to a great degree from Zirbes' work with her summer demonstration schools. These schools were her pioneer effort at demonstrating the larger role of the related arts. This early work merged with Harold Alberty's efforts to help the secondary school faculty plan and demonstrate a philosophical/theoretical rationale for its experimental K-12 curriculum. Zirbes agreed to "take me on" as a student along with Alberty, who chaired my doctoral committee.

In the several years that followed this eventful encounter with Zirbes, I came to understand how she functioned as a teacher. Foremost was her effort to involve students in a problem-solving approach. Her illustrations, anecdotes, demonstrations, discussions of readings, and reflections on classroom observations were all open ended. What are we seeing here? Can you see yourself in this situation? What would you bring to this problem? Where can we get some resources that would throw light on this? Her classes ended with students left discussing and thinking further about these matters. She insisted that we keep journals to jot down throughout the days and weeks our first-hand, unedited thoughts—not only about education, but also about our own life as we lived it from day to day. She worked hard to get students to know themselves as a first step to becoming effective teachers. Some of the early dissertations she guided were written in first person—a breakthrough from the traditional so-called "objective" third-person style of professional writing.

Years later, whenever I associated with classroom teachers, both locally and in other settings, I could invariably "spot" those who had worked with Zirbes. They pursued this kind of problem-solving attack that was her professional trademark. And equally significant, they tended to have a solid, reliable philosophical perspective on the values that they were convinced should undergird all of education.

Zirbes was an extraordinary, powerful teacher. She challenged students and her professional colleagues to rethink, revision, and reimagine their professional goals and to design methods for achieving them. As I have indicated, she did this in a setting dominated by an almost totally male faculty caught up in a larger professional world centered on instruction. She could not have taken this pioneering role without the full support of several of her colleagues—individuals like Boyd Bode, Harold Alberty, and H. Gordon Hullfish, who were on hand pursuing an extension of Dewey's thinking to provide a strong philosophical base. Fortunately for her work and that of these colleagues, the University School had the freedom by its charter to be an island protected from the dominant ethos of the College and the University, free to generate its own philosophy and to demonstrate an elementary and secondary program in the light of that philosophy. Zirbes played a significant role in that laboratory setting.

I recognize the possibility that a memoir of a favorite teacher runs the risk of being loaded with unintentional hyperbole—a look back through rose-colored glasses. I want, therefore, to turn this essay into an identification of some of the concepts that clearly were intellectual themes in Zirbes' professional career. To check myself in this effort, I reread her written work, observed again her audio-visual materials, and recalled anew my convictions about her influence on my own thinking from earlier discussions of what she stood for with two of her many doctoral advisees who later achieved national recognition—Harold Shane and Leland Jacobs—Shane at Indiana University and Jacobs at Teachers College. As a result of this checking, I believe the themes I identify here do illustrate what Zirbes stood for. Moreover, I believe that they illustrate my thesis that her thinking was a significant historical bridge between cutting-edge ideas in her post-World War II world and some of the most exciting breakthroughs now beginning to receive attention in the best reform efforts of the 1990s.

These four statements of themes follow in no special sequence and are clearly without a fully-fleshed out philosophical/theoretical discussion—perhaps the kind of notes Zirbes might have made for herself on cards when she addressed groups of educators, as she did throughout her career, at a state Association for Supervision and Curriculum Development (ASCD) conference or a national assembly audience of ACEI (Association for Childhood Education International). Her world with a national audience was not much different from her home environment with a group of elementary teachers in the

Elementary Center of Arps Hall. In Kipling's phrase, she "walked with kings" but did not "lose the common touch."

Effective curriculum planning and implementation require a democratic school setting. Zirbes' efforts, along with those of Harold Alberty, are clearly reflected in the University School's philosophy and purposes which they helped to create with the faculty of the school. "Democracy as a way of life" was the driving force of the school throughout its existence. This value position was also the basis for Zirbes' own university teaching. It involves a basic reconceptualization of relationships between teacher and student and among teachers and administrators, and indeed, between the school and a larger community.

New goals and purposes not foreseen at the outset evolve as the curriculum planning process moves ahead. Throughout her career, Zirbes warned against the linearity of curriculum planning with a technological rationale. For her, the detailed initial statements of countless specific goals, intended finally to produce specific outcomes, were bound to submerge critical new goals that would emerge in the planning process involving teachers working with students. She found support from her colleagues, Bode and Alberty, as they extended Dewey's philosophical position. She also drew on emerging conceptions of humanistic psychology and thinking that were defining new frontiers in sociology and anthropology. If you wanted to find the newest publications in these fields, Zirbes would have them before the library or any other faculty member. She would hand such books to students and always ask: "What do you think?" Her probing questions would leave no doubt but that she had thoroughly read each publication and had projected its implications for the study of education.

In problem-solving no sharp divisions exist between the cognitive and the creative. Curriculum experiences for Zirbes drew heavily on the arts—art, music, dance, and drama. She worked closely with her friend and colleague, Ross Mooney, in his research into the nature of creativity. Her leadership in the 1952 national Granville Conference on Creativity perhaps best illustrated this persistent interest in the arts. Too, this interest is reflected in the design of the University School curriculum which she influenced. It had a central core of related arts from kindergarten through grade 12. For Zirbes all good thinking was, in itself, a creative act.

Curriculum planning and design must attend to the developmental tasks of children and youth. Zirbes was always sensitive to the need to recognize developmental tasks of children and youth. The University School, early after its establishment, had Robert Havighurst as a faculty member, the individual who later proposed the concept of "developmental tasks. " Willard Olson's work on the longitudinal studies of the "organismic age" of children also provided theoretical support for Zirbes' conviction that a teacher should "move" with a group of children over a longer period of time than one school year. Otherwise, she knew, teachers could not really begin to observe and guide effectively growth and development which did not normally take place at an even, specified rate. This position also raised serious questions about clearly defined grade levels and encouraged interage grouping within the school.

There were other themes that ran through Zirbes' work, but these four give something of the flavor of her professional views as I reflect on them some 30 years after her death as an emerita professor. In 1948 when President Truman gave her the National Woman of the Year Award, he called her a "teacher of teachers." She liked that! I also think that she would have liked to be remembered in May Sarton's words. Sarton spoke of herself as a person who had "given herself away like a tree that sows seeds every spring" as a "tree's way of being—to spill out its treasure on the wind."

PART FOUR

Extending an Invitation To Share a Journey

Harold Alberty, Teacher and Guide
by Victor B. Lawhead

Florence B. Stratemeyer: Teacher Educator for a Free People
by Martin Haberman

Alice Miel: Exemplar of Democracy Made Real
by Louise Berman

The Longevity of a Good Mentor: J. Harlan Shores
by William H. Schubert

The professor's journey is one that goes to the edge of the known world. One of the aims of the journey is to push back the boundaries of that world and to discover ways of engaging others in this task and of sharing with them all its mystery and wonder. Such is the spirit of the four essays that follow—essays about Harold Alberty, Florence B. Stratemeyer, Alice Miel, and J. Harlan Shores. Each of these educators engaged different sets of questions at the edge of their world; yet, there is much commonality, not only in their aims but in the means they used to invite others to share their journey.

Using Bellah's concept of a "community of memory," Lawhead shows how Alberty sought to engage his students. The notion that students need to be introduced into such a community and to make it their own is a theme running through the four essays. Books are repositories of memory. Each mentor opened up these repositories to their students and showed them what and how to read in order to better understand the intellectual journey. Stratemeyer insisted that her students provide evidence to substantiate their views: "On what basis do you say that?," she would ask. Alberty required weekly note cards on readings. At their first meeting, Shores placed on Schubert's lap a large stack of books. That students would read and read widely was assumed.

The invitation to share a journey took other forms. Possessing their own established research agendas, each author provided formal and informal contexts within which to explore ideas with students, including special seminars and opportunities to criticize evolving drafts of articles, chapters, and books. Just as professors sought to engage students, students' ideas created new insights for professors. Recognition for such contributions was given. Various editions of Alberty's *Reorganizing the High-School Curriculum* are scattered with citations of student dissertations, and numerous publications bear his students' names. Berman observes the influence of Miel's students on *Supervision for Improved Instruction* written with Arthur Lewis. Schubert describes how his ongoing informal conversations with Shores influenced his work over two decades and continue to influence his work still. And, homes were opened as well as offices.

Responding to written work was taken as an opportunity to give careful feedback to students, to pose questions, and to sharpen thinking in ways that would ever widen the boundaries of students' own understanding. Precision in language was modeled and expected. Respectfully and carefully, professors' comments left the students with feelings of gratitude, of having been carefully guided along a potentially treacherous road rather than compared to trite evaluation standards. Possessing a prodigious memory, Stratemeyer took student ideas seriously, remembered them, and sought opportunities to gently remind authors of contradictions in their thinking. Never imposing her world view on others, she offered her beliefs for consideration and invited students to think, to participate more fully and actively in the intellectual life.

Efforts were made to connect students with other teachers who presented the possibility of enriching their journey. Lawhead studied with V.T. Thayer and Schubert with Harry Broudy, for example. As Berman states about Miel: "Her collegiality evidenced itself in . . . opening doors for students to be involved with other professors who shared a student's interests."

Joining in a journey eventually leads students to find their own paths, their own ways to the edge of what is known. These mentors understood this, and in inviting others to come along, they simultaneously provided means for their students to find their own ways.

Biographical Information

Harold Alberty [born: Oct. 6, 1890, Lockport, NY; died: Feb. 2, 1971, Columbus, OH] served as professor of education at Ohio State University from 1927-1959. He was graduated from Baldwin University (Berea, OH) in 1912 with a Ph.B.; other degrees include the L.L.B. from Cleveland Law School in 1913 and an A.M. in 1923 and Ph.D. in 1926 from Ohio State University. Other professional roles included serving as a teacher, principal, and superintendent in the public schools of northeastern Ohio from 1911-1926. Alberty's publications include *Supervision in the Secondary School* (1931) with co-author V.T. Thayer and *Reorganizing the High-School Curriculum* (1947; 1953; with co-author Elise Alberty in 1962). Professor Alberty served as a curriculum consultant for the P.E.A.'s Eight Year Study, director of the Ohio State University Laboratory School, and the "unofficial" author of the P.E.A.'s *Science in General Education* (1938).

Florence B. Stratemeyer [born: Feb. 17, 1900, Detroit, MI; died: May 10, 1980, New York, NY] served as Co-Director of the Bureau of Curriculum Research and professor of education at

Teachers College, Columbia University, from 1924-1965. She was graduated from Columbia University in 1923 with a B.S., an A.M. in 1927, and the Ph.D. in 1931. Other professional roles included serving as a teacher in the Detroit public schools from 1919-1920 and critic teacher/instructor at the Detroit Teachers College from 1920-1924. Stratemeyer's publications include co-authoring *Developing a Curriculum for Modern Living* (1947/1957) and *Working with Student Teachers* (1958) with Margaret Lindsey.

Alice Miel [born: Feb. 21, 1906, Six Lakes, MI] served as professor of education at Teachers College, Columbia University, from 1942-1971. She was graduated from the University of Michigan in 1928 with an A.B.; other degrees include an M.A. from the University of Michigan in 1931 and the Ed.D. from Teachers College in 1944. Other professional roles include serving as a high school teacher in the Michigan public schools from 1924-1930, elementary and junior high school teacher and principal in the Ann Arbor (MI) schools from 1930-1939, and a curriculum coordinator in the Michigan schools from 1939-1942. Miel's publications include *Changing the Curriculum* (1946) and *In the Minds of Men* (1970) with co-editor Louise Berman. Professor Miel has served in a number of leadership roles including as president of the Association for Supervision and Curriculum Development.

J. Harlan Shores [born: Sept. 27, 1915, Dearborn, MO; died: April 27, 1993, Champaign, IL] served as professor of education at the University of Illinois from 1941-1975. He was graduated from the University of Kansas in 1937 with an A.B.; other degrees include an A.M. from the University of Minnesota in 1938 and the Ph.D. in 1940. Other professional roles included holding a professorship in education at St. Cloud State College from 1940-1941. Shores' publications include coauthoring *Fundamentals of Curriculum Development* (1950, 1957). Professor Shores has served in a number of leadership roles including as president of the Association for Supervision and Curriculum Development.

CHAPTER TWELVE

Harold Alberty, Teacher and Guide

Victor B. Lawhead

This recollection is based on an association spanning the thirty-one years from 1940, when I first met Harold Alberty on the campus of Ohio State University, to his death in 1971. During those years I had the good fortune of being a student in most of his courses, claimed him as my graduate advisor for doctoral studies, and served as a colleague in various capacities within the scope of our continuing professional association. While most of these encounters were reasonably formal, I cherished the special but limited opportunities to come to know him as a friend and mentor. His patient effort and encouraging support brought me to a fuller understanding of what it means to work with a master teacher in the serious study of educational problems.

My earliest acquaintance with Alberty's educational ideas came in 1939, my senior year at DePauw University, when I began a two-semester sequence of "practice teaching" in the local high school. Encouraged by Professor Earl Bowman, an earlier student of Alberty's, my classmate Paul Klohr and I (along with others from art and music) agreed to teach as a team a unit of correlated studies to which my critic teacher, Glenn Skelton, had attached the unfamiliar label, "core curriculum." My class in American history was to be the point of departure for teaching a unit of study on the Civil War enriched whenever possible by the contributions of my fellow students from other subject fields. I was not to realize immediately the long-term effects of this experience, for I can recall only a few details of our joint venture; rather, I remember more vividly my looking forward to Thursday—the day for "Current Events." The war in Europe had broken loose at the end of August that year, and most of us who were about to graduate sensed a new urgency to deal with the inevitable turn of events which would soon redirect our lives in countless ways. I did not pursue further the notion of a core curriculum at the time but instead persisted in nurturing a host of unanswered questions about the value and potential of "integrating" as an essential component of the learning process. Alberty's synthesis of ideas around a core program of general education, already having its impact, was still in the formulative stage and was not to be articulated fully until the publication of *Reorganizing the High-School Curriculum* in 1947.

My first meeting with Harold Alberty himself was fairly incidental and came in the summer of 1940 when Klohr and I, still motivated by Professor Bowman's enthusiasm for Ohio State's College of Education, enrolled there as graduate students. To help some students "get started in life," DePauw in those days provided Rector Scholars upon graduation with the tidy sum of $100, ample support for a summer term in most universities. Thus replenished, we proceeded in June to Columbus to take up studies with Boyd Bode and other luminaries from our undergraduate reading list. Without having attended a full week of lectures, we were "recruited" by Professor H. Gordon Hullfish to participate in what was to be the second from the last of the well-known workshops sponsored jointly by the Progressive Education Association and the University's College of Education. It was then that I met Harold Alberty, who with other members of the College staff, participated in the workshop on an occasional basis.

Was it in spite of or because of an ominous threat of war and the totalitarian challenge to democratic values that this was a time of boundless optimism among progressive educators? Few documents of the time were more typical of the expressions of faith in democratic education than the draft report of the P.E.A.'s Committee on Philosophy, "Progressive Education: Its Philosophy and Challenge" (Alberty et al., 1941). The report sketched a bold proposal for linking democratic values to educational practice and placed particular emphasis on understanding human development and the valuing process. In seeking wide discussion of the report prior to its publication, Professors Alberty and Hullfish, as Committee chair and member, respectively, distributed mimeographed copies to Workshop participants for their reactions and comments. For me this initial skirmish with progressive thought and the exhilarating experience of the Workshop itself was to set a life course and allow me to enter upon a human relationship that was to be defined ultimately by time and circumstance.

I connect my earliest recollection of Alberty with the P.E.A. and one of its most significant documents in the same sense that Robert Bellah and his associates describe how exemplary individuals embody the meaning of a "community of memory"—a real community that does not forget its past (Bellah et al., 1985, pp. 152-155). The educational ideas of this credo, shared by Alberty and fellow progressives of his time, have provided the substance of a continuing perspective on educational practice shared successively by the stream of educators who have followed in this tradition throughout this century. In the intervening years this community of memory which ties its members to the past has been the community that now sustains our best aspirations for the future course of education. What follows in my retrospective of this distinguished member of the education professoriate is part of the narrative and history of that community.

Toward a Core Program of General Education

Students sometimes referred to Alberty in his presence as the father or perhaps the grandfather of the core program. "If so," he would retort with some levity, "it is an illegitimate child." This often could serve as his starting point for crediting the influence of others on his own ideas and theoretical positions. There is a saying that a teacher learns much from his teachers, more from his colleagues, but most from his students. Of the several influences which shaped his thought and action and which especially interested those who studied under his tutelage at the time, none seemed more pervasive than that of his graduate mentor, Professor Boyd Bode. Through conversation and published acknowledgment Alberty left little doubt but that Bode's impact was primary. Recalling the origin of their relationship, he often spoke with irony of leaving the comfortable security of school administration in Cuyahoga County,

Ohio, to come to the Ohio State University to experience intellectual devastation at the hands of Bode whose mock-serious taunting of school administrators Alberty had resented at the time. John Dewey, with whom he was associated briefly in 1928, and colleagues Max Otto of the University of Wisconsin and V.T. Thayer of the Ethical Culture Schools in New York, also served as central influences in the development of Alberty's philosophical views. Faculty colleagues of the College of Education, in the third and fourth decades of this century, with their collective involvement with others in the Progressive Education Association, presented an exciting forum where Alberty's curriculum proposals could face the test of philosophic argument. Particularly formative in shaping his curriculum ideas were his experiences as chair of the Committee of Science on General Education of the P.E.A.'s Eight Year Study and his close association with teachers in a laboratory setting at the University School, where he served as Director from 1938 to 1941.

Probably to a greater extent than with any other curriculum topic, Alberty has been identified with core programs of general education in high schools. This identification was due in part to his concern that the meaning of the term "core" had become elusive when reduced to concrete elements of curriculum structure. In his view the expression "core curriculum" was a contradiction in terms for it implied the core was the totality of the curriculum, dismissing entirely the important role of specialized education as a necessary complement to general education. Thus he proceeded to redefine what he conceived to be the organic relationship between the pair of concepts.

"You can't ride both horses at the same time," Alberty used to caution when he observed a tendency of curriculum designers to organize general education around the duality of both problems and subject matter. Although he shared with Dewey and others the necessity for making the experience of problem-solving central to the educative process, his unique contribution to educational reform rests in large measure on the insights he brought to content reorganization. Sensitive to matters of structure as well as instructional strategy, he perceived the practical necessity of defining a core program with sufficient parameters to encompass a wide range of patterns, one of which he modeled after his own preference. Thus he stressed a clarification of types of core programs recognizing roughly six patterns characterized by their differentiated use of organized disciplines and by the degree to which their respective contents were problem centered (Alberty, 1953, pp. 169-191).

In appraising the long-term impact of Alberty's proposals, one cannot escape the historic irony imbedded in the fact that higher education has been more responsive than secondary education to his suggestions for design and structure. Not only have colleges and universities addressed more directly the problem of structuring general education, but they have also preempted the term "core" to describe their innovations far more often than have the high schools. Instead of the substantive reorganization he envisaged for the secondary school curriculum, one sees today at this level of education a plethora of ill-defined practices which leave the subject-centered program largely intact. Even the connectedness of interdisciplinarity, once the hallmark of most core programs, now seems minimal in secondary curriculum. Yet within higher education one notes wider professional interest in integrative studies and, within the past few years, the publication of a rather comprehensive report on the history, theory, and practice of interdisciplinarity (Klein, 1990).

Alberty as Teacher and Guide

Turning from Alberty's legacy to core program development, which in a sense was public and shared by many, I turn to a set of personal reminiscences which will reflect the quality of experience shared primarily by his graduate students whom he influenced most directly. At the risk of exceeding the measure of indulgence one might reasonably expect of the reader of a personal narrative, I would like to depict some of the ways he worked with students toward their own self-development.

It was in the larger lecture courses, such as "The Role of the School in the Social Order," that Alberty was able to illuminate his theoretical positions on educational purposes, curriculum design, and classroom practice. Here also, due to the popularity of that particular course, he reached a mass audience which helped to create the reality and myth long associated with his reputation as a teacher. His manner of handling reading assign-ments was one such tradition.

Any account of the devices Alberty used to broaden the intellectual awareness of his students must include his success in extending their habits of reading. Despite his difference with Scott Buchanan and Stringfellow Barr over the dominant role given the "Great Books" in their curriculum proposals, he nevertheless listed prominently his own choice of classics. There was, of course, the canon of experimentalist thought—works of Bode, Dewey, James and others—which were repeated on bibliographies of all courses whatever their titles. In addition, he emphasized a reading of the comparative studies—not only Bode's *Conflicting Psychologies of Learning* (1929) but also synoptic works of such authors as Brameld, Brubacher, and Justman. However, I had the feeling that he assumed that students would read the canon without his urging, and his concern seemed less for "plowing old ground"—to use his term—than for reading the new sources that might cast educational problems in a fresh perspective. To this end he solicited each week lists of the students' "Six Best Readings," one of which would be selected randomly by number for brief critical evaluation at class time. There was always the assumption that a serious student would have read far more than listed since the assignment implied a reasonable degree of selection. This practice had not only the advantage of assessing the range and scope of a student's reading but also assured the instructor that the authors' ideas had been given a measure of critical review. The reading list with its particular critique was not always returned, but whenever it made its way back to the student, the remarks might range all the way from: "Do you really prize the *Readers Digest* as a professional journal?" to "I'm glad you found Learned Hand instructive on this topic—perhaps you would also find Justice Holmes' opinions of value." Many of Alberty's graduate students, including this writer, have been known to perpetuate the practice in their own teaching, wondering if the practice might have had its origin with Bode and whether or not in another time the students also had made "book" before class on what number might come up in this weekly academic lottery.

However instructive and intellectually engaging these
lecture courses had been at the time, and apart from the reading
exercises, I find my recollections of them far less enduring than
memories of the small doctoral seminars in which I participated
from 1948 to 1950. By that time Alberty had published the first
edition of *Reorganizing the High-School Curriculum* containing the
theoretical framework of his grand design for curriculum reform
in secondary schools. Yet there were still significant questions to
pursue and theoretical constructs to improve; these became the
focal concern of the seminars. How can the knowledge, skills,
and values endemic to subject fields be utilized optimally in a
"problems of living" core? What is the role of resource guides in
curriculum planning? What would be an effective program of
preservice preparation for core teachers? Questions such as these
with their attendant problems and issues provided the point of
departure for the seminars. Since he normally was off campus in
the autumn quarter, the seminar problems were undertaken in
the following two quarters. This usually provided sufficient time
for preparing individual and group position papers, conducting
extensive discussion and evaluation, and drafting a preliminary
report of the seminar findings. If fortunate enough to receive the
invitation, one member might enroll with Alberty for the
"Special Problems" course in the following summer to refine and
edit a final report, thus receiving special acknowledgment
among its several authors. Shared authorship of these reports
held an additional incentive because Alberty always gave special
attribution in his own writings to the unpublished work of his
graduate students. Such was the primary context in which I
remember this patient and helpful teacher.

The seminar provided the setting for examining with
Alberty the subtleties of curriculum inquiry—a place where, as
in Thomas Green's description, one learns to "attend to fact,
watch the argument, beware of certainty, be aware of possible
objections" (Green, 1982, p. 136). There his earlier legal training
came to the fore in the cross-examination of the students whose
propositions were under study. It was also there that we came to
know the meaning of Gilbran's standard for the wise teacher, to
lead ". . . to the threshold of your own mind." I recall on one
occasion arriving at what I thought was a novel insight into

general education's responsibility for nurturing specialized interests and talents in their incipient stage. After proceeding to share my newly-found wisdom with others in the seminar, I readied myself for a defense of my position. To my surprise, Alberty's reaction was of polite interest without the inducement of intellectual terror which was sometimes a possibility. My brief claim to original thought was laid to rest a few days later when *The Educational Forum* published his highly original and definitive article, "Bridging the Gap Between General and Vocational Education in the High School" (Alberty, 1949, pp. 211-217).

The Progressive era in education produced its share of partisans who leaned noticeably to one side or the other of the important dichotomies that help to describe human experience. Alberty sought to develop the capacity to use perennial ambiguity and paradox as points of departure for creative analysis and fresh synthesis of thought on educational problems. One finds this level of discernment particularly in the clarity of his definition of general and specialized education and in the complementarity he perceived in their effective relationship. "The separation (in organization) between general and special education," he wrote, "is justified at the point where special interests can no longer be effectively dealt with by groups that are organized primarily in terms of common concerns" (Alberty, 1949, p. 213). He went on to say that "general education should concern itself with the development of common ideals, understandings and abilities and with the cultivation of special capacities, abilities, and interests *up to the point of technical competence*. Special (or vocational) education should concern itself with the development of technical proficiency in a context of common ideals, understandings, and abilities" (Alberty, 1949, p. 214).

In the seminars, Alberty attached considerable importance to clarity of definitions and to the valuable distinction between carefully stated issues and loosely framed questions. Indeed, the seminars gave far greater attention to formulating coherent statements of assumptions, criteria, and generalizations than to proposals of a programmatic nature. As in the case of the article cited above, his writings were instructive models of clear prose about the salient issues to be resolved. And as is true of all seminal thought and writing, it is difficult to add form and substance in any restatement of his works.

In his attempt to bring unity to things that should never have been separated, Alberty often stressed the special role of the teacher as advisor and counselor. His own ability to assess critical educational needs and to assist in their satisfaction ranks high among the traits that make him a worthy mentor, both by precept and example. A few examples will illustrate his perceptiveness in this respect.

A common and sometimes questionable practice in most universities is to staff many sections of undergraduate courses with doctoral students and, in this respect, Ohio State was no exception in the late 1940s. Because I had completed five years of high school teaching with considerable satisfaction, I viewed the repeated invitations to teach a section of the basic principles course as a special opportunity, one which might provide me a better basis for choosing a position later. After all, a bid to teach in college seemed honorific enough even though I knew it would postpone the completion of graduate studies.

Whenever he discussed these invitations with me, Alberty's advice was never explicitly negative but rather a series of probing questions leading to considerations I had overlooked: "What makes you think teaching undergraduates would be so different from working with high school students? You have just spent four years in military service; do you think you can afford to delay your studies longer? Why not proceed with your studies and consider college teaching at a later date?" In looking back I have been forever grateful for his helping me to view such choices in a wider context and, in this instance, sparing me a needless extension of graduate study.

One exception to his advice against accepting a teaching assistantship came just prior to the summer of 1949. Having accepted a visiting professorship at the University of Southern California for that term, he recommended that I assist V.T. Thayer, who was to teach in his place "The Role of the School in the Social Order." It was an uncanny piece of advice, for he must have had some prescient idea of the tremendous impact Thayer was to have on my thinking as a consequence of our brief association. This venerable humanitarian and educator, steeped in what today's authors of *Habits of the Heart* would call the biblical tradition in its rational sense, succeeded more than anyone in fostering my abiding interest in the body of case law bearing on church-state relations and particularly the role of religion in public education (Bellah et al., 1985, pp. 28-31, 33).

In final tribute to Harold Alberty as advisor, I have him to thank for helping me choose a thesis problem not only of workable dimensions but also one which had the potential for considerable personal development on my part. Even though I had traveled widely here and abroad with the United States Navy during the war years, I had never overcome an innate tendency toward diffidence and shyness in unfamiliar social situations. Left to my own predilections, I probably would have settled on some abstract but provocative curriculum issue that offered the shelter of a year or so of research in university libraries. At this juncture in my studies, Alberty let it be known that the potential role of state departments of education in effecting curriculum improvement had by no means been examined fully and the developing core programs in Maryland deserved timely attention. Although he had a host of candidates who could have undertaken such a study, I am confident in retrospect that he saw in the necessary professional contacts with many state and county educators a tailored experience that for me would not only foster greater self-confidence but also provide the opportunity for a worthy contribution to an important facet of curriculum development. He seemed always to have a rare but necessary balance of affection for and detachment from his students.

This collection of vignettes has taken as its point of departure the contribution of Harold Alberty to the community of memory brought into existence by the education professoriate. These particular reminiscences focus on his influence on students and colleagues within that community who shared his regard for liberal educational reforms. In bringing this retrospective to a close it would be reassuring if one could find today more vestiges of Alberty's valiant attempts to unify philosophy, curriculum, and methods. Instead, one finds most high schools reflecting even greater fragmentation after three decades of atomistic tinkering. Thoughtful reflection of democratic values (if undertaken) becomes suspect as soft pedagogy. Students still have to look to the extracurricular program for a block of time and purposeful activity sufficient to realize a deep educational experience. And, as several recent studies have reported, a dominance of teacher talk seems to characterize the primary interaction of the classroom. In viewing the education scene, many of Alberty's students must kindle some illusion of deja vu; for, after having shared his long struggle for connectedness, they cannot but be disappointed with the frenetic quest for a coherent plan that was never lost—only forgotten. But in a wider sense the core values and ideas of his legacy have an independent life of their own and are realized anew wherever his students and others touched by his sensibilities choose to continue the traditions of this shared community of memory.

CHAPTER THIRTEEN

Florence B. Stratemeyer:
Teacher Educator for a Free People

Martin Haberman

For many college faculty it is not a question of publish or perish but a process of publish and perish. The legacy of a professor that can be summarized by a curriculum vita is likely to be a meager one. The greater legacy is in the students. What have the faculty helped the students become committed to and act upon? What have these students learned?

In a democratic society, knowledge is a necessary but not sufficient condition. An educated individual is one whose actions are based on reasoned judgments which can be explained and defended and which are subject to change (growth) as knowledge increases. Therefore if faculty were somehow able to teach students everything they now know, it would merely be an acceptable beginning. The great need is to educate in ways which will transcend what is now agreed-upon knowledge and prepare students to function in a world that is beyond our wildest imagination. The recognition that their students are their legacy leads faculty to appreciate that students' future behavior and accomplishments are the final test of their teaching.

The faculty's competence is manifested not only by what their students are able to do but by how well they contribute toward maintaining our democratic institutions. Have students been trained to replicate faculty understanding and know-how, or have they also been educated to think about what they know in ways which will help them deal with the nature of knowledge and their commitments to particular ideals? The need for training is universal. The need for education is the very source of life for a free people.

These concepts are my earliest remembrance of Florence B. Stratemeyer. The notion that the teacher is validated by the students and dependent on them has stayed with me for forty years. As a student in her class my initial reaction was, "Does this impressive, famous individual really believe we are more important than she is? Does she really believe we control the value of her contribution simply because we will outlive her, or because we will be teaching others, or because we will be functioning citizens, or all of the above? This must be some kind of exercise. The 'right' answer will come in the next session." But in my three years of subsequent study with her the "right" answer was never given; it emerged as students began to behave as if their ideas really did matter. Indeed, the better I knew her the more I appreciated her commitment to students and her belief in their potential. The personal courtesy and intellectual respect she showed each of her several thousand master's students and her 145 successful doctoral students spoke most eloquently of her conviction that the students' ideas and ideals and the development of the students' powers of analysis were her paramount concern.

Great teachers are not simply experts in some field of knowledge; many people are bona fide experts in a particular field or discipline without ever teaching anyone anything. Great teachers are also not necessarily great speakers; many politicians, media people, and others can hold the attention of an audience and never teach them anything. In spite of the popular stereotypes, therefore, great teachers are more than knowledgeable spellbinders. They lead students to not only comprehend new ideas but to make those ideas a basis for personal growth and a guide to future thought and behavior. The great teacher is a master of both input *and* elicitation.

This approach to students is far from the typical college teacher's perception and treatment of students. Many faculty— particularly those in the larger institutions—tend to view students as largely ignorant, disinterested, and unwilling to apply themselves. Many faculty would be overjoyed if their students would grasp even a small portion of the facts and information they regard as minimum essentials. The quip, "College teaching is throwing artificial pearls at genuine swine," still garners understanding smiles from many faculty. The way college teaching is pursued in many institutions it might be described as "the opportunity afforded the faculty to review what they think they know in the presence of students."

Stratemeyer regarded college teaching as something she did from the inside out, always guiding, showing how, and sharing the very processes she was engaged in with her students. In effect, she commented upon, analyzed, and explained what she was doing while she did it so that students would learn *both* the content of her courses and the methods she used to make the course content meaningful. The reason for this two-fold approach was her commitment to the ideal that college teachers—particularly college teachers of future teachers—should model what they advocate and even more, be aware of the developmental levels and backgrounds of experience which students bring to their college classes. This is a direct analogue of Dewey's *The Child and the Curriculum* (1902) transposed into the level of higher education. Anyone who studied with Stratemeyer came to clearly understand the need for and the ways to become a more effective college teacher as a major prerequisite for functioning as a teacher educator. It is a continuing source of amazement to me and would be of some consternation to her that in the volumes which now purport to summarize the knowledge base in teacher education there is still little or nothing devoted to the philosophy, methods, and evaluation of college teaching by which most future teachers are still prepared. The following are merely a few anecdotes which typify her ability and commitment to the practice of college teaching.

Remembering Student Ideas

Stratemeyer first came to Teachers College as a young woman from Detroit. From 1924-1965 she served on the T.C. faculty. Her ability to remember students' ideas was legendary. I can recall several instances in classes, which frequently numbered 200 in size, when she would respond to a student's comment by saying something like, "That's a very interesting comment, John. How does it reconcile with the comment you made in the paper you wrote last month in which you said. . . . " At this point the student would be sitting stunned for two reasons: first, that Stratemeyer was listening to him with sufficient care and patience to want to know the rationale for his thinking and, second, that she had read and remembered what he had written in a previous paper and then recalled a contradiction to his present view. To be able to reflect back to students *their words, their ideas, their commitments* and to ask them to justify inconsistencies in *their thinking* is the most powerful form of teaching. It elevates college teaching to a high art. Stratemeyer was the master practitioner, possibly without equal at eliciting self-reflection. The effects on students were enormous. Initially, some were devastated, others were amazed, a few were overjoyed, and most were simply complimented that an individual of such distinction would remember what they had said or written. After the initial shock wore off, the student reaction was universal: to read, write, and think harder than they had ever done before in their lives in order to explain, ostensibly to Stratemeyer but actually to themselves, what they really believed and why. This process of reflecting back students' views to push them to further clarification must have required superhuman effort. Her classes were large and her assignments included several papers per semester. To read, remember, and use this much written data and then add what students said in class required an unparalleled memory. Such unusual remembering could only be achieved by a person who truly cared about what her students thought.

The ultimate example of this ability was demonstrated for me at an AACTE meeting in the Chicago Hilton in 1959. A distinguished teacher educator, Lawrence Haskew, had just given a keynote address and was standing in the lobby chatting with Stratemeyer and a few others. One of the numerous points he had included in his speech came up and Stratemeyer said to him, "You know in the paper you wrote in ED 200 in 1934, you took the opposite point of view." A hush fell over the group as this reference to a twenty-five-year-old student paper was taken in. To his credit Haskew stopped, reflected, and promised to give the matter more thought. Stratemeyer's ability to clarify one's thinking bordered on the uncanny.

Stop the Elevator

Dean C. Corrigan, now the Distinguished Harrington Professor in the College of Education at Texas A & M, was an impecunious graduate student at Teachers College in 1957. In addition to his modest scholarship he supported his young family by running the elevator evenings in the Horace Mann Building. On one evening each week, during one of Stratemeyer's classes, he would stop his elevator on the second floor and take a seat in the balcony of the auditorium in which the class was held. There were approximately 200 students spread throughout the auditorium. Although Corrigan was not registered in the class, he was deriving a great deal of benefit from sitting in and made a regular habit of being an unregistered, "invisible" auditor. One night, after making a particular comment, Stratemeyer looked up into the balcony and said, "Provided of course that's all right with you, Mr. Corrigan." It certainly was all right with Dean, but he almost fell out of the balcony nonetheless. Stratemeyer always took the trouble to know her students, regardless of class size, but spotting and learning the name of an unregistered auditor, in this case the elevator operator, was a remarkable demonstration of her commitment to students.

I made a practice of initiating each new conference with her as if we had just left off moments earlier when in truth we might not have had a personal meeting in a month or more. I never summarized or reintroduced a topic but simply began where we had left off. She never needed a refresher on what we had discussed previously but was able to immediately pick up and continue. The same dynamic was reported to me by all her advisees. This remarkable ability to remember and use students' ideas also extended to our dissertation topics, exams, and papers for other courses. Stratemeyer modeled concern for her students as individuals and as professionals by the respect she demonstrated toward our ideas, beliefs, and commitments.

Have You a Good Story for Me?

At the time I was a doctoral student, Stratemeyer had approximately fifteen other active advisees. There were several of us supervising student teachers who were "around" much of the time. We were on assistantships and had small offices near hers. Typically, most faculty met their advisees by appointment but were also available for informal meetings as we interrupted them with endless "Got a minute?" drop-in meetings. This was not true for Stratemeyer, whose appearance combined with her reputation to intimidate many students. She was over six feet tall, amply proportioned, and had a shock of white hair. In addition, she had an intense, businesslike expression most of the time. She dressed in dark clothing and had an erect posture. The care and seriousness with which she listened made many faculty as well as students self-conscious in her presence. As a result, no student would dare to drop in or interrupt her without an appointment and careful preparation.

I had a running battle with the other full-time students who were "around," and I contended that Stratemeyer's philosophy would require her to respond to student needs. To demonstrate this I would occasionally walk into her office without an appointment when I had a genuine question of concern and would always receive a courteous and helpful response. Frequently, several students would gather in the hall to watch my unscheduled drop-ins expecting me to be thrown out. They were awed by my audacity at simply walking in on the great educator. What they didn't appreciate is that Stratemeyer truly believed in her students and, if she was presented with a serious concern, she would always take time to clarify, give advice, or suggest a resource. As a result, rather than throw me out, she pretended my concerns were of vital interest to her as well. There is no question she was there for the students; it was the students who denied themselves the great value of relating to her on an informal basis.

As a result of this behavior and the fact that I was one of the very few native New Yorkers in the doctoral program at that time, I developed a reputation for brashness among my fellow students. Being housed in nearby offices we frequently joked and told stories at a sufficiently high noise level to disturb her since the door to her office was usually open. She never complained although we frequently sensed that she believed more decorum might be called for. What we never appreciated was that she might have occasionally enjoyed being part of our group and sharing a laugh with us but could not bring herself to do so.

One day as I was passing, Stratemeyer *called* me into her office and explained she was going to speak in Troy, Alabama, and asked if I had a funny story she might use to begin her address on "Guidelines for the Development of a Teacher Education Program." I was flabbergasted. That she would want to begin a speech with a joke struck me as out of character. Even worse, my mind went blank and I could not think of a single clean story. I offered several puns I could recall from childhood but nothing that was even remotely related to teacher education. After each feeble attempt at humor, Stratemeyer would smile and say things like, "That is amusing!" or "My, my." We both sensed my failure and her lack of candor in encouraging my effort. Finally, a *New Yorker* cartoon popped into my head and I suggested she describe a funny situation rather than tell a story. She nodded and I plunged in. The situation I described was a clearing in the jungle. Natives were seated in a circle. A masked medicine man was dancing in the center. One seated woman turned to the other and proudly said, "Oh, you see my son, the doctor!" Stratemeyer smiled and looked innocently hopeful. I said, "This is a hilarious story. Trust me! The audience will love it!"

Several weeks went by before I had the opportunity to meet with her again. She casually but with her usual seriousness reported she used the story but simply could not recall whether anyone laughed. I have always carried the vision of her in Troy, Alabama in 1959 telling that story, and in my mind's eye I imagine an incredulous audience wondering what in heaven's name had possessed Florence B. Stratemeyer to do such a thing. On the other hand, who knows? Maybe they loved it!

On What Basis Do You Say That?

As students we learned to badger each other with "How do you know that?" Actually, Stratemeyer's phrase was, "On what basis do you say that?" Using this question and endless patience, she wrote all over our papers and, in the process, taught us to think. There can be no question that she spent more time and effort reading and correcting papers than many students initially spent writing them. It wasn't that students did not work hard or put forth sufficient effort; Stratemeyer applied high standards to the papers by the way in which she corrected them. She never simply graded or made approving or disapproving comments. She frequently raised questions. Most typically, she would actually rewrite whole phrases, sentences, even paragraphs and then ask, "Is this what you mean?" Before the popularity of "feedback" as the most powerful tool of instruction, Stratemeyer perfected the practice to an advanced degree. It was exhausting to read her notes. They extended far beyond questions and even beyond suggestions. If she thought the student had a sound idea and needed a clearer means of expressing it, she actually wrote in the "corrected" material in extensive marginal notes or between the lines. This extensive reaction was of genuine help and a source of real instruction. It stands in sharp contrast to many faculty who mark papers by simply using a red pencil to note errors, merely indicate a grade or, even worse, make judgmental quips. Stratemeyer helped students explain themselves by serving almost as a coauthor. This process was even more elaborate on dissertations. Here the written dialogue was almost endless, but the finished product was almost always a source of great pride and satisfaction to the advisees.

The content of many written dialogues with Stratemeyer was frequently devoted to answering the question, "How do you know that?" which when raised in a non-threatening way was probably the greatest single cause of reflection and new insights we had ever experienced. We learned to refer to six sources of support for our positions: research, theory, experience, expert opinion, logical argumentation, and common sense. The process of exposing the basis for our positions required a thoughtful analysis and one that led to genuine change and growth. In the current hubbub over how to better teach children and youth to think more effectively, the need to involve their teachers in Stratemeyer's process seems more timely than ever. This need for thoughtful analysis is even more relevant for educational leaders and policy makers.

The no-feedback practice of having graduate students write a final paper due at the end of the semester with no time for polishing and rewriting is unfortunately still typical in many institutions. She modeled a college teaching practice which involved (1) having a personal conference with each student (regardless of class size) to plan the term paper, (2) requiring a rough draft submitted sufficiently early in the semester to be read and returned with extensive, helpful comments, and (3) a final paper which had been polished and rewritten. And this was before word processing! This certainly breaks with the university tradition of having papers submitted during the last class of the semester.

Final Exams

Stratemeyer had events called "opportunities to write" rather than tests. This was not a euphemism but an authentic change in nomenclature that reflected what she believed. She taught us to respect our ideas and to become sufficiently good at expressing them—including the "How do you know that?" rationale—so that we wanted to express our ideas. Her exams were thus transformed into genuine opportunities to write. I can recall a snowstorm hitting against the classroom windows during one such occasion. Stratemeyer kept commenting on the bad weather, hoping we would stop writing such lengthy responses (which she would have to painstakingly read and edit) and go home. "It's getting deeper out there," she commented. "It's getting deeper in here too," I replied. She looked at me with what I honestly felt was genuine affection.

The Grand Ideals

Stratemeyer was an idealist in teacher education. She pointed out the most notable and noteworthy goals to which we might aspire. As a result, she was easy to write off then and even easier to ignore today if we but point to the "realities" of low budgets, overblown bureaucracies, fragmentation through overspecialization, racism, poverty, lack of public support, leaders without leadership skills, ill-advised policies and unfunded state mandates. Nevertheless, teacher education needed and still needs her scholarly laying-out of our first principles—what is it we stand for and why.

This brief overview cannot do justice to her vision of teacher education. Fortunately, these are summarized in her own voice in The Sixth Hunt Lecture, "Perspectives on Action in Teacher Education" (Stratemeyer, 1965). In this elegant address, Stratemeyer presented her analysis of the perennial issues facing teacher educators: the meaning of the teacher as scholar; the components of scholarship in teacher education; the relationship among thinking, feeling, and behaving in teacher-scholars; the addition of the professional dimension to teaching scholarship; the nature of knowledge and the generation of knowledge in teacher education; the balance of the specialist/generalist in education; the meaning of quality in direct experience; the role of the college teacher-researcher-scholar.

Before I was graduated and left for Milwaukee, where I still find myself, Stratemeyer took me aside and said, "Martin, there will be no limits to what you can accomplish if you listen to good advice along the way." I was too young to ask, "How will I separate the good advice from the bad?"

A game I played with my children and now with my grandchildren relates to the most famous people I have ever met. In my case the list is formidable if one is easily impressed. But there is no question in my mind that the greatest influence on my life as a teacher educator and as an American has been Florence B. Stratemeyer. This is indeed strange since almost everything I have done, from developing the intern model which became The National Corps to my current development of alternative certification programs, is something she would argue against. Why do I believe so strongly in her influence if this is the case? I can honestly reply that in developing my most important contributions, whether teaching, scholarship, or action, I have felt her spirit and her voice asking "Why do you say that?" "On what basis?" "What would reputable, thorough people who disagree with you say about this?" And finally, "Why is this a good idea, Martin?" I can say without hesitation she would judge my accomplishments (and everyone else's) by the thoughtfulness and usefulness of my positions and not on the basis of their similarity to her views. What greater compliment can be paid a teacher educator for a free people?

CHAPTER FOURTEEN

Alice Miel:
Exemplar of Democracy Made Real

Louise Berman

> Some scribbled notes written in the faint light of
> a movie projector; some lines vaguely repre-
> senting a tree with social learnings weighing
> down its branches; three columns headed "Do
> well," "So-so," and "Can't do" with a few lines
> under each of the latter two headings; and a few
> pages of pithy sayings and things to read—these
> comprise the notes of a doctoral student in Ed
> 233n, Social Learnings in the Elementary School.
> Noticeably absent are lists of well-formulated
> purposes or objectives, outlines of three-point
> lectures, and a date on the class calendar for a
> final exam. Is one spending her time wisely par-
> ticipating in such a class? (Berman, 1958, p. 1)

These words began a "reaction paper" found in a file of
notes and materials from a course I took with Alice Miel at
Teachers College, Columbia University. [1] Notes from other
courses in which I was either a student or, as she titled my job,
"co-instructor," are similar—snippets of what was happening in
the moment. These glimpses, however, were frequently
profound, reflecting a professor's shaping of ideas from various
persons and sources into thoughts which lingered, sometimes
hauntingly.

Many years later as I browsed through files which have
followed me from Teachers College into numerous offices, I
recalled qualities and insights which seem central to Alice Miel,
the person and professor: the importance of the perceptions of

other persons—their ways of making sense of their worlds; the acknowledgment of the creativity of others—their unique means of formulating newness, of weaving ideas, of elaborating, of questioning; the delight and yet tensions in cooperative thinking and action, whether in forming an organization, dealing with small groups, or collaborating on a book; the establishment of visions of what education, particularly in the common school, might mean for persons of various philosophical persuasions, ethnic backgrounds, and geographic boundaries; the significance of voices from the past in establishing present and future directions; the centrality of classroom teachers in the educational enterprise; the ideal of professor as ever-compassionate, growing and changing, knowledgeable, and ethical; the work of the professor as establishing settings where persons can explore fresh ideas as democratic beings.

Yes, notes from being with Alice were full of instances of new insights, of persons exploring, and of journeying together. The jottings included not only her ideas but also those of fellow graduate students. Through her being, her methods, and her procedures, Alice Miel invited us to reflect, to be active learners. Although lecturing was not her preferred way of teaching, she lectured at times when she thought a series of ideas needed to be synthesized.

Notes from classes—these tell much about the professor. But they give only a small part of the story. The complex and rich life of a highly involved professor can be partially captured through comments of fellow colleagues, friends, and students; books and articles; tributes paid at various points in a person's career; and records of collaborative efforts in moving the profession ahead. But capturing the vibrancy, the civility, the morality, and the creativity of a growing and changing person is an almost impossible task.

Recalling Alice's frequent advice to search, to think about what can be, and then to eliminate, I decided to focus on the period I have known and been involved with her from the late 1950's until the present. Because I have written about certain of her ideas elsewhere, I am excluding here her professional work (Berman, 1989, 1992). [2]

My first contact with Alice was on a Saturday morning. She met me in her office. After hearing my story and pointing out certain requirements for graduate study, she indicated she would be happy to advise me. She did indicate that she had many students, and I should feel free to work with someone else if I wished. I liked her concerned independence. In 1958, I decided to enroll in the doctoral program at Teachers College for two years of residence with Alice as my teacher and advisor. During the second year I was invited to be a "co-instructor" with her. Throughout my residence and subsequent years, I learned much from her about being a professor—the exploration of ideas, as evidenced in research and scholarship; the development of settings where others can flourish, as evidenced in teaching and advising; and the creation of collegial and collaborative arrangements benefiting the larger profession as evidenced in service. In the case of Alice Miel the arenas of the professoriate were closely interrelated, perhaps because she is an integrated, thoughtful human being.

The Context of Teachers College

The setting in which Alice resided for many years as a doctoral student, research associate, professor, and department chair was Teachers College, Columbia University. The stately old red brick buildings on the north side of 120th Street housed the oldest Department of Curriculum and Teaching in the country. Curriculum was a fledgling field when she began her career; she was instrumental in bringing to the college persons from around the world who would further the understandings of the field through research, study, teaching and informal collegial gatherings.

Within high ceilings and multi-sized rooms, flexibility in teaching was supported. Certain of the rooms reminded persons of our educational heritage, as portraits of individuals significant to the profession gazed on those seeking to better understand educational thought. Students and faculty availed themselves of a magnificent resource of the Teachers College complex, a large library which continues to house current as well as historical documents and philosophical treatises as well as school-based documents. The context was and continues to be diverse and exciting. Alice chose to live much of her life at Teachers College in a cooperative on West 123rd Street. The neighborhood had multiple kinds of dwellings from old brownstones where adults and children congregated outside to mid-rises where graduate students were often quartered. Persons of a variety of ethnic, socio-economic, and racial backgrounds lived together in a neighborhood very characteristic of New York City.

In addition to ethnic and socio-economic diversity, the area was characterized by a richness of cultural and intellectual fare. The numerous libraries and human resources of the area could cause some persons to get lost in a surfeit of choice. But not Alice! Instead, in the midst of intellectual and cultural challenge, she maintained a focus which enabled her to be open to experiences and ideas but grounded in her core ideas.

Alice Miel as Teacher and Advisor

At a testimonial dinner for Alice at the time of her retirement, Hollis Caswell read a letter from a supervisor who had worked with Alice when she was a teacher in the Michigan schools. Edith Bader wrote, "Even though she [Miel] specialized in classics, she is a wonderful human being who is primarily interested in the general growth and development of students." Caswell went on to read from the supervisor, "She not only has a basic interest in students as persons, she gives this interest a broad setting. She is always concerned that education should develop a society in which individuals can grow, each day becoming more nearly what their capacities make possible" (Caswell, 1971).

The same qualities which showed themselves as a former secondary school teacher were evident—and perhaps more so—in the university setting. She continued to have a strong interest in persons, not only as individuals but also as members of society. The commitment to worthwhile purposes and projects was invitational to students at any level to join forces in working toward something bigger than themselves. Indeed, she exemplified the significance of democracy as being created and recreated in educational settings.

In addition to her commitment to major educational and societal issues, Alice was concerned about the immediate worlds of her students. Even though classes were frequently very large, after a class session or two, she knew people's names and usually something about them. She honored individuals by not making herself center stage. In a sense, she was a member of a jazz group, each individual having opportunity to perform. As "co-instructor," I was given the various tasks of a college teacher. Students assumed responsibilities in preparing for panels, small groups, or role playing. New ideas, personal experiences, and knotty questions were valued, yet an asymmetrical relationship with the professor was apparent. At times Alice synthesized ideas, or related a person's idea to her personal experiences, or brought in pithy readings. The jazz group went on, but at times she played solo. The improvisation, change, and creativity necessary to democratic living were played out in her classes. She had the courage to withstand the criticisms of those who wanted the professor as lecturer.

Even as her classes were creative so she nurtured creative sparks in her students. For example, a group of educators from Iran were on campus to consult on aids and questions found in textbooks. Since I was interested in creative thinking, in preparation for meeting with them, Alice asked me to find examples of aids in instructional materials. Despite the wealth of elementary and secondary school texts in the resource library, I found that most aids called upon a narrow range of thinking skills. I asked if she minded if I dreamed up some aids that would invite the development of skills in thinking and valuing. Her assent to go beyond what was available helped me clarify my ideas on the purposes of tasks students are asked to perform. In addition, she honored my ideas by encouraging me to prepare them for publication (Berman, 1967).

As students shared their emerging thinking with Alice, she shared hers with students. She was continuously trying to make better sense of her field of study, to push back the boundaries. At times she brought to classes written documents. On one occasion she shared a paper on definitions of terms, including curriculum, curriculum development, guidance, supervision, and administration. The fruits of her analyses and re-analyses appeared in a later work on curriculum and supervision (Lewis & Miel, 1972). As students we learned the courage it takes to share ideas in process. We also learned that ideas collaboratively shaped can be very powerful.

Sharing her home life with students, Alice frequently entertained her advisees at her apartment for "dessert and conversation." Occasionally a resource person would initiate conversation by discussing an idea or a project. More often, the conversation was free-flowing, often providing an opportunity for students to talk about anxieties, concerns, current affairs, or just to be together. She was particularly hospitable to students from other lands. One student from Africa talked about her daily visits to him in the hospital during a period of illness. Her compassion matched the precision and thoughtfulness of her mind.

She loved language and was committed to care in using it. Interested in the total communication process—speaking, listening, writing, and editing—she listened with the intent of entering the world of the speaker and helping that person bring forth meanings which may heretofore have been silent or unclear. She listened also with a capacity to help the other tap "inner resources," knowledge, and skills ready to emerge. Even in situations where time was at a premium, her well-selected words usually provided the needed guidance, encouragement, and incentive to continue on the journey. As I taught with her, I came to know her more informally but, even in a more relaxed context, she continued to be an attentive listener. She set aside time daily for joint reflections on where classes had been and where we might go next. She helped me and other students find our own voices.

Her interest in words, their roots, their meanings was reflected in her love of foreign languages. Growing up with a Danish mother gave her some background in Danish. She later taught Latin and French and studied Spanish, Dari, and Japanese during experiences abroad. She usually searches for the right word in her speaking and writing and encourages those who work with her to do the same. She dislikes far-fetched, meaningless, or contrived language and admonishes against making up meanings. According to Alice, persons should be scholars of language, understanding the origins of words and using them thoughtfully (Berman with Miel, 1977).

Alice's life seemed to have a rhythm. Although she was intensely involved with students when classes were in session, when they were not, she ordinarily took off for the family home in Michigan or for some other point. Upon returning to campus, she shared drafts of her recent writings. She typically completed many drafts of a book, article, or speech, each time polishing the language and improving the logic. Her writing reflected careful thinking, integrity, and making of an idea her own. She very much encouraged students to do the difficult work of dealing with meaningful ideas, making them their own, and expressing them clearly.

Alice, over the course of her career, served on many doctoral committees. In addition, she usually required several papers in each of her classes. She was a concerned editor, pointing out ideas that were not carefully sculpted or shared. She tried, however, to match her style of editing to the individual. For some persons she would indicate an idea as unclear with knowledge that the individual could make appropriate changes. For others she felt she needed to rewrite unclear parts or to indicate consistent shortcomings with "you have a habit. . . . " (Miel, 1977).

When asked what advice she would give to doctoral students, she mentioned two points: (1) be precise in language and (2) have integrity (Berman with Miel, 1977). She indicated that the latter point grows out of care with language.

Realizing that those who had opportunity to study with Alice were indeed privileged, when she retired from teaching in 1971, a corps of her students and advisees founded Project Milestone. Under its umbrella, a number of projects were planned, including a conference in Puerto Rico attended by advisees, friends, family, and students. Project Milestone funds a variety of educational opportunities, frequently subsidizing students for conference participation or awarding outstanding educators for continuation of their work.

Alice's life with students reflected her caring for individuals. She invited students to join her in exploring and furthering ideas bigger than any one person. Indeed, she was and continues to be part of that larger community of educators.

Alice Miel as Colleague and Collaborator

Alice Miel was a composer of ideas but also, in a metaphorical sense, a jazz player. She could take ideas and with others create departments, organizations, publications and, indeed, a profession bigger than any one person in it. She was a collaborator in her own institution and in the larger community of educators.

Alice seemed to have the respect of her colleagues even though Teachers College was full of strong persons, each with a unique orientation and set of underlying values. To be collegial in such a setting can be tough, for academe frequently rewards idiosyncratic as opposed to cooperative efforts. Yet, Teachers College during the period that Miel was a professor was undergirded by a faith in education as a tool for dealing with societal ills and making a better life for all peoples. After all, Teachers College had a marked tradition of the power of educators in a democracy.

Alice had many contacts and friends in the College and seemed especially supportive of young faculty. Her collegiality evidenced itself in utilizing her peers as resources in classes and opening doors for students to be involved with other professors who shared a student's interests. Her working relationships with others made it easier for students to continue their studies when she was on sabbatical. For example, I was shepherded through parts of my dissertation writing by Margaret Lindsey and Harold McNally while Alice was on sabbatical.

From 1960-67 Alice chaired the Department of Curriculum and Teaching. In that capacity she sought to apply principles of democratic problem-solving she had been exploring and espousing for many years. At times ideological differences in the Department centered on the theory-practice dilemmas, yet a respect for others and a sense of civility existed.

Active in a variety of professional organizations, Alice was among the group who in 1943 participated in the merger of the Society of Curriculum Study and the Department of Supervisors and Directors of Instruction to form the Association of

Supervision and Curriculum Development (ASCD). I recall my first ASCD conference held in Washington, DC, in 1960. Alice kept a calendar which would have worn out most persons. Former students, committees, and social events crowded the several days of the conference. A quick trip back to New York allowed her to meet her evening class. In her usual way of integrating various aspects of her life, she shared with students conference topics related to the thrust of the course.

Alice was also active in Professors of Curriculum, an elected group of 100 persons, which at the time of her induction was primarily a male organization that met prior to ASCD meetings. Informal in its organization and dedicated to giving professors of curriculum a chance to share ideas about curriculum and instruction, Alice made one of her last presentations to the group at the Detroit meeting in 1979. Her humility often precluded her talking much about herself. In this presentation, however, she shared insights about herself as an educator (Miel, 1979).

During her later years, Alice has lived in Gainesville, Florida, where former professors of the University of Florida and professors selected from other universities engage in both professional and social activities. Among the projects in which Alice is involved is working with Friends of the Library; this group raises money for the university library through gathering and selling used books.

Currently residing in a retirement community where stillness, stately trees, and manicured lawns are a contrast to the concrete and activity of her New York community, she still has her gracious people-centered approach, an example of a person who continues to sustain and encourage others in their journeys.

Personal Reflections

I have known Alice Miel for most of my professional lifetime. She is an extraordinarily complex person. I admire both her wisdom and her mystery, her connectedness and her strong positions. At times she is an enigma to me, but at all times she is a person who exemplifies humanity and the professoriate at its best. Allow me to share a few ideas that I believe contribute to her genius.

First, she is a kind of leader who is called to serve, abdicating many of the privileges of leadership while engaging in the hard work necessary to getting a task done. She contributes her own wisdom while simultaneously building on the strengths of others.

Second, she has held to a set of beliefs throughout her career, at times examining her philosophy and again extending a perspective or applying it in a new setting. Yet her basic beliefs about persons, their value, the importance of unity with diversity, and the use of thought and feeling in creating better situations permeate her various undertakings.

Third, she is a person of focus, courage, commitment, passion, and kindness. Moral integrity and consistency shine through.

Fourth, she loves and respects life and finds her roots in rather basic things. I recall visiting her in Michigan—the area she calls home. We visited the small hardware store in town where Olsen knives, manufactured in her county, were sold; we looked at barns with hip roofs; we sat at the big stone hearth at her lakeside cottage. And on the Fourth of July, old-time family fun was the tone of the day as ice cream was made, canoe races held, and generations of family gathered. Although her roots are in Michigan, Alice has created a community wherever she has lived—where caring, friendships, good cooking, and hospitality abound.

Alice Miel has provided a strong voice in education around the world. The world is her village. Indeed, after her retirement from Teachers College, she spent two years in Afghanistan as a social studies specialist with the Curriculum and Textbook Project of the Ministry of Education.

Clearly Alice Miel is an exemplar of a creative and wise leader. In the words of John Fisher, former President of Teachers College:

> . . . she [Alice] has contributed a very special quality of leadership to our profession. During a turbulent time when many have had difficulties retaining a sense of educational direction, Alice has kept a clear sense of where she was going and for the soundest of reasons has returned

also the respect and esteem of her co-workers. In a very unusual way she combines high principles, genuine humaneness and firm convictions. Moreover, as an excellent teacher she had encouraged comparable qualities in her students and so has helped to set in motion influences that have already had far reaching effects and which will continue for a long time to come. Because of her contributions, Teachers College is a different and better place than it would otherwise be, and its service to the world of education has been strengthened. For what she has done and for the sort of person she is, she has our enduring admiration and gratitude. (Fisher, 1971)

Notes

1.   I am grateful to two persons for the careful reading of this chapter. My colleague Jessie Roderick of the University of Maryland gave valuable editorial advice. Alice Miel not only gave editorial help but also read for accuracy of information. I assume responsibility for the substance and organization of the chapter.

2.   Articles which give an overview of her early years include my 1989 essay, "Alice Miel: Leader in Democracy's Ways" in *Childhood Education* and Alice Miel's 1992 article, "Roaming Through a Life-space," in *The Educational Forum* .

CHAPTER FIFTEEN

The Longevity of a Good Mentor: J. Harlan Shores

William H. Schubert

"Professor Shores, just let me know if I drop into your office to ask questions at an inappropriate time."

"That will never happen."

I still remember those four words: "That will never happen." They were uttered by J. Harlan Shores to me over twenty years ago, and I recall them as if they were spoken yesterday. I recall the incredulity with which I heard them. I thought that no advisor would be that available to advisees. For me, however, the essence of J. Harlan Shores' teaching, the kind of mentorship he provided, is portrayed in that interchange we had early in my doctoral program. Throughout my doctoral studies Dr. Shores lived up to his prediction.[1] It never did happen that I was put off for stopping by. No question was too inane. No idea was scoffed at. No wish to find new readings was neglected. I learned to be a mentor by experiencing a great one. I do not choose the term "great" lightly. Even when his wife Betty was dying of leukemia, Professor Shores managed to maintain his devotion to his students. Although we knew that Mrs. Shores was ill late in 1973 and, because of this, tried to ask for little from Dr. Shores during that difficult autumn, we did not know the severity of her condition until the last few days.

I hope that the above example illustrates what I believe to be the quality that sets the best teachers, mentors, even parents apart from all others—*devotion*. Professor Shores' life in the College of Education at the University of Illinois at Urbana-Champaign was a life of devotion. He was devoted to students. His office door was open. His books were available to borrow.

His home was a place for advisees to gather. And his devotion extended to the cause of his work in curriculum. It was not merely to show students the mechanics of curriculum development but to *engage* them in considering the question of what is worthwhile to know, to be, and to do as an educator.

Professor Shores was serious about his work. He was friendly with students—cordial is a better word. He thought deeply before speaking, often pausing a rather long time. In a coversation about Shores at the Bergamo Curriculum Theory Conference some years after my Urbana days, Paul Klohr described him as a country gentleman. Klohr recalled Shores' presidency of ASCD (Association for Supervision and Curriculum Development) and other leadership roles in which they had interacted, and he talked of Shores' reserved demeanor and rural, midwestern accent and deliberate delivery of comments that moved like an arrow to the heart of an issue or problem discussed.

This was similar to the teaching style I encountered in a course that bore the same title as the classic curriculum text, *Fundamentals of Curriculum Development* (Smith, Stanley, & Shores, 1950). The book, authored by Shores with B. Othanel Smith and William O. Stanley in 1950 and revised in 1957, was an outgrowth of this course. Interestingly, however, by the summer of 1973, when I took the course, no book was required. Instead, Shores devoted each class session to an inquiry-style conversation about a single question or topic that stimulated discussion and debate. When we arrived for the class session, Professor Shores would already have been there for fifteen minutes or so, and the chalkboard would have become a bibliography that he was still writing. No reading assignments were given. Instead, it was evident that we were expected to become deeply acquainted with the broad array of literature on curriculum. Classes were both opportunities to share perspectives we had found and to have scholarly exchanges on the questions that served as our syllabus. Rephrased, these questions were the take-home midterm and final examinations as well: Who is to be educated? Educated for what? Educated with what? For whom is the content relevant? When to educate? How to educate? How to change the curriculum?

In a large sense the questions were the beginning of long-term independent study that lasted throughout my doctoral program and continues to influence my thinking and professional work. In retrospect, although I think that these questions incorporate traditional curriculum design topics, I am convinced that study and discussion of them opened doors for me to the many new issues and perspectives that have characterized the curriculum field in the past two decades. Clearly, the questions have had a lasting impact on my teaching and my writing. One aspect of Professor Shores' teaching that intrigued students and deepened their interest in topics of his class was the fact that Shores himself was actively grappling with the questions. At one point he told me that one of the main curriculum problems that plagued him was that of determining priority among the curriculum questions he had identified. (In research on reading, his other major scholarly area of study, he identified the nature of comprehension as his most nagging dilemma).

But, the teaching of classes only partially reveals the pedagogy of J. Harlan Shores. It was in stopping by his office and talking about ideas and other informal conversations in the halls of the College of Education and at his home that I gained the most from him. Through these *transactions* [to use John Dewey's term that relates a mutual process of growth (Dewey & Bentley, 1949)] we fashioned a curriculum; I learned about curriculum development by engaging fully in it to design it for my own doctoral studies. Let me now try to characterize the way this occurred.

As an elementary school teacher from 1967-1973, I had often wanted to pursue a doctorate. However, I wanted advanced graduate study to facilitate, expand, and deepen inquiry that I had been conducting as a teacher. I had a self-initiated interest in philosophy, which in some respects stemmed from my master's degree work in history and philosophy of education under the guidance of Philip G. Smith, A. Stafford Clayton, Stanley E. Ballinger, and Malcolm Skilbeck at Indiana University from 1966-67. I was particularly intrigued with the work of Dewey and what it meant to engage in reflective thought that enables the imaginative projection of answers to the perennial curriculum question of what is worth teaching and learning in different situations. So, I wanted to study curriculum, and I wanted to study it philosophically, through lenses of teaching experience.

During the time that I was looking for a place to pursue doctoral studies, it was almost universal that research in the curriculum field was empirical (interpreted usually as experimental or quasi-experimental research). Yet I wanted to philosophically connect assumptions about what is worth learning with imaginative practice. While inquiring about programs at several noted universities throughout the United States, I visited with J. Harlan Shores in Urbana in the summer of 1972. He was more willing to listen to my thoughts about what I hoped to accomplish in doctoral studies than any one else I had spoken to. At the conclusion of our conversation, he had piled several books on my lap and conveyed the distinct impression that he was interested in what I had learned from experience. This was the beginning of a very intensive period of study from the fall of 1972 through the spring of 1975. As I look back on it now, I see the seedbed of many of the scholarly projects that have engaged my attention for the next two decades.

Teacher Lore

At that initial meeting in the summer of 1972, it was clearly too late to begin doctoral studies in the fall. Moreover, Shores wanted to learn more about me and my potential as a scholar. He was interested to learn more about the ideas I was gleaning from practice, so together we developed a provocative assignment for me to pursue as I embarked on my sixth year of teaching elementary school in Downers Grove, Illinois. We decided that I should engage in a creative conversation *with* several authors (e.g., John Goodlad, Vernon Anderson, Jerome Bruner, John Dewey). Of course I added Smith, Stanley, & Shores and A. S. Neill, John Holt, Herbert Kohl, and others who spoke directly to my teaching. The point was to read these works and let them respond dialogically with the values derived from my teaching experience that continued to guide my work as an educator. This I did in a paper set up as my voice in conversation with literature. Reflecting on it now, I see what Shores asked me to do was a form of what today I would call "teacher lore" (Schubert & Ayers, 1992; Schubert & Lopez-Schubert, 1993). I did not enroll for credit to do this work but simply did it with the understanding that Shores would read it to help him decide if it would be worthwhile for him to advise me in doctoral studies. He told me that if I were accepted in the program, he would later count the paper as an independent study. He did so when I studied for the qualifying examination.

Curriculum Bibliography

When I actually began my Ph.D. program in the summer of 1973, one of the first pieces of advice Dr. Shores gave to me was to immerse myself in the literature, get stacks of index cards on which to record what I found that spoke to my interests, and keep complete citations (including pages for any quoted materials). Though the advice seems straightforward enough, to have that kind of organization from the beginning of my study was an invaluable asset to my future writing projects, especially the dissertation. Dr. Shores told me that I could obtain a locked library carrel. Because the Downers Grove Schools generously gave me a sabbatical leave at one-half salary and I could combine this with pay for an assistantship, I could be a full-time student. I relished the chance to spend extensive amounts of time in the library. I often wandered through the stacks gazing at thousands of the five million volumes housed in the University of Illinois Library. I felt surrounded by the giants of my field—not only my field but the whole panoply of arts, sciences, humanities, social sciences, and practical and professional literatures. The sights, sounds, and smells of those days remain a fond memory. Even today when I am in a large library those sensations revive. I recall peering out of my tenth-floor carrel window at the activity on the campus lawn between the library and the Education Building. I felt as if I was a small part of the mind of humankind, privileged enough to have time to contemplate how I might learn something valuable enough to somehow enrich the lives of others.

Symbolically (elitist though it may seem), at certain moments I fancied myself as having opportunity to see beyond the shadows of Plato's cave into the sunlight, having responsibility to somehow return it to others. So I packed my "light" in the form of a steadily growing supply of index cards and took them into the world! My increasingly bulging briefcase in fact did become a source of reference for many who would stop to ask for one kind of citation or another. My index cards (at least those on curriculum) became the primary source material for my first book, *Curriculum Books: The First Eighty Years* (Schubert & Lopez-Schubert, 1980), a bibliographical history of the curriculum field, 1900-1979. Shores supported this effort to trace the roots of curriculum, an expanded development of his (Shores, 1949) bibliographical history of research on elementary curriculum organization. Interestingly, Shores did not ask that I read this work; it was merely one that I found in my reconnoitering through the stacks, following my interests from one volume to the next.

Synoptic Texts

From the mid-thirties when Caswell and Campbell (1935) wrote the first synoptic curriculum text, such synoptic texts often included the term "development" in their title. Today, most have dropped this label from the title, symbolizing a broader cultural and philosophical area of inquiry known as "curriculum studies," "curriculum inquiry," or simply "curriculum." Nevertheless, even if the field is more inclusive than the act of developing curriculum, that act remains a significant part of the field which must be taught.

The broad perspective (social, cultural, philosophical, and historical) provided by the Smith, Stanley and Shores book had helped me as a teacher. In doctoral studies it was helping me to integrate my thoughts on curriculum as a budding scholar. I found other texts that attempted to do this in many eras (too many to note here). These books helped orient curriculum leaders in schools. I later referred to such books as "synoptic curriculum texts." Authors of synoptic texts tried to be encyclopedic and at their best they provided novel lenses through which to view the emergent field. By encouraging my continuous independent study in the library and by the example of his synoptic text, Shores inspired me to want to create a synoptic text in a subsequent era which I called *Curriculum: Perspective, Paradigm, and Possibility* (Schubert, 1986).

Out-of-School Curriculum and Student Lore

Not until now, while reflecting on what to say for this chapter, did I think of Shores' influence on my call for attention to the impact of curriculum outside of school. He did this not by pronouncements about what I ought to do nor even by the example of his own scholarly work. Instead, he did so by the example of his mentorship of me. He took time to get to know me as a person. He knew my family, he learned about my teaching experience; he sent flowers and extended sympathy when my father died (even though it was only a month after his own wife passed away), and he discussed ideas with me. In short, he knew the lore of my life—what today I have called "student lore" (Schubert & Lopez-Schubert, 1994). And he used this lore, in Deweyan fashion, to build a curriculum, not just for me in my doctoral studies, but with me.

Facilitating and Enabling as a Mentor

Professor Shores played a key but subtle role in my attempt to do these unusual variations in developing my curriculum of doctoral study. Interestingly, perhaps ironically, despite the excellent reputation of the University of Illinois faculty in the curriculum field from the 1950s onward, there was no distinct doctoral program in curriculum. Instead, students of curriculum enrolled in elementary or secondary education or even policy studies or educational psychology. The choice depended on their related interests. However, in any case the student worked closely with an advisor to tailor make a program of courses. Depending on the advisor, this program was more or less fit to the expressed interests and needs of the student.

On numerous occasions, Shores exercised his advisory role by discussing my hopes for study and my rationale or justification for them. When he was convinced of the worth of my aspirations, he would make necessary contacts with those who could help my pursuits through courses, audits, tutorial arrangements, or conferences. In one instance he noted my frustration at not being able to study educational classics with Harry S. Broudy because the class was canceled due to low enrollment. Dr. Shores knew that I had long admired Broudy's work in philosophy of education. I vividly recall that it was on July 6, 1973 (my birthday) that Dr. Shores called Dr. Broudy and arranged for me to study educational classics as a tutorial. I considered it a fine birthday gift! On other occasions, Dr. Shores enabled me to pick up the necessary work in educational administration to obtain Illinois administrative and supervisory certificates by taking work with professors Fred Raubinger and Thomas Sergiovanni. These turned out to be good contacts as well because their interests facilitated my inquiry into the place of imagination in teachers' curriculum decision-making, the topic of my dissertation (Schubert, 1975). In fact, Raubinger joined J. Myron Atkin, Bernard Spodek, and Shores as my doctoral committee members. Shores also encouraged these professors to join him in writing questions for my written qualifying examination that pushed my thinking in new directions, rather than having it be the usual exercise in recall and analysis. Because of his work with me to develop the general topic of these questions, I was able to read and reflect carefully for several weeks in preparation for a challenging learning experience, despite the traditional examination setting in which it had to be taken.

Teaching

Knowing that one of my principal goals in doctoral study was to join a faculty of education, Dr. Shores arranged from the start for me to gain experience in college teaching. For two semesters I taught a general methods course for undergraduate elementary teacher candidates. Through this experience I was able to draw upon my elementary teaching experiences and integrate them with the curriculum ideas I encountered in my reading and courses. Since the methods course was in a state of being revised, I worked with professors Peter Shoresman, James Raths, Shores, Spodek, and doctoral students to experiment with possibilities, assess their effectiveness, and enact revisions. This experience spoke directly to my interest in the relations of theory and practice as had the supervisory role that I also performed in the practicum aspects of the course.

After taking a deep interest in theoretical underpinnings and historical roots of open education in a course with Dr. Spodek, I refined an elaborate theoretical paper on the history of educational thought that influenced the open education movement. In consultation with Shores, Spodek invited me to teach his course on open education for graduate students in the summer of 1973, when he was on leave. It was a rare opportunity for me, a doctoral student, to teach an advanced course at the master's degree level.

Scholarship

Professor Shores taught me to value the scholarly inquiry in many phases of my life as an educator. He conveyed to me that a good dissertation is not just a demonstration of research capability. At its best a dissertation should grow from interests and inquiries lived in experience. He made me feel that it was admirable to do a dissertation that grew from my reflections as a teacher. In fact, it was from the start a meta-reflection, an attempt to reconstruct and examine the complex array of contexts that shaped the views that enabled my curriculum enactments with students. He helped me be able to draw upon philosophical classics, the history of progressive education, and literary sources to reconstruct a perspective on teacher reflection in (and about) action. He permitted the use of classroom ethnographies and empirical studies as research methodologies that helped illuminate different dimensions of my area of inquiry. To quote from Dewey's concluding image of educational science or research, Professor Shores helped me experience that

> education is by its nature an endless circle or
> spiral. It is an activity which includes science

within itself. In its very process it sets more problems to be further studied, which then react into the education process to change it still further, and thus demand more thought, more science, and so on, in everlasting sequence. (Dewey, 1929, p. 77)

Conclusion

To draw upon Dewey again, Harlan Shores helped me have a doctoral experience that illustrated a progressive definition of education, because it was a "reconstruction or reorganization of experience which adds to the meaning of experience, and which increases ability to direct the course of subsequent experience" (Dewey, 1916, p. 76). Ideas that are central to my work now, over twenty years since my doctoral studies, are ideas that J. Harlan Shores helped me reconstruct and experience with greater meaning. Clearly, his influence is lasting—his mentorship has longevity. Many of the ideas that I now try to develop and refine in my writing, teaching, and consulting were powerfully influenced by the mentoring I received in my doctoral studies. I continue to discover this. As with any worthwhile ideas, however, the origins are multiple and develop throughout a lifetime. When a mentor perceives what is emergent and provides the wherewithal for its growth and refinement, an invaluable service of teaching is provided. J. Harlan Shores gave me such an experience and I remain grateful for it. I have tried to build on his example in mentoring my own students, with the hope that the essence of what was shared with me will pass along to subsequent generations of curriculum scholars.

Notes

1. I frequently refer to Harlan Shores as Dr. Shores or Professor Shores. That is how most of his students thought of him. He was friendly, cordial, and a scholar worthy of the respect that we thought was conveyed by the title "Professor" or "Doctor."

PART FIVE

Mutuality, Dignity, and Generosity of Spirit

Hollis Caswell and the Practice of Education
by Arthur W. Foshay

Memories of Harold Rugg
by Kenneth D. Benne

William Heard Kilpatrick: Respecter of Individuals and Ideas
by William Van Til

William Van Til: The Consistent Progressive
by John A. Beineke

Mentoring is not limited to formal teacher-student relationships. Sometimes, mentors come at crucial periods in life, often after formal education has ended or perhaps when professional or personal doubts have set in—when the value of one's work is doubted or unappreciated. Three of the four essays that follow describe relationships of mature-to-younger men and how those relationships grew to include elements of mentoring: Kenneth Benne and Harold Rugg; William Van Til and William Heard Kilpatrick; and John Beineke and

William Van Til. The exception is the first essay, by Arthur Foshay about his doctoral advisor and mentor, Hollis Caswell. What links this essay to the others is that Foshay joined Caswell's faculty at Teachers College, Columbia University, and theirs evolved into a more mature relationship, one characterized by mutuality and respect. Each essay strongly illustrates how such relationships benefit both participants, younger as well as older professionals.

Three of the four relationships resulted in joint book authorships, indicative of the high regard the more senior person held for the junior. Foshay became a coauthor of Caswell's *Education in the Elementary School*; Kilpatrick surprised Van Til by telling him to include his name on the title page as coeditor, with Kilpatrick, of the ninth yearbook of the John Dewey Society, *Intercultural Attitudes in the Making*; and Harold Rugg's wife, Elizabeth, asked Kenneth Benne to finish an unpublished manuscript of her husband's that became *Imagination*. Caswell and Kilpatrick's actions were generous, as was Benne's in accepting the formidable task of completing Rugg's study. Mentor relationships are generous, and generosity is not always onesided.

Beineke's essay differs from the others. His relationship with Van Til began because of the desire to write a book on Kilpatrick and his need to better understand the man behind the words. As Van Til's essay suggests, he was a good choice to interview. What developed from their initial meeting was a special relationship, evident in what and how Beineke writes about Van Til who stands, for him, larger than life. These were the same feelings of profound respect for an elder statesman that prohibited Van Til from rushing up to greet a wheelchair-bound and fragile Professor Kilpatrick when seeing him on Morningside Heights shortly before his death.

Biographical Information

Hollis Leland Caswell [born: Oct. 22, 1901, Woodruff, KS; died: Nov. 22, 1988, Santa Barbara, CA] served as professor, dean, and president of Teachers College, Columbia University, from 1937-1966. He was graduated from the University of

Nebraska in 1922 with an A.B.; other degrees include an A.M. in 1927 and the Ph.D. in 1929 from Teachers College, Columbia University. Other professional roles included serving as a principal and superintendent in the Nebraska public schools from 1922-1926 and holding a professorship in education at the George Peabody College for Teachers from 1929-1937. Caswell's publications include *Curriculum Development* (1935) with Doak Campbell, *Education in the Elementary School* (1942, 1950/57) with Arthur W. Foshay, and *Curriculum Improvement in Public School Systems* (1950).

Harold Rugg [born: Jan. 16, 1886, Fitchburg, MA; died: May 17, 1960, Woodstock, NY] served as professor of educational foundations at Teachers College, Columbia University, from 1920-1951. He was graduated from Dartmouth College in 1908 with a B.S. and a C.E. in 1909; other degrees include the Ph.D. from the University of Illinois in 1915. Other professional roles included holding a professorship in civil engineering at James Milliken University (IL) from 1909-1911 and the University of Illinois from 1911-1915, and a professorship in education at the University of Chicago from 1916-1919. Rugg's publications include *Statistical Methods Applied to Education* (1917), *The Child-Centered School* (1928) with Ann Shumaker, *American Life and the School Curriculum* (1936), *The Teacher in the School and Society* (1950), *The Teacher of Teachers* (1952), and *Imagination* (1963).

William H. Kilpatrick [born: Nov. 20, 1871, White Plains, GA; died: Feb. 13, 1965, New York, NY] served as professor of educational philosophy at Teachers College, Columbia University, from 1909-1938. He was graduated from Mercer University in 1891 with an A.B.; other degrees include an A.M. from Mercer University in 1892 and the Ph.D. from Teachers College in 1912. Other professional roles included serving as a teacher and principal in the Georgia public schools from 1892-1897 and professor of mathematics at Mercer University from 1897-1906 (and acting president from 1903-1906). Kilpatrick's publications include *Foundations of Method* (1925), *Remaking the Curriculum* (1936) and editor/coauthor of *The Educational*

Frontier (1933). Professor Kilpatrick served in a number of leadership roles including founding member of Bennington College, the John Dewey Society, and the *Social Frontier*.

William Van Til [born: Jan. 8, 1911; Corona, NY] has served as the L.D. Coffman Distinguished Professor Emeritus of Education at Indiana State University from 1967. He was graduated from Columbia University in 1933 with a B.A.; other degrees include an M.A. from Teachers College, Columbia University, in 1935 and the Ph.D. from Ohio State University in 1946. Other professional roles include holding professorships in education at Ohio State University from 1934-1943, the University of Illinois from 1947-1951, George Peabody College for Teachers from 1951-1957, and New York University from 1957-1967. Van Til's publications include *Economic Roads for American Democracy* (1947), *The Making of a Modern Educator* (1961), *Modern Education for the Junior High School* (1961), *Education: A Beginning* (1971), and *Writing for Professional Publication* (1981). Professor Van Til has served in a number of leadership roles including terms as president of the Association for Supervision and Curriculum Development and the John Dewey Society.

CHAPTER SIXTEEN

Hollis Caswell and the Practice of Education

Arthur W. Foshay

It was the summer of 1945 at Teachers College, Columbia University. I looked through an open door into a spacious office. Seated at an orderly desk at the far end was the man I had come from California to see—Hollis L. Caswell. He was reputed to be the leader in curriculum development in the country. I wanted to study with him, to become acquainted with his approach to curriculum problems. I was not to be disappointed. In the course of time, he became my advisor, mentor, colleague, and friend.

At this first meeting, Caswell's professional formality and quiet dignity inspired my confidence. We talked only briefly but I departed with clear instructions: take certain tests, sign up for the courses we had discussed, and come back to talk some more. I did.

The summer's work was rewarding and I decided to return. I set in motion arrangements to take a leave of absence from my job as an elementary school principal in Oakland and to pursue doctoral study at Teachers College. Late in the fall, a letter arrived from Caswell inviting me to serve as his course assistant. When I arrived in New York in June of 1946, he offered me the position of assistant principal of the Horace Mann-Lincoln School, thus making it possible for me to continue as a student for two years rather than the single year I had provided for. When I finished the doctorate, Caswell recommended that I be appointed to the Teachers College faculty. Later, he invited me to work as coauthor of the revision of his *Education in the Elementary School* (Caswell & Foshay, 1950, 1957) and in many other ways nurtured my career. It was an inspiring forty-year association.

The principal thing I learned from Caswell was to take education and myself as an educator, seriously. During the ten years I worked as a teacher and school administrator and studied at the University of California, I had accumulated techniques—"tricks of the trade," if you will—for dealing with the variety of people and problems that exist in a public school. Like many a beginner, I saw professional education as an array of techniques. However, technique in itself was not enough. My professional life seemed to lack the high seriousness I wanted for my career. Caswell projected high seriousness.

Education, he obviously believed, had to deal not only with cognitive development but also with the solving of social problems and the building of civic morality. His extensive work on state and city curriculum programs during the heart of the Great Depression of the 1930s had no doubt deepened these convictions, which were shared by many others in those times. The difference between Caswell and the others of that time— such people as George Counts and Harold Rugg—was that Caswell got into the field and made things happen.

In the process of building state and city programs, Caswell developed certain ideas that became the core not only of his 1935 book, *Curriculum Development*—which gained him national attention immediately—but also the core to the course he was offering in 1946 with the help of William Alexander. The course was a generation ahead of its time. If only the foundation and federal officials of the 1950s and 1960s had taken it, school reform in those decades would have been far more effective.

I remember well some of the hard-won wisdom Caswell passed on to us in class. "The individual school is the unit for curriculum development," he preached. To be successful, the curriculum developer must work with the individual school staff, not primarily with the central office of the school district. He also taught that curriculum development works from the classroom out, not from the top down or the outside in, though of course the "top" and the "outside" must concur. In addition, he pointed out that the way schools are organized—for example, into 6-4-4 plans, departments, teaching teams—has relatively little to do with the quality of instruction. Also, he had observed that elaborate revisions of printed courses of study common in the 1920s, with the attendant expensive committees of teachers and others, got you nowhere, since the printed course of study usually "gathered dust on the shelves."

Caswell's course also offered an historical perspective on curriculum development during the 20th century. He introduced us to the 26th Yearbook of the National Society for the Study of Education, *Curriculum Making: Past and Present* (Rugg, 1927), but in teaching from it, Caswell offered a view of the major curriculum efforts as actions, not merely as proposals or exhortations. Several class sessions were devoted to the history of commissions and committees which were intended to make curriculum policies and proposals. Only a few of these bodies had a lasting effect. Caswell suggested reasons: if they proposed concrete action, it often happened. If they stopped with pointing out failures and pleading for change, they merely passed on the problem and had little effect.

Consistent with Caswell's view of education as a field of action as well as a field for academic study was his tendency to offer action as evidence. He rarely relied on authorities for his recommendations. This marked him off from many others who quoted Dewey and Kilpatrick as their ground for making curriculum proposals and from some other students of education who would turn professional education into the study of pedagogy, thus abandoning professional action to others (Foshay, 1970; Whitehead, 1925). The blend of academic and professional work that marks the best of the education schools today was in Caswell's mind from the beginning.

Cooperative action research embodied what Caswell had learned from the beginning of his work in curriculum design in Florida (Seguel, 1966, pp. 137-175). He had learned that teachers would either distort an innovation or ignore it if they and the other people in their organization had not had a hand in designing it. They had to "own" it (Foshay, 1994). It follows that the teacher must be placed at the center of school experimentation; a university consultant's function is to be available to assist in designing the research and in evaluating the consequences of the action. This approach has been rediscovered more recently, although the recent "action research" takes many forms, some of which do not require the gathering of systematic evidence. A great deal of recent educational reform ignores Caswell's warning; it is from the "top down" and is therefore likely to disappear as its many predecessors have.

In working directly with people, Caswell's way had always been unobtrusive. He did not call attention to himself in the manner of the other "stars" of his time. He sought to change people from the inside—to help them think differently—not to overwhelm them with techniques or to make them conform to his image. One of his bits of wisdom was the observation that an education makes people different from one another, not more alike. He believed so deeply in the principle of education as self-realization that he was the kind of subtle teacher who led one to develop one's own skills. His students didn't copy him; they grew under his intellectual and idealistic influence.[1]

For this reason, many ideas and projects Caswell originated are credited to others. He must have expected this, since he viewed teaching as a task of leading others toward self-realization and, more specifically, toward the translation of ideas into action. For example, Florence Stratemeyer et al.'s *Developing a Curriculum for Modern Living* (1947) was the result of two years' "pressure" from Caswell. The notion of building a curriculum in the context of "persistent life situations" which became the theme of that book can be found in an earlier publication of Caswell's. But no acknowledgment of Caswell's gentle prodding and encouragement appears in the book.

In addition to being a leader in curriculum development, Caswell was a bold and practical administrator. When he was brought to Teachers College in 1937, he formed the first Department of Curriculum and Teaching over the severe objections of some members of the Teachers College faculty but with the backing of the then Dean, William F. Russell.

By the end of World War II, Caswell had seen that the university laboratory schools were no longer producing educational experiments (their reasons for being), so he decided to close the expensive but very good Horace Mann-Lincoln School of Teachers College. The opponents of this decision took it to court and lost. The school was closed, and during the ensuing decade many other universities closed their laboratory schools for the same reason.

He saw that the NEA Department of Supervision and the newly formed Society for Curriculum Study could help each other if they joined forces, so he led in the combination of the two into the Association for Supervision and Curriculum Development (ASCD), which now leads the country in its field with a membership of 65,000+.

Later, when I was an official in ASCD, Caswell suggested in a conversation that ASCD should ask the NEA to form a group to devote itself to the quality of instruction. I carried the message, and the Center for the Study of Instruction was formed. It still continues with a vigorous program of publications, conferences, and activities that have proved influential.

When he was dealing with individuals, Caswell's advice was brief, direct, and subtle. Once when I was to consult on the curriculum for a large city, the air was full of "back to basics." I asked Caswell for suggestions. "The people of that city know perfectly well what they mean by 'basics,'" he said. "Don't try to redefine the word for them." That single comment—and that's all there was to it—catches up the whole problem. You don't start by redefining terms. You start by trying to suggest actions—after you have listened carefully—that are likely to solve the problems as they are seen by the people who have them. Then they may wish to see their problems differently. Caswell knew me well. I needed that reminder.

Caswell never joined any "school" of educational theory. While he did promote the core curriculum, he did not do it as a "Progressive"; he did it because it made sense to him and others and because the crisis of the 1930s called for the building of a population that could take responsibility for solving social problems without violence.

Caswell's personal beliefs are expressed in his actions and sometimes in his speech. An old friend of his once pointed out to me that Caswell's small-town upbringing in Nebraska had filled his speech with metaphors from the farm. Ideas are "plowed in"; there is a "harvest" from one's actions; things go "as far as you can see," and so on. Caswell's approach to curriculum development may well have grown out of the society and culture of the midwestern small town, with its insistence on mutual respect and integrity. Certainly these values form an integral part of his character and have shaped his approach to his professional work and to the world.

Caswell thought in large terms, always with actions to be completed. He defined the field of curriculum with his first book. He invented the field of curriculum development with his innovative state and city curriculum development programs. He led in the formation of the major professional organization in the field. [2] Caswell saw education primarily as a field of action. He therefore saw the professoriate in education as an attempt to clarify and to induce action. Theories exist to clarify reality, and Caswell's notion of education reality lay in attempts to educate students. This view of education is somewhat like a physician's view of medicine: it's a clinical profession; it attempts to improve the lot of clients.

The clinical view of education does not correspond with the views of their academic fields held by many professors in universities. For them, prestige (the basic reward of the professoriate) is awarded not for excellent clinical behavior or performance but for excellent theorizing about clinical behavior, whether it be concerned with social issues, the arts and the humanities, or science. It follows that departments of education, from the university point of view, ought to be departments of the study of pedagogy, not centers of action. Applied fields, such as pharmacy or nursing or the performing arts or even clinical medicine and law, have difficulty being recognized as being at the heart of the meaning of the university. In the classical university, we study performance, but we do not teach performance. The performing arts and the practical disciplines tend to be relegated elsewhere.

Caswell's personal unobtrusiveness grew out of his discomfort with the "star system" he found at Teachers College as a student. The society he found there consisted of stars and acolytes, he once told me. As a new faculty member, one either competed with the stars and found a place in the firmament, or one became a follower of one of the stars. Caswell's style, described here, probably grew out of his disapproval of this educational practice and with his experience in the field. He paid a price for these beliefs; when he was president of TC, he was attacked in the pages of a prominent magazine; he was accused of presiding over an "extinct volcano," and he resigned the presidency shortly after this attack.

What does this mean to today's professoriate? One result of this situation has been this: during the past generation, professors have changed their loyalty from their institutions to their disciplines. What matters to professors these days is their reputation with their peers in their discipline, not with their colleagues in the university. They break tenure readily to go to another institution. They take part in the building of their own institution only up to a point; their primary concern is to build their personal reputation. If things displease them and they have an offer, they will leave without looking back.

From the point of view of the current professoriate, Caswell was unique. His devotion to the practice of education and his idealistic attempts to improve the offerings in the lower schools by rising above his own needs for recognition and power probably seem anachronistic to some now. They aren't though. They are being rediscovered by those who would improve the schools. "Cas" must look down on all of this with a chuckle.

Notes

1. Caswell had a number of outstanding students. They, too, could write their own accounts of his influence and ideas. Those I have known include William Alexander, Marcella Lawler, Alice Miel, A. Harry Passow, and Galen Saylor. There are many others.

2. Caswell's papers are collected at the University of Wyoming. More detailed accounts of his professional contributions can be found in *The Curriculum Field: Its Formative Years* (Seguel, 1966) and in *Schooling and Innovation: The Rhetoric and the Reality* (Fraley, 1981).

CHAPTER SEVENTEEN

Memories of Harold Rugg

Kenneth D. Benne

I first met Harold Rugg in the fall of 1936. I had come to Teachers College, Columbia University, as one of the first group of scholars in the Advanced School of Education there. All doctoral candidates at Teachers College became members of the Advanced School with a desk for each and a library browsing and meeting space for all. Paul Mort, the School's first director, had an image of building a universally respected teachers' "university," perhaps an American equivalent of L'Ecole Normale Superieure at the University of Paris.

Nearly all members of the Teachers College faculty attended a reception for the Advanced School Scholars that fall—Harold Rugg among them. My first impression of Rugg was that of a dandy. He was meticulously dressed with a silky, color-coordinated handkerchief in the upper pocket of his well-fitted, tweedy jacket. His short beard and mustache were carefully trimmed and his nails manicured. As we greeted each other, his pronounced stammer became evident, deepening into a stutter when speaking words with a *ch* or *sh* beginning. After a brief chat, my overall impression of him became that of a self-assured yet cordial and friendly person.

I did not enroll in any of Harold Rugg's classes. I was told by several students who did that one could gather Rugg's ideas as well or better by reading his already voluminous writings than by attending his classes. I did read several of his books—*Culture and Education in America* (1931), *The Great Technology* (1933) and *American Life and the School Curriculum* (1936). And I, of course, read *The Child-Centered School* (1928), written jointly with Ann Shumaker. I also scanned his social science textbooks written for junior high school students. I believe that six volumes of the series, eventually 17 in number, had been published in 1936.

Rugg was still working on further volumes in the series, many of these for students in elementary schools. Because of his writing regimen, he spent little time at Teachers College on days when he had no teaching responsibilities there.

I learned of Rugg's early academic career from an older educational statesman then on the Teachers College faculty— Professor William C. Bagley. He was proud of having enrolled Harold Rugg, somewhat inadvertently, into the education professoriate. During World War I Bagley had been dean of the College of Education at the University of Illinois. Rugg was then a young instructor in the College of Engineering at Illinois who became dissatisfied with the quality of his own teaching and went to Bagley to get suggestions for improving his teaching methods. At that time, the University of Illinois had recently launched a graduate program of studies leading to a doctorate in education. In talking with Bagley, Rugg became interested in this program, enrolled in it, and was the first person to earn a Ph.D. in educational studies from Illinois. For those who know only of Rugg's later work, it may seem strange that Rugg's first book was on statistical methods in the study of education.

While Bagley was proud of his recruitment of Rugg as a professor of education, their philosophies of education were very different. Rugg had become a social reconstructionist in his conception of the mission of education. Schools along with other agencies of deliberate education, he believed, should take the lead in changing our social and economic systems in keeping with democratic values. This would require the focusing of school studies on social and economic issues and a crossing of traditional and conventional subject matter boundaries in the process. Bagley was a conservative, both politically and educationally. He advocated a school curriculum which followed the lines of traditional academic disciplines, a curriculum planned and managed by expertly trained teachers. Rugg's own social texts drew from several different disciplines in seeking to illuminate various problematic aspects of the drastically changing life and culture in America and the world— "Our Country and Our People, "Changing Governments," Man at Work: His Arts and Crafts," etc.

From 1938 to 1941, I taught in Columbia's Teachers College while completing my doctoral dissertation. I taught one of the four sections of a course in the foundations of education which, at that time, was a requirement for all master's degree candidates. Each of several sections of the course was taught by a team of faculty members drawn from several academic disciplines—history, philosophy, sociology, economics, psychology and religion, and from several professional fields—curriculum and administration among others.

The first semester of the course centered on crucial problems of American culture, national and international. In the second semester, basic criticisms of American and world culture and economy, developed in the first semester, were applied to problems of reconstructing curriculum, patterns of instruction, organization and administration in American schooling. Since faculty and students were required to utilize and integrate ideas and information from diverse specialized fields of study, appropriate reading materials of high quality were difficult to find in any one or two books. The faculty—twenty-one in number—set out to prepare its own book of readings. Harold Rugg was the general editor of the project, and I served as one of six members of the editorial committee. Our project resulted in two volumes of *Readings in the Foundations of Education* (Rugg et al., 1941), each with more than six hundred pages of text. During three years' work on this committee, I became much better acquainted with Harold Rugg both as a person and scholar and as an advocate of social change through education.

I have already noted that Rugg believed that educational programs and, more specifically, those of schools, should be designed to widen and deepen the democratic way of life in America. His voluminous writings for educators as well as his "model" books for children and youngsters were dedicated to this mission. He had been a member of the now-legendary Kilpatrick discussion group which met from time to time during the late 1920s and early 1930s to discuss historic changes occurring in civilizations and cultures and the meanings of these changes for refurbished educational policies and programs. It was this group which conceived the interdisciplinary study of educational foundations by teachers, a program already

discussed. And it was out of this group that the idea of a
left-liberal or radical educational journal, the *Social Frontier*, came
to fruition during the economic depression of the 1930s.

Rugg came to share with other members of the Kilpatrick
discussion group the belief that, in order to achieve an abundant
and just economy, an unregulated market-steered economy must
yield to some sort of planned economy. But he differed with
other prominent social reconstructionists in education—Counts
and Childs, for example, in two major ways.

First he adopted Howard Scott's idea of technocracy.
Planning for the production and distribution of economic goods
was seen, by Scott, as a "technical" process. It was, therefore, to
be carried out by technical experts—engineers, economists, and
others with requisite knowledge and skill. I have no doubt that
Rugg's embracing of technocratic planning was related to his
engineering background. He shared with Thorstein Veblen an
admiration for engineers as modern bearers of the ethic of good
workmanship which had once characterized craftsmen working
in various media—stone, wood, and metal. Their virtue lay in
envisioning and enacting honest and elegant solutions to
production problems—the "instinct of workmanship" as Veblen
named it. Economic planning was for Rugg primarily a *technical*,
not a *political* process. Counts and Childs, and I along with them,
saw it as both political and technical. Ideally, we wanted all
citizens to participate in forging economic policies. This was a
necessity in a culture committed to participative democracy.
Rugg embraced the values of political democracy. But this was
not fully consistent with his advocacy of a meritocracy of
engineers and economists as planners of economic production
and distribution for all Americans. The task of enlightened
citizens which, as noted before, he was interested in educating,
was to serve as a power to offset the power presently exercised
unilaterally by the predators of big business and finance and
thus to legitimize technocratic planning for a democratic
economy of abundance. It seems that Harold Rugg never
grappled seriously with the *political* and *moral* aspects of his
recommendations for fundamental social and economic change.
He appreciated deeply the power for good, potential in our
"Great Technology" as he called it. Louis Henry Sullivan,

architect, engineer and teacher of Frank Lloyd Wright and others, was for Harold Rugg a cultural hero, a prophet of the integrative American culture which, Rugg believed, would eventually encompass and reconcile the technical and the beautiful aspects of culture in a distinctively American manner. He praised Emerson and Whitman, poets of an emerging great and good America but gave no great kudos to Jefferson and Madison, political prophets of the American democratic experiment. And America's great novelists, Hawthorne and Melville, who probed and portrayed the tragic depths of American life and culture, he ignored completely.

The second way in which Rugg differed from many other social reconstructionists among American educators was in his advocacy of a central role for "the fine arts" in the education of whole and integrated citizens in America. He appreciated and lauded the excellence of American science and technology and believed that the philosophy of John Dewey and other American pragmatists was an accurate abstraction from and portrayal of this excellence. But he did not find in this philosophy a clarion call to create a beautiful and integral way of life in America and to appreciate and celebrate the creations of distinctively American artists—poets, painters, dancers, architects, and workers in the crafts.

When Rugg moved from the University of Chicago to Columbia University and New York City, he became "converted" to the vision of "America's Coming of Age" under the leadership of artists in all the arts. (Van Wyck Brooks had just published a "prophetic" book by that name.) Among those whose vision he came to share were Van Wyck Brooks, Waldo Frank (for a time the editor of a new magazine, *The Seven Arts*), Lewis Mumford, and Georgia O'Keefe. All of these were associated with the studio of the great photographer and friend of the arts, Alfred Stieglitz, at 291 Fifth Avenue, New York City. All of these artists and critics saw a renaissance emerging in the American arts and a central role for such arts in creating integrity and maturity in Americans and in their culture.

In the 1930s Rugg saw a wide gap between the education of students in methods of critical problem-solving as a goal of schooling and their concurrent education in processes of creative

discovery and awareness of beauties in their own work and that
of others. He accepted John Dewey's "complete act of thought"
as an adequate model for the former. He sought in the fine arts
(and later in the practices of Taoists, Yogis, and Zen Buddhists)
for guidelines of a discipline in creative discovery, appreciation,
and awareness. Rugg's interest in bridging this perceived gap
persisted and became a central focus in his studies between his
retirement from the Teachers College faculty in 1951 and his
death in 1960. (I will say more of these studies later.)

The nature of this gap in educational terms was formulated
just a few weeks before his death in a 1960 address to the
Philosophy of Education Society.

> We must build the foundations for the school of
> Freedom. While keeping the dynamic power of
> the theory of the active school, we face the
> incredibly difficult task of finding the way to
> match it—in theory and in practice—with the
> quiet school of intense concentration and
> intuitive identification. The cue to the quiet
> mind is the creation of conditions which favor
> the ancient commonplace of concentration of
> attention. . . . Under Parker, Dewey and the
> artist teachers we built the School of the First
> Freedom—freedom from external restrictions.
> Now we must build the School of the Second
> Freedom—that of the inner freedom of the
> relaxed, threshold mind of intuitive discovery.
> The concept of discovery will revitalize our
> freedom to investigate.

It was a tribute to Rugg's inveterate optimism for him to
state that the "freedom to investigate" had been "established" in
American life and schooling. His own experience might well
have taught him how precarious this establishment actually was.
In 1941, his textbook series in social studies was condemned as
"subversive" by super-patriotic groups at various places in
America and actually publicly burned in a few of these places.
Rugg was genuinely puzzled by this reaction to his many years
of concentrated and devoted study and writing.

I believe this puzzlement is evidence of his naiveté about human morals and politics, particularly in their irrational and tragic manifestations, even while he developed and demonstrated enormous sophistication in the affairs of the intellect and the arts. I believe Rugg actually believed that his textbooks were *descriptions* of American history and society. Actually, of course, they were written from a left-liberal, social-democratic point of view and invited readers to consider serious deficiencies in our economy, society, and culture and to commit themselves to correcting these deficiencies. Others saw his work as subversive of American capitalist values. He wrote out of a moral and political outlook that tended to regard conflicting moral and political outlooks as corrigible by accurate information, "enlightened" thought, and aesthetic sensitivity. He assumed rather than "advocated" or "argued" the moral and political values inherent in his analysis of American culture and his advocacy of its reconstruction.

During the nine years between his retirement from Teachers College, Columbia University, and his death in Woodstock, N.Y., Harold Rugg and I became closer friends and intellectual companions than we had been before. There are probably two reasons for this convergence. One was the need in both of us for dialogue with other "social reconstructionists" in American educational theory and practice. We had all built on John Dewey's left liberalism in social philosophy. Dewey came to be increasingly neglected by educational philosophers both of the "left" and of the "right," beginning in the 1950s. Younger "leftists" among educational thinkers became Marxists. The "rightists" cultivated the task and methods of philosophizing exemplified by the later Wittgenstein in his *Philosophic Investigations*. These philosophers only analyzed language and concepts used in education and usually avoided any clear value-laden recommendations to practicing educators. Avoidance or neglect of problems of social and political philosophy by educational theorists was safer during the rising tide of McCarthyism in the years during and following World War II.

Two university centers maintained a social reconstructionist stance during the 1950s—the University of Illinois and Boston

University. I was at Illinois until 1953 and at Boston in the
following years. Rugg became a fairly frequent visitor in both
places for formal conferences and informal conversations.
Between 1951 and 1960, he visited and spoke at the University of
Illinois at least two times and at Boston University at least three
times. I visited Rugg in his home at Woodstock at least four
times between 1951 and 1960.

I mentioned earlier that Rugg found few social
reconstructionists who shared his left liberalism in socio-
economic outlook and his strong interest in a fuller place for
experiences in the arts in school programs. I was one of these
few. I wrote a piece on "The Functions of Art" for the Teachers
College *Readings in the Foundations of Education*. I published in
Art Education Today and spoke to several art teachers' workshops
at the Museum of Modern Art in New York City. I did not share
Rugg's view of the "redemptive" power of the arts, already
discussed, or his conviction that John Dewey neglected the arts
in his conception of thinking. Rugg and I did share a belief that
the inner and outer conditions required for creative imagination,
the organismic and environmental variables which foster and
which impede the cultivation of a creative approach to life's
problems, had been neglected by scholars in education.

Harold Rugg spent a major part of his time between 1951
and 1960 in studying and writing on this problem. And I carried
on a parallel study during several of my years at Boston
University. A good bit of our conversation when we met during
those years had to do not with social-cultural criticism but with
our hunches and findings about creativity and how persons
learn to approach life's puzzles and conflicts creatively.

A number of our discussions of creative imagination took
place in the house Rugg had designed and helped to build in
Woodstock, New York. This house was in some large part the
product of Rugg's own imagination. Before Woodstock became
synonymous with hippies and rock and rollers, it was widely
known as a colony of artists in various media. A number of
painters, sculptors, composers, and authors lived and worked
there. This plethora of artists influenced Rugg's decision to make
a home in Woodstock.

He bought a hilltop plot of land and employed a local builder who worked with fieldstone as a building material. Rugg liked to tell the story of how he located the place to build his house on its hill. He went with the builder to the hilltop, carrying a desk chair. He moved the chair from spot to spot until he found a place where, resting from his writing, he could best see the view of surrounding hills, forests, and fields. When he found this place, he asked the builder to make the immediately surrounding space into a study with a window toward the view and to arrange the rest of the house around this study. Rugg's stone hilltop house in Woodstock did more than fit its surroundings; it helped these surroundings to fulfill and express their potentialities for homely beauty and life-friendliness which they could not have done without it. Rugg's house was an artifact which helped to actualize beauties previously unnoticed in that environment's forested hills. It was a well-imagined and well-placed artifact—a Ruggian work of art.

Rugg's studies and thought came to focus on finding and expressing the conditions evocative and supportive of human acts of creative imagination. He studied the reflective accounts of discoveries in science, mathematics, and art written by the discoverers themselves. He came to find the "locus" of creative imagination in the off-conscious mind—not the fully conscious mind or the deeply unconscious mind. This led him to the study of off-conscious states of mind as in hypnotism, in-trance states, in Taoist, Yogi, and Zen Buddhist practices of Eastern sages, in the "Tao of the West," as he named it, in William Blake and the mystics, and in processes of symbolization and symbolic transformation of meanings.

He was still writing and rewriting his manuscript on the creative process when he died quietly in his Woodstock garden on a summer morning in 1960. His widow, Elizabeth Rugg, asked me to edit his unfinished manuscript and to see it through the process of publication. The book acquired the name *Imagination* and was published by Harper and Row in 1963. I undertook this task both because of my friendship with Harold Rugg and because I believe that the study of the processes and conditions of creative imagination is fundamentally important to all persons in our high-technology world but perhaps especially to those who would educate others for living a human life in that world.

I wrote in my editor's preface to Harold's last book that he had not achieved a "theory" of the imagination but that he had bravely brought into conceptual relationship fields of study usually hermetically sealed off one from the other. And he had demonstrated that mastery of ideas from diverse fields of thought and practice was necessary in order to achieve a credible and adequate "theory" of the creative process in human beings. Actually, this observation can be accurately applied in an evaluation of all of Rugg's voluminous writings on education. Harold Rugg was not a systematic theorist. But he had the intuitive wisdom and the courage to locate the important ingredients of an educational theory adequate to his day, concepts often segregated one from another in our specialized and departmentalized academia, and to work to shape these ingredients into meaningful interrelationships. We need more Harold Ruggs in educational studies today.

CHAPTER EIGHTEEN

William Heard Kilpatrick: Respecter of Individuals and Ideas

William Van Til

This is a memoir about William Heard Kilpatrick, his style as a master teacher and his style as a leader of educational organizations. It is also a memoir about the relationship of an old man and a young man. Look elsewhere for Kilpatrick's biography; look elsewhere for appraisals of his contributions to philosophy of education. My memoir is simply a recollection of a great person I was privileged to know.

Our first encounter was inauspicious. It was 1934, one of the deep Great Depression years. I was just out of Columbia College, proud of my liberal arts credentials, abysmally ignorant of the field of education, and employed as a teacher in a reform school that had no books, no pencils, no paper, no course of study, no anything except delinquents. On weekends I rode with a fellow teacher from rural Warwick to New York City to take courses at Teachers College toward an M.A. So I found myself in the old barn-like Horace Mann auditorium with hundreds of others in the presence of an old man with a lion-like mane of white hair, an unlined pink face, and the voice and bearing of a benign Southern gentleman. As I rode back to New York State Training School for Boys, I might have been heard muttering skeptically concerning his ideas, "I'd like to see him try to teach that way at Warwick!" I wanted to believe yet I was unable to believe.

Born on November 20, 1871, William Heard Kilpatrick was 62 when I first saw him. He was becoming known to the press as Columbia's "million dollar professor." Not that Kilpatrick's total lifetime earnings remotely approached a million dollars. The press gave him the sobriquet because his gigantic classes limited(!) to 465 students were in the process of bringing in more than a million dollars in tuition fees.

Twenty-five years later I asked Kilpatrick to tell reporters assembled in his apartment how he, the exponent of Progressive education, the prophet of meeting the needs of the learner, the advocate of recognizing individual differences, could reconcile his philosophy of education with the task of teaching these mammoth classes. The year was 1959 and the occasion was a press interview with Kilpatrick as part of the John Dewey Centennial Year observances. Here is his explanation, unedited, just as I tape-recorded it:

> I'll tell you what I tried to do with my class. It demonstrates what I think Dewey would stand for. I had a large class, so we had to do the thinking largely in advance. Then I asked a number of questions. I tried to ask those questions so they couldn't tell how I would answer them. I gave a number of statements (which might or might not be true) for them to criticize. I tried to arrange them so they couldn't tell which way I would criticize the statement. In other words, they would have to think.
>
> The class was divided into discussion groups and they had to meet an hour outside for every hour they met inside. The discussion group must be not more than eight nor less than five, so they could talk things over together. Each group was to have a person of the group to report what the group thought on each question in each statement. Mr. A would report on question one, Mr. B on question two, and so on. Then when I met the class I would plan to say, "Question one, groups 7, 28, 35 will answer it, question two. . . . " I would go right on through. Then when we came into the class, I would say, "We will take question one. Now number 7, what do you say? What did your people think?" He gets up and tells it. "Twenty-eight, what did

> your people think? Thirty-five, what did your
> people think?" If they disagreed, then I had
> them argue it out and it was thrown open for the
> whole class to take part in the argument. If they
> all agreed and I agreed, then we went on to the
> next question.

After the reform school year, I taught for almost a decade at
the University School of Ohio State University. University School
was one of the more experimental schools of the Eight Year
Study of the Progressive Education Association. I learned to be a
professional educator during that period; as the Kilpatrick
phrase puts it, "We learn what we live." My reading included
several of Kilpatrick's books such as *Foundations of Method* (1925),
Education and the Social Crisis (1932), *The Educational Frontier*
(which Kilpatrick edited, 1933), and *Selfhood and Civilization*
(1941). I looked forward eagerly to each issue of the *Social
Frontier*, the lively and controversial journal which he and other
change-oriented educators had founded. I grew.

Once at a Progressive Education Association convention I
attended a special meeting called to protest Kilpatrick's coming
mandatory retirement. The protest had his support, for
Kilpatrick, always ahead of his time, also opposed age discrimination. But ageist policies prevailed and he retired. I assumed
that I would never see Kilpatrick again, not knowing the number
of years he had yet to live and that I was to work with him
following his supposed retirement.

One of his leadership roles was as chairman of the board of
the Bureau for Intercultural Education, a pioneering organization that worked for better human relations among
Americans of all races, religions, and ethnic backgrounds. In the
mid-1940s the board of the John Dewey Society asked him to edit
a yearbook on intercultural education to be published by
Harpers. Since I was then director of publications and learning
materials for the Bureau for Intercultural Education, I became his
legman in the development of *Intercultural Attitudes in the
Making* (1947).

His way of creating a yearbook was unique. I have always
wondered why other editors of yearbooks haven't copied it. First

he called together in the Bureau offices in New York a group of intellectual leaders in human relations education to plan the structure and central thrusts of the book and to suggest possible authors. Then he invited writers who were skillful in communication to prepare the chapters. Kilpatrick knew that intellectual leaders in a field are not necessarily the best writers and, conversely, that the most skillful writers are not necessarily the best planners of structures or proposers of seminal ideas. So some carried through one role and some the other and a few did both.

In 1946 Kilpatrick was in his mid-seventies and I was in my mid-thirties. Never physically powerful, he was becoming frailer. So, as his right-hand man for the yearbook, I traveled weekly from midtown Manhattan uptown to the Kilpatrick apartment on Morningside Heights. His home was a large, comfortable, wide-windowed, old-fashioned apartment within walking distance of the Columbia campus. The apartment building was perched on a cliff that overlooked the roofs of a teeming city area where Puerto Ricans, African Americans, and Italians were concentrated.

I recall vividly my first visit. Marion Y. Ostrander, Kilpatrick's third wife, greeted me warmly and ushered me into the big living room where Kilpatrick awaited me. I am not much good at small talk. But I felt the occasion demanded some so I talked about the view. Kilpatrick listened patiently and contributed little. I mentioned that I had been in one of his large classes. "What year?" "1934, the spring." He excused himself and disappeared into another room. He returned and said, "And you got a B+." Somewhere in his apartment he still kept all the names and grades of uncountable thousands of students who had been in his mammoth classes.

I returned week after week as author correspondence developed and as manuscripts eventually arrived. I soon discovered that Kilpatrick tolerated rather than welcomed small talk. The man was innately courteous, dignified, formal, reserved, intent. His mind worked like a Swiss watch, precise, accurate, orderly. He raised the important questions, suggested good procedures as to problems, gave careful instructions. After an hour or two, I would return to my office with a week of editorial work ahead. Kilpatrick would turn back to looking over another yearbook chapter or writing another book or to the affairs of the Urban League or the League for Industrial Democracy.

Eventually the entire manuscript was ready to send to Ordway Tead at Harpers. I brought to Kilpatrick the stack of pages topped by the title page which read "Intercultural Attitudes in the Making edited by William Heard Kilpatrick." He thumbed through. He waited until I had risen and was on my way to the door.

"Mr. Van Til." (I was always Mr. Van Til to him.)

"Yes, Dr. Kilpatrick." (I would no more have called the Dalai Lama by his first name than call Dr. Kilpatrick Bill or Heard.)

He said, "I want you to make a change on the title page. It is to read, 'edited by William Heard Kilpatrick and William Van Til.'"

I was thunderstruck. The 35-year-old legman had become the co-editor of *Intercultural Attitudes in the Making* with the eminent philosopher of education born six years after the end of the Civil War.

"Thank you," I gasped.

"If I make any other changes, I'll call you," he said. And the door closed.

Never, I vowed to myself, no matter how long I live, will I ever fail to give full credit to anyone who ever works with me on a publication or a project. I have kept the pledge.

I had other occasions to watch him work. At the Bureau I edited a book by a young Fieldston School teacher, Spencer Brown. *They See for Themselves* (1945) described the documentary approach to learning which proceeded through student interviews and discussions and which culminated in student-written documentary plays. One play was critical of Father Charles Coughlin and his magazine, *Social Justice*. (Of Coughlin, the *New Columbia Encyclopedia* reported, "In the nineteen thirties he made radio addresses in which he criticized such diverse groups as U.S. bankers, trade unionists, and Communists" as well as New Deal policies . . . "Coughlin also published, *Social Justice*, in which he expressed pro-Nazi opinions and made increasingly anti-Semitic remarks . . . Father Coughlin was . . .

silenced by his superiors.") In 1945 a group of supporters of
Father Coughlin met with Kilpatrick and Bureau staff members
to protest the material dealing with Father Coughlin. Kilpatrick
was subjected to tirades, veiled economic threats, and thinly
disguised abuse. He heard the censors out. At the close of the
meeting he reaffirmed the right of young people to use the
method of intelligence. He said courteously, "You have given me
an insight into the sensibilities of some persons that I have not
had before." Distribution of *They See for Themselves* by the Bureau
and Harpers continued.

For years he presided over board meetings of the John
Dewey Society for the Study of Education and Culture, for he
served as president of the organization from 1938 to 1957. As a
long-term board member, I marveled at his leadership skills
even as I did while a Bureau staff member. He would listen to
conflicting opinions by people of good will who were debating
policy with the passion that only the dedicated can bring to bear.
He often helped them clarify proposed alternatives. Then, with
scrupulous regard for all that had been said, he would reconcile
proposals and create a synthesis. Amazingly enough, his new
common ground usually seemed reasonable and acceptable even
to those who had earlier been disputants.

He grew older and frailer. I remember an occasion at his
dinner table, presided over graciously by Mrs. Kilpatrick, when
he told me that he had received recently a newspaper clipping
from a friend on the West Coast. It spoke well of Kilpatrick and
Progressive education. He had responded to his friend that he
was especially appreciative since, as far as he knew, this was the
only good thing being said about him by the press of that section
of the country. Along with John Dewey, George S. Counts,
Harold Rugg, and other Progressive educators, he was under
constant attack by reactionaries.

During the McCarthy era I was attempting to fight the
reactionary educational McCarthyites through a 1953 ASCD
yearbook, *Forces Affecting American Education*. I talked to
Kilpatrick once and expressed my despair at the success the
reactionary forces apparently were having in destroying modern
programs of education. He said, "The attacks on education
simply show that the kind of education in which we believe is

becoming more effective. They only fight us bitterly when we are making a real difference. Otherwise they ignore us."

In the 1960s when I was teaching and administering at New York University, I would very occasionally drop in at his apartment when events brought me to the Columbia campus. Kilpatrick was then in his nineties. One day a sad-faced Mrs. Kilpatrick told me at the door that he no longer wanted to see visitors. "He's a proud man, you know. He doesn't want people to remember him as he is now." As I walked back toward the campus I saw him. He was in a wheelchair which was being pushed along Morningside Heights by a young man. I watched for a long while. But I did not approach him. I never saw him again. William Heard Kilpatrick died on February 13, 1965. On behalf of the John Dewey Society, I arranged a memorial service which was held a short time afterward.

Since I first encountered Kilpatrick, I have become well acquainted with many professors. But seldom have I met one who rivals him in representing the enduring principles which should guide the educational professoriate. While the editors define these principles in their introduction to this book, I would propose one additional characteristic: to write out of conviction and dedication and with observance of scholarship in order to communicate with others on what needs to be known. When I once asked Kilpatrick how a professor could most make a difference, he replied, "Through writing and a few graduate students."

As I review my experiences with Kilpatrick which stretched across decades, I realize how many of our encounters illustrate the tradition. For instance, his tape-recorded description, quoted above, of how he enabled all students in his classes of hundreds of students to participate is a classic account of how a well-read and thoughtful professor can help students to approach ideas with a sense of exploration. The magic of his leadership of board member discussions of policy for the John Dewey Society and the Bureau for Intercultural Education also testified to his skill in exploring ideas.

His dedication to his institution, Teachers College, and to his profession, education, was manifest to me as a student in 1934 when I first heard his voice, through the time in 1937 when I joined the protest against the ageism which forced his retirement, into the 1950s when I was working with both the Association for Supervision and Curriculum Development and the John Dewey Society on yearbooks against McCarthyism, and into the 1960s, the last years of his life, when we discussed strategies for fostering Progressive education.

His sense of moral responsibility went well beyond academe and into service to such organizations as the Urban League as well as those in which I was a neophyte participant, the John Dewey Society, and the Bureau for Intercultural Education. As to writing, Kilpatrick's production was remarkable and went well beyond the books mentioned in this essay. Always his writing grew out of his commitment and dedication and scholarship. Were he alive he would condemn today's too-common professorial turning-out of routine prose designed to impress tenure and promotion committees and university administration bureaucracies.

Of all the characteristics of the educational professoriate, the one that stands out from my experiences with him is the tradition of civility. To me, an unforgettable instance of his respect for the worth and dignity of each person is his naming me, the young legman, as coeditor of *Intercultural Attitudes in the Making*. Still another illustration of his civility is his response to abuse from the reactionary religious right of his day with thanks for the insights into their sensibilities.

The man was not perfect: some found him forbidding and some thought him vain. He had his persistent intellectual perplexities. For instance, he was never able to completely reconcile his early Progressive curriculum commitment to education based on children's needs and interests with his later Progressive curriculum emphasis on the need for reconstruction of society in the interest of achieving a better social order.

Yet clearly Kilpatrick stands as one of the Mountain Men of education. He was a professor whose credo embraced the basic principles which should shape the educational professoriate in the years ahead.

CHAPTER NINETEEN

William Van Til:
The Consistent Progressive

John A. Beineke

This, too, is a memoir about the relationship of an emeritus professor with a young man. To paraphrase this professor, look elsewhere for a William Van Til biography or for an appraisal of his work. This essay is a discussion of a great person; as he was treated with respect, he treated me with the same. I had read William Van Til's books on curriculum and foundations of education as a teacher and graduate student during the 1970s. I knew him to be a modern exponent of the Progressive principles of a generation before mine which had a brief reprise during the tumultuous sixties and during my early days of teaching which began in 1972. Then came the Reagan era and with it the apostles of a new essentialism including William Bennett, E. D. Hirsch, and others who were highly critical of Progressive theorists and practitioners. It was during the height of this conservative resurgence that I first met Dr. Van Til.

I had begun my initial research for a biography of William Heard Kilpatrick. An administrative appointment at a southern Indiana university had brought me within a two hour drive of Dr. Van Til's home, and a fellow dean gave me a formal introduction to the veteran educator and writer. I was pleasantly surprised when I first met him. Here was an individual who was articulate, intellectually disciplined, and widely read beyond the field of education. When I arrived for my first interview with Dr. Van Til on his association with Kilpatrick, he was full of anecdotes on this grand old man of Progressive education. The thoughtfulness and care with which Dr. Van Til discussed Kilpatrick's work was quite striking and served as an added incentive for my biographical research. Clearly, Dr. Van Til was doing more than merely recounting one's life; he was bringing me into a tradition (lived by Kilpatrick and himself) and treating me as others had treated him. I was being introduced to more than a set of beliefs and convictions; I was receiving the thoughtfulness and courtesy from an academic who was saying thanks to others—to former advisors, teachers, and colleagues in academe. This is quite important to underscore since I do not write as a former student of Dr. Van Til's. He was not my doctoral advisor nor did I meet with him to research *his* work. Yet, he gave of his time freely and generously to me—a young, aspiring researcher. His kindness and thoughtfulness were stunning and permitted me to realize that mentoring and the loyalty to the professoriate rests first and foremost upon ideas and not just on a sense of "academic genealogy." Dr. Van Til recognized my beliefs and brought me into the Progressive tradition.

After my first interview, I quickly brought myself up to date on the remarkable career of William Van Til. And as I think of his work I am not surprised by the additional characteristic he added to the nature of the professoriate, that being "to write out of conviction and dedication and with observance of scholarship in order to communicate with others on what needs to be known." This could be viewed as a guiding tenet for Dr. Van Til's career for I now see him as a writer first and foremost who wrote out of conviction to the ideals of Progressive education and with the dedication for those who helped to shape these ideals and beliefs. Dr. Van Til had displayed to me more than a historical sense or a gesture to the importance of history for history's sake. He saw himself as a writer and, while writing out of conviction, he placed himself within a larger context—a context that linked him with not only the leaders of Progressive education but also with the intellectual leaders of the 20th century. Yet, he also saw scholarship as a way "to communicate with others what needs to be known." Combined with this career of high ideas and convictions is also his eternal struggle of a writer longing to be heard.

Graduation in 1933 from Columbia College merely added Van Til to the ever growing lists of unemployed. He wrote unpublishable prose, applied unsuccessfully to all the print outlets in New York City, and heard nothing regarding teaching positions. Though he had aspired to be a journalist, he had taken a few teacher education courses as insurance. Then on a dreary November day in 1933, he began to teach at the New York State Training School for Boys at Warwick in rural New York. The position paid $70 a month, and Van Til's task was to teach and supervise what was known in those days as juvenile delinquents.

Even at this initial stage of his teaching career, Van Til began to employ the approach of Progressive education. The strategy worked, and while Warwick was a challenging and potentially dangerous environment, Van Til proceeded, not by force or coercion but through honest and open efforts, to develop the potential of each student. It was at this time that Van Til traveled regularly from Warwick to a course at Teachers College under William Heard Kilpatrick.

Summer courses completed and an M.A. in civic education in hand, Van Til applied in 1934 for a position at the University School on the campus of Ohio State University. With the endorsement and strong support of the two Teachers College faculty members in charge of his student teaching, Verna A. Carley and Harold Hand, he was appointed as a teacher of English and social studies. One of the more intriguing vignettes in Van Til's autobiography, *My Way of Looking at It* (1983), relates to the time his beliefs in the mission of Progressivism were tested by a group of high school students at University School on his first day of teaching. It is an episode I always share with my classes and in talks I give on education. Since Van Til had come to the school with a modest reputation as a "reform school teacher," he was immediately given a class of boys who were, to put it kindly, "having problems." By his own self-description he was at the time "a primitive Progressive," attempting to follow Dewey's advice to employ "interest and effort" and Kilpatrick's suggestion of "purposeful activity." He began, innocently enough, by asking the boys what they wanted to study. The boys responded that they wanted to study about "crooks." "I was at a crossroads," Van Til later wrote. He could have obfuscated the issue, claiming that crooks were not in the English-social studies curriculum. Instead he followed the Frostian "road less traveled."

After a fateful pause, Van Til acquiesced and the students undertook a problem solving curriculum of real life problems using the city of Columbus, Ohio, as their classroom. They visited a police station, examined demographic data, made maps, read widely, looked over dissertations by sociologists, and photographed troubled inner-city neighborhoods. Their findings were placed in written form and, with the assistance of the art teacher, placed on display for the other students at the University School to view and examine. The experience proved both profitable and productive for the young men and the student body. The inquiry approach led to history, sociology, creative writing, extensive reading, photography, and research.

The young teacher had tested the Progressive theory and became a lifelong convert to its tenets. But Van Til still had a deep-seated longing to be a writer. For him it was not enough to write his first post-college article "But Should We Indoctrinate?" which differed with George S. Counts' views, or to publish articles about University School teaching experiences such as "The Student Council," "Youth Visits Industrial Detroit," or "Youth Hosteling in Ohio." He still wanted to be a writer of "literature," a free-lance journalist. So in the summer of 1937, when they were 26, he canoe-kayaked down the Danube River with his wife, Bee. *The Danube Flows Through Fascism* (1938) was accepted and published by Maxwell E. Perkins, the legendary editor of Charles Scribner's Sons.

It would be writing, in fact, that took Van Til temporarily away from the classroom and the world of academics. Although he had begun work on his doctorate at Ohio State, the opportunity to write full time arose in the 1943, first in Washington, D.C., for the Consumer Education Study, and then in New York City where he worked with the Bureau for Intercultural Education.

In 1946, Van Til completed his doctoral dissertation, *A Social Living Curriculum for Post-War Education*, an approach to curriculum development through centers of experience derived from the interaction of values, social realities, and needs. It was his independent synthesis of much that he had learned from a decade of teaching in Ohio State's University School and from such Progressive educators as his advisor Harold Alberty and teachers Boyd H. Bode and H. Gordon Hullfish, from Kilpatrick in person, and from Dewey, Caswell, Counts, and others through print. He incorporated the curricular synthesis into his first chapter of the first yearbook of the new Association for Supervision and Curriculum Development, the 1946 *Leadership Through Supervision*. These crucial theoretical formulations were to guide his applications to schooling throughout his entire life.

Dr. Van Til returned to academia in 1947. Although he had never been an associate professor, Van Til was offered full professorships at Teachers College, Columbia University, and at the University of Illinois. Native New Yorkers who had spent a decade in the Midwest, he and his wife chose the latter offer, deciding to rear their family in Champaign-Urbana, Illinois. At the University of Illinois from 1947 to 1951, the professor of social studies education (termed "social stew" by his history department colleague Arthur E. Bestor) taught undergraduate and graduate classes, served for the first time as a doctoral advisor, and worked with school systems in the Illinois Secondary School Curriculum Program, all the while enjoying collegial interactions with the talented university faculty.

After leaving the University of Illinois, Van Til spent six years as one of the four Divisional Chairpersons at George Peabody College for Teachers spanning the years 1951 to 1957. This distinguished group of chairpersons was collectively known as the "Four Horsemen." In addition to Van Til, the other well-known educators included Harold Benjamin, Nicholas Hobbs, and Willard Goslin. Following the Peabody years, there was a decade of teaching, administration, and writing at New York University from 1957 to 1967. Throughout his professorships Van Til regarded social activism as an integral responsibility of an education professor. For instance, after Governor Adlai E. Stevenson appointed him to the Illinois Interracial Commission, Professor Van Til mediated a potentially explosive racial situation in the Alton, Illinois, public schools. He also mobilized a coalition of organizations to kill in committee a McCarthyite legislative bill which would have mandated the censorship of textbooks and other materials used in Illinois schools. At Peabody he chaired Nashville's first community meetings on school segregation and co-organized the Nashville Community Relations Conference which contributed to the desegregation of schools and colleges. At New York University, his letter published in the *New York Times* urged establishment of an American Conscience Fund for the college education of the students who defied segregation at Central High School, Little Rock, Arkansas.

One of the more significant aspects of Van Til's career has been his ability to transcend the world of professional journals, frequently read by a narrow audience within a discipline, and to write for a larger constituency in widely-read magazines. The best example of this phenomenon was Van Til's 1962 article, "Is Progressive Education Obsolete?" in the *Saturday Review*. By the 1960s the philosophically-consistent Van Til and other like-minded Progressives had weathered the difficult 1950s, where not only liberal politicians but also liberal thinkers in education were scarred by the McCarthyite attacks on modern education. In addition, Hyman Rickover, Arthur Bestor, and other critics of the schools laid the perceived problems of public education at the doorstep of John Dewey and his followers—most notably Kilpatrick, Bode, and Counts. Van Til turned the tables on the commentators in his article by neatly categorizing Dewey's successors into three distinct ideological strands, demonstrating their intellectual, pragmatic, and lasting contributions to the world of education. Van Til saw in Kilpatrick the emphasis on the needs of the individual learner, the necessity for classroom planning and activity, and the importance of intrinsic student motivation. For George Counts, it was the need to meld the social and economic aspects of society into the school milieu with teachers in the vanguard of a movement to reconstruct the world in which they lived and taught. Finally, Van Til identified Boyd Bode as a voice calling for the development of intelligence within the context of democratic values which would inevitably lead to democratic schools. Van Til repeatedly drove home the key point that Progressivism, far from leading the country astray, had actually bolstered a number of positive societal and school practices. These "Mountain Men," as Van Til labeled them in the *Saturday Review*, were in need not of exclusion and derision but re-examination and rediscovery.

In 1967, Van Til stepped down from his administrative duties at New York University and accepted a new role at Indiana State University. With a relatively light teaching load and ample opportunity to write, Van Til became the Coffman Distinguished Professor of Education. He would spend much of the decade prior to his retirement at Indiana State University teaching graduate classes, holding doctoral seminars, and sharing his expertise on writing with colleagues and students.

Supposedly retired in 1977, an event about which Van Til enjoys saying, "I didn't retire, university mandatory age policy retired me; I just kept on working," the writer continued his voluminous output of scholarly titles. While the list of publications was lengthy and impressive at the time of his retirement, the flow has continued on unabated. The latest count on publications was nearing the three hundred mark, including authorship (or collaboration) of 25 books and 13 yearbooks. The last decade has seen an autobiography, *My Way of Looking at It*, retrospectives and memoirs on ASCD and the John Dewey Society.

Throughout these various works, the consistency of Van Til's thinking serves as a testimonial to Progressive tradition. He has stood valiantly with the Progressives in their ideas of change, growth, and optimism regarding students and the educational process. Yet his loyalty to the basic tenets of Progressive educational philosophy, in a field which frequently swings to and fro, has led to his criticisms of innovations and reforms which owe allegiance only to novelty. Such consistency and commitment have been the hallmarks of Van Til's professional life, remaining so for more than half a century.

Dr. Van Til held true to his wishes to write and to his convictions in Progressive education. However, he saw himself within a larger tradition—one who was treated with kindness and one who treats others with the same. Dr. Van Til's devotion to the Spring Conference (an informal meeting venue providing educators an opportunity to talk to one another about significant issues) and his regular returns to high school reunions of the Ohio State University Lab School, his continual contact with alumni and colleagues of former institutions, and his tireless willingness to give interviews to young professors and various doctoral students—these all display the acts of a great professor. Yet he has done this because he knows he must—indeed, the consistent Progressive never lost sight of ideas. Moreover, Dr. Van Til never forgot the importance of people—colleagues, students, advisors, senior coauthors—and the acts of kindness that exemplify what it means to be a Progressive and a professor.

An attempt to catalog and capture the essence of Van Til the man could be attempted: writer, scholar, teacher, philosopher, advocate, inspiration, model, intellectual, communicator, leader. The terms all fit, and yet the list remains incomplete. But such an effort, even utilizing such distinguished nouns, limits rather than defines. When some became too worshipful of John Dewey, this pragmatist warned in a 1949 *Educational Leadership* column called "John Dewey's Disciples," that to take his ideas and set them apart as the definitive and irrevocable philosophic truth would be a disservice to both Dewey and what he stood for. That is why clones, imitators, and ideologues have never been welcomed by the Progressive pioneers, nor do they provide messages that last. This is also why Van Til's contribution has remained distinctive and singular. He embodies the grand Progressive tradition in education, yet has been able to retain his own voice, his own counsel, his own contribution. He has always known that the schools and society are inseparable entities, that the curriculum devoid of application to real issues and problems in today's world is ineffectual, that intelligence and democracy must be wed together for either to survive, and that the needs of the learners must be met for any true learning and meaning to emerge from the schooling process. Van Til is unique, as Dewey would have all educated men and women be, and therefore his legacy remains fresh, vibrant, and enduring.

PART SIX

Civility, a Project
Pertaining to the Public World

George S. Counts as a Teacher: A Reminiscence

by Lawrence A. Cremin

The Dignity and Honor of Virgil Clift

by Francine Silverblank

Educating Civility: The Political Pedagogy of James B. Macdonald

by Bradley J. Macdonald

Bradley J. Macdonald sets the context for the three essays that follow when he remarks that civility, in its "deeper root meaning [is] a project pertaining to the public world—to 'politics' in an expansive sense—and to the attempt to bring about changes in personal and social conditions so that we could truly develop as humans." This is precisely the sense in which civility permeated the lives of Macdonald's father, James, and the lives of George S. Counts and Virgil Clift.

Each educator's particular expression of civility took different forms, but the intent was nonetheless very much the same. Cremin recounts aspects of Counts' political journey, from his leadership of the American Federation of Teachers to helping found the New York State Liberal Party. Amazingly, while running for the United States Senate in 1952, Counts never missed a single class at Teachers College. Politics, for Counts, was an expression of his effort to improve the public world and, as such, was an extension of his life as an educator. Professing was more than mere word play; the professorial role was to engage the burning social issues of the day but to engage them in a certain hopeful way.

As an African American man from rural Indiana, Virgil Clift faced a special set of challenges. Constant experience with discrimination might have embittered Clift, but it did not. As Silverblank explains, inspired by ideals drawn from Abraham Lincoln, Clift sought the moral high ground and encountered each challenge with determination to "foster behaviors and views that encouraged respect for the rights and dignity of all people." He responded to prejudice courageously, and he responded with civility.

Writing of his father, Bradley Macdonald speaks of his "moral compass that helped lead one from the personal to the political and back again." For James Macdonald, as for Counts and Clift, "the personal was the political." One lives one's politics. These mentors profoundly understood that the quality of their relationships with students spoke most eloquently for their political and moral commitments; the results were transformative. As Cremin observes, through his carefully prepared courses and in his thoughtful work with students, Counts—and the power of his ideas—changed lives "repeatedly and profoundly." Silverblank says the same of Clift. As Bradley Macdonald states: "Indeed, a true political pedagogy is one that at once engages with the familiar and the dissimilar, the commonsensical and not-yet-known, in the process taunting one to critique our everyday life and to dream of the future." It is in this sense that the work of mentors encompasses civility.

Biographical Information

George S. Counts [born: Dec. 9, 1890, Baldwin City, KS; died: Nov. 10, 1974, Belleville, IL] served as professor of education at Teachers College, Columbia University, from 1927-1956. He was graduated from Baker University (Kansas) in 1911 with an A.B. and the Ph.D. from the University of Chicago in

1916. Other professional roles included education professorships at Delaware College in 1916, Harris College (St. Louis) from 1918-1919, University of Washington from 1919-1920, Yale University from 1920-1926, and University of Chicago from 1926-1927. Counts' publications include *The Selective Character of American Secondary Education* (1922), *Dare the Schools Build a New Social Order* (1932), *The Social Foundations of Education* (1934), *Education and American Civilization* (1952), and *Education and the Foundations of Human Freedom* (1962).

Virgil Clift [born: May 1, 1912, Princeton, IN] served as professor of education at New York University from 1963-1978. He was graduated from Indiana University in 1934 with a B.A.; other degrees include an M.A. from Indiana State College in 1939 and the Ph.D. from Ohio State University in 1944. Other professional roles include holding a professorship in education at the Agricultural and Technical College of North Carolina (Greensboro) from 1948-1963 and at Morgan State College from 1948-1963. Clift's publications include the editorships of the 16th yearbook of the John Dewey Society *Negro Education in America* (1962) and *The Encyclopedia of Black America* (1981).

James B. Macdonald [born: March 11, 1925, Delavan, WI; died: Nov. 11, 1983, Greensboro, NC] served as professor of education at the University of North Carolina, Greensboro from 1972-1983. He was graduated from the University of Wisconsin-Madison in 1949 with a B.S.; other degrees include an M.S. in 1951 and the Ph.D. in 1956 from the University of Wisconsin-Madison. Other professional roles included holding professor-ships in education at the University of Texas-Austin from 1956-1957, New York University from 1957-1959, University of Wisconsin-Milwaukee from 1959-1963 and 1967-1972, and University of Wisconsin-Madison from 1963-1966. Macdonald's publications include the works *Reschooling Society* (1973) and *Schools in Search of Meaning* (1975) with Esther Zaret.

CHAPTER TWENTY

George S. Counts as a Teacher: A Reminiscence

Lawrence A. Cremin

[This essay was previously published in 1988 in *Teaching Education*, Volume 2, No. 2, pp. 28-31 and is reprinted with permission of *Teaching Education*.]

George S. Counts was a magnificent teacher, and I had the pleasure of studying under him at the very peak of his powers. I knew him over a quarter century, first as a lecturer, seminar leader, and dissertation advisor, and later as a mentor, faculty colleague, and treasured friend. He was extraordinary in every one of these roles, as I shall try to convey in the reflections and reminiscences that follow.

I first went to see Counts in his office during the spring of 1947. He was widely known as one of the outstanding scholars in the foundations of education as well as a former president of the American Federation of Teachers and a founding member of the New York State Liberal Party, and he was surely one of the preeminent members of the Teachers College Faculty. I had recently been graduated from the College of the City of New York, where I had come to believe, for better or for worse, that to bother a professor in his office was some kind of tacit admission that one was too stupid to grasp what had gone on in class. The widely accepted goal was to get through four years of undergraduate education without ever having to see a professor in his office, and I had managed to do so. At Teachers College it was different. One was supposed to go to see the professors in their offices. But I had no idea of what one did after one got there. So I asked my friend Gordon Lee, who was a year ahead of me in the doctoral program, how to set about doing it. Gordon said, "It's simple: you go and ask a question." I thought up a question and rehearsed it on Gordon and it seemed sensible to him, so I arranged to see Counts in his office. We started to talk and had a very pleasant conversation and after about an hour I left, feeling very good about the whole venture. That evening I saw Gordon, who asked how it had all gone, and I replied, "Splendidly." Gordon inquired, "How did the question go?" "My God," I responded, "I never asked it!"

Eventually, I went back many times and asked many questions, and the reaction was always the same. I would put the question and Counts would respond, "Well, what do you think, Larry?" And the discussion would be off and running. When it was all over, I would indeed have an answer but it would be my own answer. Counts was a Socratic teacher, who played midwife to his students' ideas. He loved the give-and-take of conversation in his office, and stopping by to see him was always a warm and exhilarating experience.

Counts's office was the perfect site for the Socratic teacher. The walls were crammed with books, pamphlets, and periodicals arranged on shelves that rose to the ceiling, while the tables held stacks of recent publications, especially newspapers and magazines. Counts worked at a rolltop desk, with pictures of Abraham Lincoln and John Dewey above it. He smoked incessantly, mostly a pipe and occasionally a cigar; the pipe seemed always to be going out, with the result that it was constantly being relighted. As one entered the office, Counts would swing away from his desk and turn in his swivel chair, rise, and warmly welcome his visitor. In my experience, the conversation that followed was invariably an animated exchange of ideas and opinions, frequently punctuated by Counts's reaching for a book or magazine or newspaper with the recommendation that I consult it as soon as possible for illumination. Counts seemed to me to have read everything on every side of every educational issue; and, as he made his recommendations, I would dutifully note them, with every expectation of turning to them promptly. But I never came close to catching up. The longer I knew him and the more we talked, the greater the gap between the burgeoning list and my actual achievement.

Counts's favorite lecture course was called "Education in Industrial Society." He taught it once each academic year and frequently during the summer session as well. The enrollment was usually somewhere between 75 and 100, but Counts never used a teaching assistant. An extensive syllabus was handed out during the initial session, listing topics dealing with the history, sociology, and political economy of industrial society, in Europe and North America, from the eighteenth century to the present, with exploration of the bearing of each topic on educational theory, policy, and practice. For each topic there were lengthy bibliographical suggestions. The examination, also handed out during the initial session and due at the final session, was to formulate five or six questions that seemed to go to the heart of the course and to answer one or two of them at length. Counts made no discernible effort to "cover the ground." When I took the course, he managed to get through roughly a third of the topics, and I doubt whether he ever got through more than half; but, one way or another, he did manage to touch the substance of all of them. His lectures were a marvelous melange of up-to-date information, bibliographical commentaries, personal experiences, anecdotes, and aphorisms. There were invariably questions from the students. They were always treated seriously, and there was always enough time to deal with them. It seemed more important to Counts to engage students in the material that was covered than it was to cover more material. Lecture courses rarely change lives, but Counts's did, repeatedly and profoundly. The most common recollection was that students never looked at education quite the same way after completing the course: the "civilizational approach" Counts taught was often compelling.

Counts also gave a seminar each year on the role of interest groups in the development of educational policy. Each student was expected to choose an interest group (I chose the American Association of University Professors) and write a paper on the nature and substance of the group's educational policy recommendations and the strategies and tactics employed to gain acceptance of those recommendations. Counts used the first third of the course to introduce the students to the literature of the politics of education as developed by Howard K. Beale, Charles E. Merriam, Bessie Louise Pierce, Robert Bruce Raup, and others (characteristically, he never mentioned his own pioneering work of the 1920s, *School and Society in Chicago*); the remainder of the course was devoted to presentations of the students' works-in-progress. Counts made every effort to involve students as critics of one another's work but always as constructive critics. He himself was constantly encouraging, full of suggestions, and ready with assistance; the occasional student who had patently gotten off course was invited to the office for special help. By the end of the term, no one could miss the lesson being taught: There was the formal structure of local school boards, state legislators, and the like, but it was impossible to understand the making of American educational policy apart from the constant interaction of interest groups in the educational policy process.

Incidentally, even after years of experience, Counts took his teaching as seriously as any of his activities. He made no appointments and permitted no visitors on the afternoons of scheduled classes; his assistant, Nucia Lodge, would smile graciously, bar the door, and remark, "Mr. Counts is preparing for class." As a result, the substance of his lectures and discussions was always fresh, apropos, well organized, and up to date. And, whatever the tempo of his external political activities, his teaching always came first. He actually managed to campaign for the United States Senate in the autumn of 1952 without ever missing a class.

I early concluded that I wanted Counts to sponsor my doctoral dissertation, but I was unclear as to what I might take as a topic. With characteristic generosity, Counts handed me a file of five-by-eight cards one day, saying that he had long meant to undertake a study of foreign travelers' views of American education during the nineteenth century but despaired of getting down to it and suggesting that he would be pleased to give me some notes he had made on the topic and have me proceed on my own. I worked for a time on the foreign travelers—Alexis de Tocqueville, Sir Charles Lyell, Charles Dickens, Francis Grund, Frances Trollope, and others—and got quite interested in them but eventually turned the study into what became *The American Common School: An Historic Conception* (1951). Counts followed my progress with interest but rarely interfered; he readily replied to questions but never prodded. When I gave him a draft to read, he returned it to me in two or three days with just the right balance of encouragement and constructive criticism. Later, when the dissertation was published, he wrote a generous foreword. Throughout the process, he managed to criticize without demanding any sort of compliance with his ideas.

I was appointed to an instructorship at Teachers College in 1949 and to an assistant professorship in Counts's department two years later. Part of my teaching assignment was to participate with Counts, John L. Childs, and Robert King Hall in a panel course called "Education in American Society." The senior professors could not have been more generous in making a place for me, although they had for several years taught the course by themselves, and Counts himself yielded several of his lectures to "the new kid on the block." Beyond that, when it was suggested that I might teach "Education in Industrial Society" during one of the summer sessions, Counts not only acquiesced but encouraged me to offer my own version of the course.

I also remember the first time I was on my way to teach my very own class at the exalted rank of instructor. Counts appeared in the hall and asked, "Where are you going, Larry?" I replied, "To teach my class, sir. " "Say, Larry, I've never given you any advice about teaching, have I?" Counts inquired. "That's correct, sir," I responded. Counts proceeded to tell me how his friend Ralph Linton, the anthropologist, had once studied to become a medicine man of the Tanala tribe in Madagascar during the 1920s. When Linton had finished his studies and was formally inducted as a full-fledged doctor, he was advised that he was now qualified to teach the arts and mysteries of the medicine man to others who would learn it. And the advice his mentors gave him was, "Don't tell the newcomers everything you know in the first class; spin it out slowly." That was Counts's advice to me as I made my way to my first class in 1949.

Having joined the faculty, I continued to be Counts's student, but the great good fortune of my relationship with him was the symmetry he insisted upon at all times. I could cite dozens of instances, but one stands out in my mind. During Counts's last year at Teachers College, he was talking with me one afternoon and remarked that he had always wanted to give a course on the relationship between education and liberty but had never gotten around to it and wondered what I would think of his giving such a course during his final year at TC. I replied that I thought it was a splendid idea and suggested that if he did indeed offer it I would want very much to be allowed to sit in. Nothing more was said for several weeks and then I received a call from President Hollis L. Caswell, saying that Professor Counts had proposed a new course entitled "Education and the Foundations of Liberty," which the college very much wanted to have offered but that Professor Counts had insisted that he would only give the course if Larry Cremin could be persuaded to teach it with him. It was one of the memorable experiences of my life, especially the last session, in which every one of Counts's former doctoral students living between Washington, D.C., and Boston attended. The junior member of the teaching team joined them out in the audience, and we all listened to one of the finest summations of the relationship between education and liberty ever given.

Every teacher's style has its underside, which is often the obverse of its virtues, and Counts was no exception. An occasional lecture could go awry as the mix between exposition and anecdote got out of balance, and the teacher gave way to raconteur. A seminar session on a weak paper that was too gently criticized could prove a total waste of time. And a wordy dissertation draft that probably needed one more revision could be approved for a defense, where it would be rather mordantly dealt with by one or another of the examiners. In the case of *The American Common School*, Henry Steele Commager was sharply critical of my verbosity, and the 528-page manuscript that went to the defense eventually boiled down to the 265-page manuscript that went to the publisher, without the loss of a single idea, merely superfluous words. Later I came to disagree rather fundamentally with Counts on the nature of the foundations of education and how they should be studied and taught—he tended to view them as a discipline in their own right while I saw them as a congeries of disciplines, including the history of education, the philosophy of education, the sociology of education, and others. Yet, however much one might take issue with Counts or note occasional imbalances between gentleness and rigor in his style, those of us who were his students respected him profoundly. He was no saint to be venerated but rather a wise, learned, and dedicated teacher, who professed the field of education superbly. His example remains lively in my mind even today.

CHAPTER TWENTY-ONE

The Dignity and Honor of Virgil Clift

Francine Silverblank

Virgil Clift was recognized as an important leader in education long before 1963 when he came to New York University where I met him, studied with him, and worked with him. Over the years I learned to appreciate him as a fine teacher, a valued colleague, and a good friend. Most importantly, my recollections are of a thinker and investigator who knew how to stand alone, a gentleman of the old school for whom the terms dignity and honor had meaning.

There are many people who will tell you that their lives are forever different because of Virgil Clift. In particular, I remember a young black student, a 1960s Don Quixote, who dashed wildly about pressing for campus reform that stressed "a personally relevant and meaningful education." I guess my course didn't fit the bill because his work was less than adequate, and when he received a C- on a term paper, he objected to this outrage and in loud and clear language let me know that I was a biased, warped, bigoted, twisted racist.

Now you have to remember that the late 1960s and early 1970s were times of staggering upheaval on campuses, and the voices of many students were strident, anti-intellectual, and anarchistic. In the spirit of the times, I suggested that he ask Professor Clift to grade the paper because, given his point of view, Professor Clift's credentials were unimpeachable and beyond all question. A few days later a chastened and reasonable fellow showed up at my office and, with a sheepish grin, told me that Professor Clift said, "Did it ever occur to you that you are a C- student?"

Many years later the student and I met again at Virgil's retirement dinner. He recalled the incident and explained how it had changed the direction of his life. He took courses with

Professor Clift, engaged in "rap sessions" with him, and most importantly, found an open and honest mentor. Professor Clift taught him to understand how his own insights, perceptions, ideals, and experiential background shaped his thoughts, feelings, and beliefs.

I mention this incident because it epitomizes Virgil Clift's commitment to teaching students *how* to learn. In a society dominated by hierarchical approaches and authoritarian solutions to problems, Virgil's humane tact—with its faith in the potential development of all human beings—encouraged a problem-solving procedure through which students learned to define a problem, then consider and test possible answers. He welcomed the opportunity to bring students to a growing love affair with ideas. He cherished this role as matchmaker and performed it very well indeed. What he had in his possession was a great gift, and he took joy in the giving.

His writing reveals a deep concern for the role of schools in furthering democratic values. When confronted with any problem or issue related to desegregation or integration of schools, he tried to place it within a framework that included a philosophical position consistent with democratic ideals in America. He also considered the historical perspective out of which our democratic ideas and institutions have emerged—the most sacred of these ideals being respect for the individual and the opportunity for each person to develop to the fullest of his or her capacity in order to contribute to the general welfare and common good.

During our years together at New York University, Virgil often referred to three quotations by Lincoln that he thought very important. Interestingly, these quotes or the ideas contained in them have received more consideration during the 1990s than they did when he used to cite them in the 1960s.

- You cannot further the Brotherhood of man by encouraging class hatred.
- You cannot build character and courage by taking away initiative.
- You cannot help men permanently by doing for them what they could and should do for themselves.

I was always impressed with the fact that Virgil was ready to challenge many of the clichés that far too many educators had come to accept as immutable axioms. I recall one particular departmental meeting, at the end of which, some of us were discussing what was happening in Bedford-Stuyvesant. We argued about desegregation and busing versus local control and improvement of segregated schools. Certainly, it was a hot topic—one had only to look in the journals which were filled with research studies, position papers, assorted facts, and endless opinions. Virgil listened with amusement and charitably suggested that what was called for was a modest amount of sorely needed understanding. Each position had worth, but it also had its own can of worms. Schools as well as districts were disparate, and the political, intellectual, and moral climate of each was not always equivalent. Therefore, solutions might also have to vary. Intellectually we all knew this to be true, but it was Virgil who gently focused the debate and allowed us to move beyond our own beliefs.

That day he also talked about change, and what he said I would hear in my mind many times over the next two decades. He reminded us that change was synergistic, not additive, and by citing concrete examples went on to show how each element was an integral part of the whole which worked as a unit. If one part of the system was changed then, planned or not, the whole system changed.

He always taught by using examples. On one occasion I mentioned that he was really quite lucky because, as a professor at New York University, he didn't have to confront bigotry and intolerance. With patient conviction he helped me understand the truth of his life (and that of other educated, upper-middle-class African Americans). He suggested that if we tried a little experiment the reality of a long heritage of prejudice and neglect would become apparent, and I would not have to be persuaded that subtle forms of discrimination plagued him each and every day of his life.

This was the experiment. I was to choose an inner-city school. Then, he would go into the main office, identify himself as a professor from N.Y.U., and ask to meet with the principal. He predicted that he would be invited cordially to sit down and would be assured that as soon as the principal was available, which wouldn't be long, they could meet. A few minutes later I was to show up with the same request I, too, would be treated graciously and asked to wait. At no point would we acknowledge each other. After ten minutes or so passed, I, not Virgil would be shown into the office first. No book, tome, study, or treatise could teach me such a painstaking lesson about the prevalence of covert discrimination and the potent, effective, and influential force that it could be.

I look back upon another time when I had to bring some papers to his apartment and, after depositing them on the table, we settled down for some friendly gossip about the curious, peculiar, and sometimes laughable happenings at the university. My eyes settled on a lovely, small portrait of a young farm boy which was pleasant to look at and much to my liking. I mentioned that it reminded me of the work of Thomas Hart Benton who, with paint and brush, recorded the rural American heartland. "What you're looking at," he told me, "is a young Virgil Clift."

He talked about growing up on his grandfather's and father's farm in southwest Indiana. The farm which was just over 500 acres was considered large in that section of the country during the early part of the 20th century. He spoke of the rewarding life that farming offered a young person and how it strengthened the family unit because everything and everybody played a role in the achievement of family purposes. He noted how the country changed from an animal or man-powered society to one that was power driven by steam and gasoline. He commented on the transformation of the United States as population centers moved from rural to urban settings and how this metamorphosis affected families, homes, schools, and ways of earning a living.

He recalled his one-room, one-teacher school which had thirty students in grades one through eight and remembered how the teacher spent ten to fifteen minutes each day teaching arithmetic to each grade and, when it made sense, grouped two or more grades together for any number of subjects. He recollected how younger children learned from listening to the older ones being taught. But he also carried in his thoughts memories of hickory switches that were used thoughtlessly and often.

Eventually Virgil's mother transferred him to a predominantly black school that to her mind offered higher-quality instruction because a couple of its graduates went on to college, if only for a little while. The high school that Virgil attended was located in Princeton and was all black, had two teachers and forty-five students. From here he went on to Indiana University and the first real challenge of his life, for now he had to learn how to take responsibility for his decisions and solve problems without family support. He also learned that a person could overcome his shortcomings and lack of opportunities. It was a lesson that deeply impressed him and one that he passed along gratuitously to his students.

After graduation he was admitted to law school but was mindful of the fact that his minority status would limit both his income and opportunity to pursue various areas of the law. He reasoned that college teaching offered a more satisfactory alternative and would allow him the luxury of pursuing truth and the knowledge that supports it. With that goal in mind he started graduate work at Indiana and continued at Ohio State where he received his doctorate. After a forty-five-year career, in 1991, Ohio State's College of Education recognized his many accomplishments and honored him with its Hall of Fame Award. Also of great significance was the Citation for Distinguished Alumni, an award presented to encourage minority students to pursue graduate and professional studies at Ohio State and go on to make similar distinguished contributions to society.

Clearly, when Virgil retired from New York University, he was not put out to pasture, for his was a deeply ingrained heritage that demanded intellectual curiosity, a sense of ethical duty, devotion to the profession, and efforts to foster behaviors and views that encouraged respect for the rights and dignity of all people. In short, he continued to engage in a multitude of undertakings which included writing, consulting, serving on many state and national committees concerned with the improvement of human and race relations, and teaching.

Virgil typified the intellectually inquisitive professor who had seen many changes take place during his lifetime and who made it his business to understand these changes. He embraced those that were compatible with his convictions and rejected those that did not conform to his standards. His overriding interests and considerations remained the excitement generated by ideas, the responsibility for social action, and the display of good manners to all human beings, regardless of their opinions or station. For him academe was a treasured way of life where arrogance, egotism, and chicanery had no place. It was an environment that prized speculation and reflection—not financial balance sheets. It was an institution that venerated dignity and honor.

In a sense Virgil has come full circle. He is back on the farm in Princeton, Indiana, raising cattle and still very much involved with the land, learning, and civic service.

CHAPTER TWENTY-TWO

Educating Civility:
The Political Pedagogy
of James B. Macdonald

Bradley J. Macdonald

To discuss the character of James B. Macdonald's pedagogy is a difficult task for me: not only was I not a student of his in the traditional sense, but I was also his son. What this means is that I never actually knew him in the traditional teacher role, as one who engages in a practice in which there are structural situations of learning, reading, writing, thinking, and dialogue. That is not to say that this role didn't seep into our relationship, for it did. But it does mean that my experience with him as "teacher" was always overlaid by the fact that I was his son, someone who was related to him in an intimate way, biologically, socially, and culturally. Indeed, the fact that he was my father means that attempting to define his pedagogical style becomes even more difficult: it was, still is, and will always be, too intimate, not in the sense of emotionally close (and thus possibly traumatic) but rather in terms of being hidden within the recesses of my being as a "tacit dimension" (or even more relevantly, a "hidden curriculum"). As my father was wont to urge curriculum thinkers and workers, this task of uncovering the tacit dimension to our lives—be it associated with schooling or our personal lives—should be foremost in our projects. It is my hope that the foregoing process of personal discovery, one that must be unique, has a public dimension as well.

In a way, it could not be more fitting than to put my father into a section devoted to "civility" in pedagogical matters. In saying this, though, I must explain what I mean by the term. I do not mean "civility" in the sense of being courteous and polite (though he could be that) but rather in terms of the deeper root meaning of "civil": that is, a project pertaining to the public world—to politics in an expansive sense—and to the attempt to bring about changes in personal and social conditions so that we could truly develop as humans. As my father said on many occasions, both personally to me and in written form, his interest in curriculum arose only because it allowed him to engage and, he hoped, to change the larger macrocosm within which education was situated. He was thus "civil" in his pedagogy to the extent that he forced students to come to terms with the social and political world around them, to lay bare the values that they came to world with, and to critically think about the possibilities of a new world. This task, as may seem apparent, means that he was sometimes not "civil" in the conventional sense of the term—in dealing with core issues, values, and emotions, one can't help but take a stand that may offend.

His devotion and commitment to students was unerring, but so was his impatience with any attempt to sidestep what he considered to be important moral issues. This also was evident in his relationship to his children. As Alex Molnar, one of his former doctoral students, recounts, my father had no problem calling one's hand if he felt, rightly or wrongly, you approached your life from a morally suspect position:

> Jim wasn't incapable of expressing anger. I remember once I gave a presentation at a meeting that Jim attended and I thought I had been witty and clever and erudite and the audience had received what I had to say very well indeed. Afterwards, when I went up to Jim and I asked him how he liked it, he looked at me rather scornfully and his only comment was, "They loved it." (Molnar, 1985, p. 38)

In this sense, then, what guided my father's pedagogy was a moral compass that helped to lead one from the personal to the political and back again. We might even say, using a term developed by feminists in their struggle against patriarchy, that for him, "the personal" was "the political." In many places in his writings, he observed that not only could individuals never escape the political structures and choices that they must confront as socially-embedded human beings, but that when they inevitably attempted to transform their conditions of existence, the goal of the political project must be the development of the unique individual person. And, the personal was the political for me. I am a political theorist today not only because of my father's deep devotion to theory (I not only had many occasions to discuss theory with him but also acquired a taste for theory through environmental osmosis), but also because he called upon all of us to come to terms with our "civility," our basic values and orientations from which we situate ourselves in the political world. It just so happened that I melded the two together into my vocation.

If I may recount a particularly vivid incident that relates to his pedagogical style: I remember shortly before his death sitting with him as he excitedly discussed a particular theoretical point. At the time I was reading Thomas Pynchon's *Gravity's Rainbow*, and he quickly snatched up the text and in the back he drew a diagram to illustrate his position. In looking at the diagram today, I honestly cannot remember exactly what the discussion was all about. But what I do remember is that it was a truly "dialogic" situation, one in which we both were in the process of clarifying our ideas, each recognizing the validity and importance of the other, situating ourselves in the interstices between our theoretical beings in the mutual process of self-discovery. And, I am sure this was not a wholly unique experience. My father's excitement and openness in the dialogic process was something that all of his students encountered.

If the process of discovery was part of his pedagogical approach, so too was the sheer excitement about ideas themselves. All too often, as teachers, we become immune to the energy that ideas have in our lives, possibly because we have already been there and have had to portray them in innumerable situations of learning. For my father, ideas always continued to live and, by that very dynamic life, animate and excite. This meant that one could not slouch off their force but must recommit to them daily. This did not mean, though, that one must have an *idée fixe*. Dogmatism was not only an anathema to him in his prescriptions for educational change, but it also escaped him in his own theoretical journey. Indeed, there is no clearer example of this conceptual ebb and flow— the development and growth of thought along divergent though ultimately converging lines of flight—than my father's œuvre itself. In an autobiographical statement published in 1975, he notes that his life and work involved "the struggle for personal integration, educational integrity, and social justice," a project which demanded "the constant reevaluation of oneself, one's work and one's world—with the hope that whatever creative talent one may possess will lead toward something better that we may all share, each in his own way" (Macdonald, 1975, p. 4). In this context, we can understand why he felt that ideas themselves have a role in this constant self-evaluation and why we must be open to the siren call of new ideas if we are to continue along the path of our personal and social betterment.

If I were to try to encapsulate the character of my father's pedagogy, I might call it "moral realism." In using this term, though, I do not mean an attachment to the status quo or an unthinking commitment to that which practically works. Rather, I mean by the term what E.P. Thompson meant when he used it to describe the unifying ethos behind the work of artist-turned-revolutionary William Morris: the unerring attempt to raise the issue of hope and desire, the expression of alternative values and commitments, within the confines of our existing institutions (Thompson, 1976). My father always felt that thinking about the practicalities of curriculum was not to be given over to the technicians and behavioralists, a forfeiture that would undoubtedly dissipate one's goals and actions into mere tinkering for the sake of our bureaucratic and techno-logical realities. Nor should we necessarily allow our utopian ideals to overshadow the real practical possibilities within the world of schooling. Rather, what must take place is a dialectical process of desire and necessity—of expressing hope and engaging in real possibilities—for the sake of our own unfolding as unique individuals. As he said in one of his last published writings, curriculum theory must be a "prayful act," a constant attempt to bring about the transcendent within the imminent (Macdonald, 1981; B. Macdonald, 1996). All of those who encountered him as a teacher could not but be transformed in some way, whether they liked it or not. Indeed, a true political pedagogy is one that at once engages with the familiar and the dissimilar, the commonsensical and not-yet-known, in the process taunting one to critique our everyday life and dream of the future. In so doing, one becomes part of the process of creating "civility," at once disturbing but a part of the circle of life in our individual development.

EPILOGUE

Professorial Dreams and Mentoring: A Personal View

Robert V. Bullough, Jr.

Young people often dream of what they will become. Dreams take form through the lives of admired others. Physicians often beget physicians; teachers beget teachers. But dreams come from other sources as well. Sometimes they come in the form of "distant teachers" (John-Steiner, 1985), deceased individuals whose lives and work inspire emulation. Neighbors, relatives, religious leaders, public, and even mythological figures may in one way or another invite imitation. Dreams of this kind facilitate the transition from adolescence into the adult world and into the world of work (Levinson et al., 1978). For the three editors, the dream took the form of professing and along the way we have had many good teachers and a few, a precious, small handful of mentors who picked us up and, drawing on Robert Coles' imagery, handed us along.

Immature Dreams

Our professorial dreams were and are closely tied to a shared mentor. We met as graduate students at the Ohio State University in the middle 1970s, each carrying his own incipient professorial dreams along with a bundle of open questions and self-doubts. Our dreams reflected our youth and inexperience and relied heavily and unashamedly upon images of ivory towers, places of refuge and safety. One telling of our tale goes this way: Disillusioned and disappointed from the political backwash of the 1960s that culminated in Watergate, we sought a quiet place from which to begin making sense of what had become of America and ourselves, a place of peace purified

from the taint of practice. Theory was the "exalted state to be
devoutly wished."

Purified from practice, we dreamed of a quaint university
life: non-political and free from the nasty competition that
characterized business; professors who were above petty
jealousy and beyond the little ideas that enthralled tiny
minds. Resistant to bureaucracy and collegial and communal in
nature, surely the university was a realm where *big* ideas
mattered. In this respect we differed little from others of our
generation who seemed to foolishly but fervently believe that
social change would come by wishing for it, by wishing hard.

Despite our fantasies, graduate school proved to be highly
political and often nastily competitive. Occasionally we were
given glimpses of how petty some professors could be and how
"little" was on their minds. We witnessed comparatively few
demonstrations of professor collegiality. No utopia, here. Yet
somehow, from the safety of the student's side of the desk,
portions of our dreams remained intact, and subtle and
significant changes took place as they were enlivened.

A Shared Mentor

Given two decades' worth of hindsight, we now know that
a very large portion of the dream that we eventually carried
with us from graduate school and into our first academic
positions came as a result of our advisor, Paul R. Klohr, whose
essay on Laura Zirbes is included in this collection. He was our
mentor, and perhaps that says it all.

The themes identified in this collection resonate with our
experience as students of Professor Klohr's. Rather than restate
them, which would smack of hyperbole and only result in a
lifeless listing, we will share a few illustrative experiences of
the sort conveyed in other essays. The sense of what we want to
say, a portion of it, in any case, is nicely captured in
Oakeshott's description of the "intellectual virtues":

> How does a pupil learn disinterested curiosity,
> patience, honesty, exactness, industry, con-
> centration and doubt? How does he acquire a
> sensibility to small differences and the ability

> to recognize intellectual elegance? How does he
> come to inherit the disposition to submit to
> refutation? How does he not merely learn the
> love of truth and justice, but learn it in such a
> way as to escape the reproach of fanaticism?
> And beyond all this there is something more
> difficult to acquire: namely, the ability to
> detect the individual intelligence which is at
> work in every utterance, even those which
> convey impersonal information. . . .
>
> The intellectual virtues may be imparted
> only by a teacher who really cares about them
> for their own sake, and never stoops to the
> priggishness of mentioning them. Not the cry
> but the rising of the wild duck impels the flock
> to follow him into flight. (Auspitz, 1991, p.
> 355)

Klohr's commitment to students meant that unlike some of his
colleagues he did not seek followers; his was not a quest for
converts—there was no cry, just an abundance of "flying," often
into distant, unfamiliar territories. Groupies we were not, for
he would not have them. On some issues it was unclear where
he stood; what was important was where we stood and how we
came to our positions and how those positions related to others'
thinking and writing. He posed questions, pointed in the
direction of possible answers, and nudged us to engage issues
that might otherwise have gone unnoticed. He listened a lot
more than he talked, which proved frustrating at times for
those socialized, as were we, to expect answers. There were,
however, better and worse answers, of this we were certain.

In the early 1970s the curriculum field along with teacher
education was comfortably wrapped in the straitjacket of
management by objectives. The talk was of competency-based
teacher education: certainty in outcomes and rigor in
evaluation. Educators sought to make the messiness of education fit the neatness of systems thinking. It did not; it could
not. Similarly, philosophers of education were caught up in
concept analysis with the result that the field became

increasingly esoteric and irrelevant to the moral and practical
issues faced by educators. Such were the times.

Klohr knew better. Our first classes with him were messy
and challenging, genuinely counter-cultural. Reading lists were
long and included items from diverse disciplines and included
obscure writers working well outside the mainstream of education along with more than a sprinkling of forgotten but
important works from earlier periods. Klohr took seriously the
charge of Joseph Schwab that the curriculum field was
"ahistorical." On his reading list, Hadley Cantril's *The 'Why'*
of Man's Experiences (1950) followed Jerome Bruner's *The*
Relevance of Education (1971) and preceded Thomas Cottle's
Time's Children: Impressions of Youth (1971); Stephen Corey's
Action Research to Improve School Practices (1953) followed
Dean Chamberlin et al., *Did They Succeed in College?* (1942);
Paulo Freire's *Pedagogy of the Oppressed* (1970) preceded Jules
Henry's *Culture Against Man* (1963). These are but a few of the
many titles on the suggested reading list for the introductory
graduate curriculum course. Never had we thought of education
so broadly, nor had we before realized that the study of
education is the study of all that is human and all that humans
hope for. It is an arena within which the disciplines come
together and, in hoping to find place, find added meaning.

Before this insight settled into our minds, there was a time
of uncertainty. What, pray tell, did reading Philip Rieff's *The*
Triumph of the Therapeutic (1966) or Hampden-Turner's
Radical Man (1970) have to do with education? The answer
was everything when education is understood as more than
schooling, more than getting and keeping control over a
classroom of rambunctious students—when education is
understood as an expression of humanity's highest aspirations
and hopefulness for a brighter future. Klohr introduced us to a
range of unfamiliar ways of thinking about education and
education-related issues. In the curriculum field, his con-
ceptualization of the diversity of work being done—a
conception built around what he called "gestalts"—and his
understanding of the potential to provide new foundations for
educational studies residing in work being done on the edges of
the disciplines, particularly in continental philosophy and

sociology, led him to nurture and to move along behind the scenes what became the Reconceptualist movement (Pinar et al., 1995).

Klohr organized special seminars that met in his office to enable small clusters of students to encounter some of the topics and ideas that were engaging him—the nature of lived experience, alternative states of being, cultural change, and the foundations of education, among them. Participation was by invitation ("private" yet unconditionally open to whomever asked), and the seminar was taught without thought of course load. As with the other students, the three of us read, wrote, and conversed. Outside of class we often met for lunch—Klohr's treat, often as not. And the conversation continued. The seminars and lunches provided the opportunity to engage in what Klohr called "middle range theorizing," which in his judgment was sorely lacking in education. Curriculum was to bridge the foundational studies and educational practice.

Following a day's walking and talking in the Hocking Hills area of southern Ohio a book, *Centering: In Pottery, Poetry, and the Person* by Mary Caroline Richards, was found on one of the authors' desks, then just outside of Klohr's office. In it was a card—Klohr's cards are always unusual, tasteful, pointed, interesting, carefully selected—expressing appreciation for the time spent together. Then it was hard to believe a senior professor could actually feel appreciative for spending a day with a student, but he genuinely did. In the book, Richards writes:

> When we say that education works toward freeing the person, we are saying more than we can implement. Here as elsewhere, we serve an ideal. The ideal works through the polarities of release and discipline. The energies continuously play, spending and husbanding themselves, expanding and contracting like a huge bellows playing upon a fire. We do not want libidinal exhaustion, nor do we want superego constipation. We don't want social confusion and cultural frivolity, nor do we want

> pedantic tidiness and pious propriety. We have
> to keep the energies alive and playing; this is
> part of our pedagogy. (Richards, 1964, p. 118)

Mentoring is two sided; students helped keep Klohr's energies
alive and playing, and he was grateful. In turn, he helped
channel our considerable libidinal energies and protected us
from superego constipation as best as he could.

Other books followed. Suggestions for reading, often
selections from books marked with paper clips, reflected
Klohr's sense of our unfolding as students; we were guided
gently, almost imperceptibly toward new possibilities for
gaining understanding and insight. It was impossible to read all
that we should have, but read we did. Recommendations not
only were designed to push our thinking in directions that we
seemed to be moving but also to help us become part of a
"community of memory." The importance of this community to
Klohr manifested itself in many ways. A sadness crossed his
face when on yet another trip to Hocking Hills, he mentioned
that he'd read in the *New York Times* that George Counts had
just died. The community of memory had lost one of its
statesmen; the full import of this loss to a young outsider would
only be understood later, from the inside of the community.

Klohr read our papers with care, balancing encouragement
with measured criticism. Before word processors, he reworked
sections of our dissertations until they made sense, until both he
and we were satisfied. He read what became our first
publications, and his remains a most respected opinion even
though generosity sometimes blunts his critical edge. His
classes were generally very large and, without the help of an
assistant, he read and gave feedback on so many papers and
served on large numbers of dissertation committees that this
undoubtably limited his own writing. But, he made the decision
knowingly; students came first. Only later did we realize how
rare was his commitment to those who studied with—not
under—him.

He took us to our first professional conferences. At the time
professors did not receive support from the college to attend
professional meetings. Klohr took each of us, at his expense,

introduced us to some of his colleagues, made jokes about the pretentiousness of some of the "young Turks," as he called them, aggressive junior professors overflowing with libidinal energy, on the move professionally, and a few of the senior "statesmen" who seemed to have become overly enamored with the view from the top. He advised us on our first conference presentations and then suffered through them as though hearing them for the first time. On one occasion, in Chicago, after a presentation he was irritated by the apparent arrogance of the questions directed to one of us by a junior professor who wanted to score points. Disturbed and puzzled by what he saw and heard—he knew the questioner and thought him a sensitive and thoughtful man—at the next break in the meeting he suggested visiting a nearby coffee shop. His intention was partly to console a somewhat shaken academic hopeful. What was offered was a lesson on the professoriate, about the importance of maintaining another's dignity and one's own humanity even when disagreeing openly, and an opportunity to think seriously about the future. Striving to get ahead, this eristic young professor deeply disturbed and offended Klohr's sense of professor propriety.

After graduation, we came to realize that just as we had chosen Klohr as mentor, he had chosen us, and in the process we had changed. Perhaps he changed as well. We came to realize that what we belonged to was more than a small circle of friends bound together by their involvement with a grey-haired, tweed-jacketed man from Mattoon, Illinois. We belonged to a fragile tradition, a community; inadvertently we had caught hold of portions of Klohr's professor dream. Like all traditions, this one had been reformed and recreated by each generation and then presented to the next. It was presented but not given. Traditions cannot be given; instead they are lived and in the living are offered. Just as Professor Klohr made his dream available to us, it was recreated and enlivened and then offered to him by his mentors, Harold Alberty and Hank Hullfish who encountered it in their mentor, Boyd H. Bode.

A Fragile Tradition

The tradition Klohr represented was fragile not because he was fragile, but because his conception of the professoriate had fallen out of institutional favor. He was a teacher, first and foremost. He did not entertain; he was no showman; instead he sought and quietly nurtured talent. Institutions show preference for some dreams and not for others; only later would we come to fully understand this.

In 1980 Klohr retired. We were initially perplexed by the decision. We knew he had grown increasingly unhappy with some aspects of his work, yet we sought ways to convince him to change his mind. He was, after all, only 62 years old and was playing a pivotal role reshaping curriculum studies in this country. Nevertheless, he was steadfast in his decision; he was tired of fighting bureaucracies. Entrepreneurs of ideas, we realized, had gained the upper hand throughout higher education. Scholarship had become a matter of counting publications, a manifestation of professorial careerism, while teaching often had become little more than an accepted nuisance that promised a few gratifying moments. As we noted earlier, the merchants had invaded the Temple. Other professors have slipped into cynicism by fighting a losing battle; he decided to retire. There was nothing more for us to say. Yet, after retiring, Klohr continued to take on advisees, especially foreign students representing a range of disciplines who needed a great deal of help, to engage in service of various kinds, including volunteering in an elementary school, and to serve the wider professional community in quiet ways. For us, he remains a trusted advisor and friend.

Teaching as Calling

The essays in this collection are about people for whom professing is or was a "calling," not merely a "career" and certainly not just a "job." Some teachers, as Mattingly (1975) describes, have felt called to teach. As a calling teaching is a moral enterprise, a form of testifying for the good, and a sacred trust. This is the tradition we were offered by our mentor. We have come to understand the decision to leave higher education as partially a result of a clash between competing conceptions of the professorship: those whose work is written about in this collection as a "calling" and the now-common and institutionalized view of professing as a "career." Sadly, as Bruce Wilshire observes, in virtually every professional arena, careerist ambitions are triumphing:

> Profession is an old word, but it took on new meaning when it was disconnected from the idea of a "calling" and came to express the new conception of a career. In the context of a calling, to enter a profession meant to take up a definite function in a community and to operate within the civic and civil order of that community. The profession as career was no longer oriented to any face-to-face community but to impersonal standards of excellence, operating in a context of a national occupations system. Rather than embedding one in a community, following a profession came to mean, quite literally, "to move up and away." The goal was no longer the fulfillment of a commonly understood form of life but the attainment of "success," and success depended for its very persuasive power on its indefiniteness, its open-endedness, the fact that whatever "success" one had obtained, one could always obtain more. (Wilshire, 1990, p. 199)

Distinctions between "job," and "career," and "calling" are fundamentally important to our point of view and to our conception of mentoring represented in the themes we have chosen to highlight in this collection. Regarding these distinctions, the work of Robert Bellah and his colleagues is especially helpful.

> In the sense of a "job," work is a way of making money and making a living. It supports a self

defined by economic success, security, and all
that money can buy. In the sense of a "career,"
work traces one's progress through life by
achievement and advancement in an occupa-
tion. It yields a self defined by a broader sort of
success, which takes in social standing and
prestige, and by a sense of expanding power and
competency that renders work itself a source of
self-esteem. In the strongest sense of a "calling," work constitutes a practical ideal of
activity and character that makes a person's
work morally inseparable from his or her life.
It subsumes the self into a community of
disciplined practice and sound judgment whose
activity has meaning and value in itself, not
just in the output or profit that results from it.
But the calling not only links a person to his or
her fellow workers. A calling links a person to
the larger community, a whole in which the
calling of each is a contribution to the good of
all. (Bellah, 1985, p. 66)

As a calling, to teach is to be morally centered, to engage in
practice that is, as Bellah and his colleagues assert,
inseparable from life. It is life. It is to be linked to others in a
community where standards of excellence are grounded in
relationships and are profoundly personal and practical and
where, further drawing on Wilshire, self-development does not
take one away from the community but deeper into it.

There are teachers of various kinds. Some are driven by
careerist ambitions and testify boldly of indefinite success.
Others see their work and the purpose of their lives differently, more broadly, as bound to community building and to
the pleasure of nurturing talent to find its own best expression
and place. We return now to the question we posed in the
Introduction to *Teachers and Mentors*: "What do we stand for; of
what do we testify?" Career? Job? Calling? Our authors
testified eloquently to us, just as do the lives of the educators
presented in this collection, of the value of getting deeper into

our communities. We add additional questions: What is the driving passion behind our ambitions? Where is our *axis mundi*? What kind of professional community are we passing along to our students? To be sure, all actions are social, and each and every one speaks of our conceptions of the good, our commitments, what we care for and about, and each reverberates outward in time and across generations. The mentors whose lives and work are described in these pages invite careful consideration or reconsideration of these questions. Each challenges us to embrace hope, and to, in Wilshire's words, "nurture our young and identify with them." In the process, we will be taking good care of ourselves as well. In an age of growing careerism, where the moral moorings of mentoring first expressed in Odysseus' charge to Mentor can so easily be forgotten, ours is a sacred obligation and an opportunity to preserve and extend a fuller and richer conception of professing, one linked to mentoring. Such was the vision given to us by our mentor, and such is the dream we seek to share. Much is at stake in how we answer these few questions and especially in how we live our answers, for ultimately professors have stewardship over the soul of higher education.

BIBLIOGRAPHY

Aikin, Wilford M. (1942). *The Story of the Eight-Year Study.* New York: Harper & Brothers.

Alberty, Harold & Thayer, V.T. (Ed.) (1931). *Supervision in the Secondary School.* Boston: D. C. Heath & Co.

Alberty, Harold & Bode, Boyd (Ed.) (1938). *Educational Freedom and Democracy.* New York: Appleton-Century.

Alberty, Harold et al. (1941). Progressive Education: Its Philosophy and Challenge. *Progressive Education, 18,* pp. 1-26.

Alberty, Harold (1947/1953). *Reorganizing the High-School Curriculum.* New York: Macmillan Co.

Alberty, Harold (1949). Bridging the Gap between General and Vocational Education in the High School. *The Educational Forum, 13,* pp. 211-217.

Alberty, Harold B. & Alberty, Elise J. (1962). *Reorganizing the High School Curriculum.* New York: Macmillan Co., revised.

Altick, Richard D. (1975). *The Art of Literary Research.* New York: W.W. Norton & Co., revised edition.

Anderson, Lorin & Sosniak, Lauren A. (Eds.) (1994). *Bloom's Taxonomy: A Forty-year Retrospective.* Chicago: University of Chicago Press.

Anderson, Martin (1992). *Impostors in the Temple.* New York: Simon & Schuster.

Anderson, R. T. & Ramey, P. (1990). Women in Higher Education: Development through Administrative Mentoring, in *Women in Higher Education: Changes and Challenges,* edited by L. B. Welch (pp. 183-190). New York: Praeger.

Antonelli, George A. (1972). Ralph W. Tyler: The Man and his Work. *Peabody Journal of Education, 50*, pp. 68-74.

Auspitz, Josiah L. (1991). Michael Oakeshott: 1901-1990. *The American Scholar, 60*(3), pp. 351-370.

Barzun, Jacques (1991). *Begin Here*. Chicago: University of Chicago Press.

Bellah, Robert N. et al. (1985). *Habits of the Heart: Individualism and Commitment in American Life*. Berkeley: University of California Press.

Berger, Bennett M. (1992). *Authors of Their Own Lives*. Berkeley: University of California Press.

Berman, Louise M. (1958). Should a Course in "Social Learnings in the Elementary School" Be Taught at the Undergraduate Level? Unpublished class paper. Teachers College, Columbia University, New York.

Berman, Louise M. (1967). *From Thinking to Behaving*. New York: Teachers College Press.

Berman, Louise M. with Miel, Alice (1977). Contributors to Curriculum: An Interview with Alice Miel. Videotape. College Park, MD: University of Maryland.

Berman, Louise M. (1989). Alice Miel: Leader in Democracy's Ways. *Childhood Education, 66*, pp. 98-102. Reprinted in ACEI Later Leaders Committee (1992). *Profiles in Childhood Education: 1931-1960*, pp. 104-112. Wheaton, MD: Association for Childhood Education International.

Bloom, Benjamin S. (1953). Thought-processes in Lectures and Discussions. *Journal of General Education, 7*(3), pp. 160-169.

Bloom, Benjamin S. (1954). The Thought Processes of Students in Discussion, in *Accent on Teaching: Experiments in General Education*, edited by S. J. French. New York: Harper Brothers.

Bloom, Benjamin S. (1964). *Stability and Change in Human Characteristics*. New York: John Wiley Co.

Bloom, Benjamin S. (1968). Learning for Mastery. *Evaluation Comment, 1* (2), entire.

Bloom, Benjamin S. (1972). Innocence in Education. *School Review, 80*(3), pp. 329-349.

Bloom, Benjamin S. (1976). *Human Characteristics and School Learning.* New York: McGraw-Hill.

Bloom, Benjamin S. (1981). *All Our Children Learning: A Primer for Parents, Teachers, and Other Educators.* New York: McGraw-Hill.

Bloom, Benjamin S. (1985). *Developing Talent in Young People.* New York: Ballantine Books.

Bloom, Benjamin S. (Ed.), Engelhart, Max D., Furst, Edward J., Hill, Walker H., & Krathwohl, David R. (1956). *Taxonomy of Educational Objectives, The Classification of Educational Goals, Handbook I: Cognitive Domain.* New York: David McKay Co.

Bloom, Benjamin S., Davis, A., & Hess, R. (1965). *Compensatory Education for Cultural Deprivation.* New York: Holt, Rinehart and Winston.

Bode, Boyd (1927). *Modern Educational Theories.* New York: Macmillan Co.

Bode, Boyd (1929). *Conflicting Psychologies of Learning.* Boston: D.C. Heath & Co.

Bode, Boyd (1937). *Democracy as a Way of Life.* New York: Macmillan Co.

Bode, Boyd (1938a). *Progressive Education at the Crossroads.* New York: Newson & Co.

Bode, Boyd (1938b). Dr. Childs and Education for Democracy. *Social Frontier, 5*(39), pp. 39-40.

Bode, Boyd (1940). *How We Learn.* Boston: D.C. Heath & Co.

Boyer, Ernest L. (1992). *Scholarship Reconsidered: Priorities of the Professoriate.* Princeton: The Carnegie Foundation for the Advancement of Teaching.

Brown, Spencer (1945). *They See for Themselves*. New York: Harper & Brothers.

Bruner, Jerome (1960). *The Process of Education*. New York: Vintage Books.

Bruner, Jerome (1971). *The Relevance of Education*. New York: W. W. Norton & Co.

Caldwell, B. J. & Carter, E. M. A. (Eds.) (1993). *The Return of the Mentor*. London: The Falmer Press.

Cantril, Hadley (1950). *The "Why" of Man's Experience*. New York: Macmillan Co.

Carruthers, J. (1993). The Principles and Practice of Mentoring, in *The Return of the Mentor*, edited by B. J. Caldwell & E. M. A. Carter (pp. 9-24). London: The Falmer Press.

Caswell, Hollis L. and associates (1950). *Curriculum Improvement in Public School Systems*. New York: Teachers College Press.

Caswell, Hollis L. (1971). Testimonial Dinner Program for Alice Miel. New York: Teachers College, Columbia University.

Caswell, Hollis L. & Campbell, Doak S. (1935). *Curriculum Development*. New York: American Book Co.

Caswell, Hollis L. & Foshay, Arthur W. (1942, 1950, 1957). *Education in the Elementary School*. 2nd ed., 3rd ed. New York: American Book Co.

Chamberlin, Dean et al. (1942). *Did They Succeed in College?* New York: Harper & Brothers.

Clift, Virgil (Ed.) (1962). *Negro Education in America*. New York: Harper & Brothers.

Clift, Virgil (Ed.) (1981). *Encyclopedia of Black America*. New York: McGraw-Hill Co.

Coles, Robert (1993). *The Call of Service*. Boston: Houghton Mifflin Company.

Conant, James B. (1970). *My Several Lives: Memoirs of a Social Inventor.* New York: Harper.

Converse, Philip E. (1994). Director's Report. In 1994 Annual Report, Center for Advanced Study in the Behavioral Sciences. Stanford, CA: The Center.

Corey, Stephen (1953). *Action Research to Improve School Practices.* New York: Teachers College, Columbia University.

Cottle, Thomas (1971). *Time's Children: Impressions of Youth.* Boston: Little, Brown.

Counts, George S. (1922). *The Selective Character of American Secondary Education.* Chicago: University of Chicago Press.

Counts, George S. (1928). *School and Society in Chicago.* New York: Harcourt, Brace & Co.

Counts, George S. (1932). *Dare the School Build a New Social Order?* New York: The John Day Co.

Counts, George S. (1934). *The Social Foundations of Education.* New York: Charles Scribner's Sons.

Counts, George S. (1952). *Education and American Civilization.* New York: Teachers College, Columbia University.

Counts, George S. (1962). *Education and the Foundations of Human Freedom.* Pittsburgh: University of Pittsburgh Press.

Cremin, Lawrence (1951). *The American Common School: An Historic Conception.* New York: Teachers College, Columbia University.

Daloz, Laurent A. (1986). *Effective Teaching and Mentoring.* San Francisco: Jossey-Bass Publishers.

Dewey, John (1902). *The Child and the Curriculum.* Chicago: The University of Chicago Press.

Dewey, John (1916). *Democracy and Education.* New York: Macmillan Co.

Dewey, John (1929). *The Sources of a Science of Education*. New York: Liveright.

Dewey, John (1934/1958). *Art as Experience*. New York: Capricorn.

Dewey, John (1956/1900). *The Child and the Curriculum and the School and Society*. Chicago: The University of Chicago Press (Phoenix Books).

Dewey, John & Bentley, A. F. (1949). *Knowing and the Known*. Boston: Beacon.

Drucker, Peter F. (1993). *Post-capitalist Society*. New York: HarperBusiness.

Eisner, Elliot W. (1968). Educational Objectives: Help or Hindrance? *Education Digest, 33*, pp. 23-26.

Eisner, Elliot W. & Vallance, Elizabeth (1974). *Conflicting Conceptions of Curriculum*. Berkeley, CA: McCutchan Publishing.

Eisner, Elliot W. (1979). *The Educational Imagination*. New York: Macmillan Co.

Eisner, Elliot W. (1982). *Cognition and Curriculum*. New York: Longman.

Eisner, Elliot W. (1991). *The Enlightened Eye*. New York: Macmillan Co.

Epstein, Joseph (1981). *Masters: Portraits of Great Teachers*. New York: Basic Books.

Epstein, Joseph (1985). *Plausible Prejudices: Essays on American Writing*. New York: W. W. Norton.

Etzioni, Amitai (1993). *The Spirit of Community: Rights, Responsibilities, and the Communitarian Agenda*. New York: Crown Publications.

Fisher, John (1971). Testimonial Dinner Program for Alice Miel. New York: Teachers College, Columbia University.

Foshay, Arthur W. (1970). Advanced, Graduate, Professional Education and the Centrality of the Act, in *The Professional as Educator*, edited by Arthur W. Foshay (pp. 113-128). New York: Teachers College Press.

Foshay, Arthur W. (1994). Action Research: An Early History in the United States, *Journal of Curriculum and Supervision, 9*(4), pp. 317-325.

Fraley, Ann E. (1981). *Schooling and Innovation: The Rhetoric and the Reality.* New York: Tyler-Gibson Publishers.

Freire, Paulo (1970). *Pedagogy of the Oppressed.* New York: Herder and Herder.

Getman, Julius (1992). *In the Company of Scholars: The Struggle for the Soul of Higher Education.* Glenview, IL: Scott, Foresman and Company.

Green, Thomas F. (1982). Evaluating Liberal Education: Doubts and Exploration. *Liberal Education, 68*(2), pp. 127-138.

Greene, Maxine (1965). *The Public School and the Private Vision.* New York: Random House.

Greene, Maxine (1973). *Teacher as Stranger.* New York: Wadsworth.

Greene, Maxine (1978). *Landscapes of Learning.* New York: Teachers College Press.

Greene, Maxine (1988). *The Dialectic of Freedom.* New York: Teachers College Press.

Greene, Maxine (1995). *Releasing the Imagination.* San Francisco: Jossey-Bass Publishers.

Hampden-Turner, Charles (1970). *Radical Man.* Cambridge, MA: Schenkman Pub.

Henry, Jules (1963). *Culture Against Man.* New York: Random House.

Herrnstein, Richard J. (1994). *The Bell Curve.* New York: Free Press.

Hiatt, Diana Buell (1994). No Limit to the Possibilities, An Interview with Ralph Tyler. *Phi Delta Kappan, 75*, pp. 786-789.

Hullfish, H. Gordon(1926). *Aspects of Thorndike's Psychology in Their Relation to Educational Theory and Practice.* Columbus: The Ohio State University Press.

Hullfish, H. Gordon (Ed.) (1953). *Educational Freedom in an Age of Anxiety.* New York: Harper and Bros.

Hullfish, H. Gordon, & Smith, Philip G. (1961). *Reflective Thinking: The Method of Education.* New York: Dodd, Mead and Co.

Hutchins, Robert M. (1970). Dedication of a Building. *University of Chicago Magazine, 40*, pp. 10-11.

Jackson, Philip W. (1968). *Life in Classrooms.* New York: Holt, Rinehart and Winston.

Jackson, Philip W. (1986). *The Practice of Teaching.* New York: Teachers College Press.

Jackson, Philip W. (1992). *Untaught Lessons.* New York: Teachers College Press.

Jackson, Philip W. (Ed.) (1992). *Handbook of Research on Curriculum.* New York: Macmillan Co.

Jeruchim, Joan & Shapiro, Pat (1992). *Women, Mentors, and Success.* New York: Fawcett Columbine.

John-Steiner, Vera (1985). *Notebooks of the Mind: Explorations of Thinking.* Albuquerque, NM: University of New Mexico Press.

Judd, Charles (1915). *Psychology of High-School Subjects.* Boston: Ginn & Co.

Judd, Charles (1916). *Measuring the Work of the Public Schools.* Cleveland: Survey Committee of the Cleveland Foundation.

Judd, Charles (1918). *Introduction to the Scientific Study of Education.* Boston: Ginn & Co.

Judd, Charles (1932). Charles H. Judd, in *A History of Psychology in Autobiography*, edited by C. Murchison (pp. 207-235). Worcester, MA: Clark University Press.

Judd, Charles (1934). *Education and Social Progress.* New York: Harcourt, Brace.

Judd, Charles (1936). *Education as Cultivation of the Higher Mental Processes.* New York: Macmillan Co.

Judd, Charles (1938). *Educational Psychology.* Boston: Houghton Mifflin Co.

Keister, Edwin Jr. (1978). Ralph Tyler: The Educator's Educator. *Change, 10*, pp. 28-35.

Kilpatrick, William H. (1925). *Foundations of Method.* New York: Macmillan Co.

Kilpatrick, William H. (1932). *Education and the Social Crisis.* New York: Liveright.

Kilpatrick, William H. (Ed.) (1933). *The Educational Frontier.* New York: The Century Co.

Kilpatrick, William H. (1936). *Remaking the Curriculum.* New York: Newson.

Kilpatrick, William H. (1941). *Selfhood and Civilization.* New York: Macmillan Co.

Kilpatrick, William H. & Van Til, William (Eds.) (1947) *Intercultural Attitudes in the Making.* New York: Harper & Brothers.

Klein, Julie T. (1990). *Interdisciplinarity: History, Theory, and Practice.* Detroit: Wayne State University Press.

Kram, Kathy E. (1985). *Mentoring at Work: Developmental Relationships in Organization Life.* Glenview, IL: Scott, Foresman and Company.

Krathwohl, David R. (1994). Reflections on the Taxonomy: Its Past, Present and Future, in *Bloom's Taxonomy: A 40-Year Retrospective*, edited by Lorin W. Anderson &

Lauren A. Sosniak (pp. 181-202). Chicago: University of Chicago Press.

Krathwohl, David R., Bloom, Benjamin S., & Masia, Bertram B. (1964). *Taxonomy of Educational Objectives, The Classification of Educational Goals, Handbook II: Affective Domain.* New York: David McKay Co.

Langer, Susanne (1957). *Problems of Art.* New York: Charles Scribner's Sons.

Levinson, Daniel et al. (1978). *The Seasons of a Man's Life.* New York: Knopf.

Lewis, Arthur & Miel, Alice (1972). *Supervision for Improved Instruction.* Belmont, CA: Wadsworth Publishing Company, Inc.

Lie, Suzanne S. & O'Leary, Virginia E. (1990). *Storming the Tower: Women in the Academic World.* New York: Nichols/G. P. Publishing.

Macdonald, Bradley J. (Ed.) (1996). *Theory as a Prayerful Act: The Collected Essays of James B. Macdonald.* New York: Peter Lang Publishers.

Macdonald, James B. (Ed.) (1973). *Reschooling Society.* Washington, D.C.: Association for Supervision and Curriculum Development.

Macdonald, James B. (1975). Biographical Statement, in *Curriculum Theorizing,* edited by William Pinar, pp. 3-4. Berkeley: McCutchan Publishing.

Macdonald, James B. & Zaret, Esther (Eds.) (1975). *Schools in Search of Meaning.* Washington, D.C.: Association for Supervision and Curriculum Development.

Macdonald, James B. (1981). Theory, Practice, and the Hermeneutic Circle. *Journal of Curriculum Theorizing,* 3(2), pp. 130-139.

Madaus, George F. & Stufflebeam, Daniel (Eds.) (1989). *Educational Evaluation: Classic Works of Ralph W. Tyler.* Norwell, MA: Kluwer.

Mager, Robert F. (1962). *Preparing Instructional Objectives.* Palo Alto, CA: Fearon Publishers.

Mattingly, Paul H. (1975). *The Classless Profession: American Schoolmen in the Nineteenth Century.* New York: New York University Press.

McCloskey, Donald (1992). Alexander Gerschenkron. *American Scholar, 61*(2), pp. 241-246.

Miel, Alice (1946). *Changing the Curriculum: A Social Process.* New York: D. Appleton-Century Company, Inc.

Miel, Alice (1979). *The Curriculum Field: A View.* Paper prepared for the 1979 Meeting of Professors of Curriculum, Detroit, MI. Typewritten.

Miel, Alice (1992). Roaming through a Life-space. *The Educational Forum, 56*(4), pp. 457-463.

Miel, Alice & Berman, Louise (Eds.) (1970). *In the Minds of Men: Educating the Young People of the World.* Washington, D.C.: Association for Supervision and Curriculum Development, NEA.

Molnar, Alex (1985). Tomorrow the Shadow on the Wall Will Be Another. *Journal of Curriculum Theorizing, 6*(3), pp. 35-42.

Morrison, Henry C. (1926). *The Practice of Teaching in the Secondary School.* Chicago: University of Chicago Press.

Murray, Margo with Owen, Marna A. (1991). *Beyond the Myths and Magic of Mentoring: How To Facilitate an Effective Mentoring Program.* San Francisco: Jossey-Bass Publishers.

Neff, Frederick C. (1954). Boyd Henry Bode: Philosophy of Democracy. *Educational Administration and Supervision, 40*(4), pp. 229-233.

O'Leary, Virginia E. & Mitchell, J. M. (1990). Women Connecting with Women: Networks and Mentors, in *Storming the Tower: Women in the Academic World,* edited by S. S.

Lie & V. E. O'Leary (pp. 58-73). New York: Nichols/G. P. Publishing.

Orwin, Clifford (1991). Civility. *American Scholar, 60*(4), pp. 553-564.

O'Shea, Joseph A. (1985). A Journey to the Midway: Ralph Winfred Tyler. *Educational Evaluation and Policy Analysis, 7*, pp. 447-459.

Patterson, D. (1991). The Eclipse of the Highest in Higher Education. *The Main Scholar: A Journal of Ideas and Public Affairs, 4*, pp. 7-20.

Phillips, Kevin (1994). *Arrogant Capital: Washington, Wall Street, and the Frustrations of American Politics.* Boston: Little, Brown & Co.

Pinar, William F., Reynolds, William, Slattery, Patrick, & Taubman, Peter (1995). *Understanding Curriculum.* New York: Peter Lang.

Progressive Education Association's Commission on Secondary School Curriculum. (1938). *Science in General Education.* New York: Appleton-Century Co.

Rainey, Homer P. (1937). *How Fare American Youth?* New York: Appleton-Century.

Reid, Anthony (1993). *Towards Creative Teaching: The Life and Career of Laura Zirbes.* Columbia: University of South Carolina, unpublished doctoral study.

Richards, Mary C. (1964). *Centering: In Pottery, Poetry, and the Person.* Middletown, CT: Wesleyan University Press.

Rieff, Philip (1966). *The Triumph of the Therapeutic.* New York: Harper & Row.

Rose, Phyllis (1984). *Parallel Lives.* New York: Vintage Books.

Rubin, Louis (1994). Ralph W. Tyler, A Remembrance. *Phi Delta Kappan, 75*, pp. 784-785, 789.

Rugg, Harold (1917). *Statistical Methods Applied to Education*. Boston: Houghton Mifflin.

Rugg, Harold (Ed.) (1927). *Curriculum Making: Past and Present*. Twenty-sixth Yearbook of the National Society for the Study of Education. Bloomington, IL: Public School Publishing Company.

Rugg, Harold (1931). *Culture and Education in America*. New York: Harcourt, Brace & Co.

Rugg, Harold (1933). *The Great Technology*. New York: John Day Co.

Rugg, Harold (1936). *American Life and the School Curriculum*. Boston: Ginn and Co.

Rugg, Harold et al. (1941). *Readings in the Foundations of Education, Vol I & II*. New York: Teachers College, Columbia University.

Rugg, Harold (1950). *The Teacher in the School and Society*. Yonkers-on-Hudson, NY: World Book Co.

Rugg, Harold (1952). *The Teacher of Teachers*. New York: Harper & Brother.

Rugg, Harold (1963). *Imagination*. New York: Harper and Row.

Rugg, Harold & Shumaker, Ann (1928). *The Child-Centered School*. Yonkers-on-Hudson, NY: World Book Co.

Rumjahn, Miriam C. (1984). A Chronicle of the Professional Activities of Ralph W. Tyler: An Oral History. Dissertation Abstracts International, 45, 1664A. (University Microfilms No. AAC 841859).

Ryan, Kevin (1977). Ralph Tyler: Education's Mr. Fix-it. *Phi Delta Kappan, 58*, pp. 540-543.

Ryle, Gilbert (1966). *Dilemmas*. London: Cambridge University Press.

Schubert, William H. (1975). *Imaginative Projection: A Method of Curriculum Invention.* Urbana-Champaign, IL: University of Illinois, unpublished doctoral study.

Schubert, William H. (1986). *Curriculum: Perspective, Paradigm, and Possibility.* New York: Macmillan Co.

Schubert, William H. & Ayers, William C. (Eds.) (1992). *Teacher Lore: Learning from our own Experience.* New York: Longman.

Schubert, William H. & Lopez-Schubert, Ann L. (1980). *Curriculum Books: The First Eighty Years.* Lanham, MD: University Press of America.

Schubert, William H. & Lopez-Schubert, Ann L. (1993). Teacher Lore as a Basis for In-service Education of Teachers. *Teaching and Teachers' Work, 1*(4), pp. 1-8.

Schubert, William H. & Lopez-Schubert, Ann L. (1994). Students' Curriculum Experiences, in *International Encyclopedia of Education*, edited by T. Husen & N. T. Postlethwaite (pp. 5813-5818). Oxford: Pergamon.

Seguel, Mary Louise (1966). *The Curriculum Field: Its Formative Years.* New York: Teachers College Press.

Shores, J. Harlan (1949). *A Critical Review of the Research on Elementary School Organization, 1890-1949.* Urbana, IL: College of Education Bureau of Research and Services, University of Illinois.

Smith, B. O., Stanley, William O., & Shores, J. Harlan (1950/1957). *Fundamentals of Curriculum Development.* Yonkers-on-the-Hudson: World Book.

Smith, Eugene R. & Tyler, Ralph W. (1942). *Appraising and Recording Student Progress.* New York: Harper & Brothers.

Stivers, Richard (1994). *The Culture of Cynicism: American Morality in Decline.* Oxford, UK: Blackwell.

Stratemeyer, Florence B. (1965). *Perspectives on Action in Teacher Education.* Washington, D.C.: AACTE.

Stratemeyer, Florence B., Forkner, Hamden L., & McKim, Margaret G. (1947). *Developing a Curriculum for Modern Living.* New York: Teachers College, Columbia University.

Stratemeyer, Florence B., Forkner, Hamden L., & McKim, Margaret G., & Passow, A. Harry (1957). *Developing a Curriculum for Modern Living* (2ⁿᵈ ed.) New York: Teachers College, Columbia University.

Stratemeyer, Florence B. & Lindsey, Margaret (1958). *Working with Student Teachers.* New York: Teachers College, Columbia University.

Taba, Hilda (1932). *The Dynamics of Education.* New York: Harcourt, Brace and Co.

Taba, Hilda et al. (1949). *Curriculum in Intergroup Relations: Secondary School.* Washington, D.C.: American Council on Education.

Taba, Hilda & Havighurst, Robert (1949). *Adolescent Character and Personality.* New York: J. Wiley.

Taba, Hilda et al. (1950). *Elementary Curriculum in Intergroup Relations.* Washington, D.C.: American Council on Education.

Taba, Hilda et al. (1951). *Diagnosing Human Relations Needs.* Washington, D.C.: American Council on Education.

Taba, Hilda (1962). *Curriculum Development: Theory and Practice.* New York: Harcourt, Brace and Co.

Taba, Hilda (1967). *A Teacher's Handbook for Elementary Social Studies.* Reading, MA: Addison-Wesley Pub.

Tanner, Daniel (1991). *Crusade for Democracy: Progressive Education at the Crossroads.* Albany: State University of New York Press.

Thompson, E. P. (1976). *William Morris: Romantic to Revolutionary.* New York: Pantheon Books.

Thorndike, Edward L. (1903). *Educational Psychology.* New York: Lemcke & Buechner.

Thorndike, Edward L. (1906). *Principles of Teaching.* New York: A. G. Seiler.

Thorndike, Edward L. (1921). *The New Methods in Arithmetic.* Chicago: Rand, McNally & Co.

Thorndike, Edward L. (1922). *The Psychology of Arithmetic.* New York: The Macmillan Co.

Thorndike, Edward L. (1927). *The Measurement of Intelligence.* New York: Teachers College, Columbia University.

Thorndike, Edward L. (1940). *Human Nature and the Social Order.* New York: The Macmillan Co.

Tyler, Ralph W. (1934). *Constructing Achievement Tests.* Columbus: Ohio State University.

Tyler, Ralph W. (1949). *Basic Principles of Curriculum and Instruction.* Chicago: University of Chicago Press.

Vandiver, Frank E. (1986). Biography as an Agent of Humanism, in *Biography as High Adventure,* edited by Stephen Oates (pp. 50-64). Amherst, MA: University of Massachusetts Press.

Van Til, William (1938). *The Danube Flows Through Fascism.* New York: Charles Scribner's Sons.

Van Til, William (1947). *Economic Roads for American Democracy.* New York: McGraw-Hill.

Van Til, William (1961). *Modern Education for the Junior High School.* Indianapolis: Bobbs-Merrill Co.

Van Til, William (1961). *The Making of a Modern Educator.* Indianapolis: Bobbs-Merrill Co.

Van Til, William (1971). *Curriculum: Quest for Relevance.* Boston: Houghton Mifflin.

Van Til, William (1971). *Education: A Beginning.* Boston: Houghton Mifflin.

Van Til, William (1981). *Writing for Professional Publication.* Boston: Allyn and Bacon.

Van Til, William (1983). *My Way of Looking at It.* Terre Haute, IN: Lake Lure Press.

Whitehead, Alfred N. (1967/1925). *Science and the Modern World.* New York: The Free Press.

Wilshire, Bruce (1990). *The Moral Collapse of the University: Professionalism, Purity, and Alienation.* Albany: State University of New York Press.

Wirth, Arthur (1963). H. Gordon Hullfish and a Vision of Teaching. *Educational Theory, 13*(3), pp. 207-211.

Zirbes, Laura (1959). *Spurs to Creative Teaching.* New York: G. P. Putnam's.

Zirbes, Laura (1960). *Focus on Values in Elementary Education.* New York: G. P. Putnam's.

Zirbes, Laura (1961). *Guidelines to Developmental Teaching.* Columbus: Ohio State University.

CONTRIBUTORS

Lorin W. Anderson is the Distinguished Carolina Professor of Education at the University of South Carolina.

William Ayers is an Associate Professor of Education in the Department of Curriculum and Instruction at the University of Illinois, Chicago.

Thomas E. Barone is Professor of Education in the College of Education at Arizona State University

John A. Beineke is Associate Director of the Kellogg National Fellowship Program of the W.K. Kellogg Foundation.

Kenneth D. Benne, who died in 1992, was an emeritus professor of education at Boston University.

Louise Berman is Professor Emeritus of Education in the Department of Education Policy, Planning, and Administration at the University of Maryland, College Park.

Elizabeth Hall Brady is Professor Emeritus in the Department of Educational Psychology and Counseling at California State University, Northridge.

Robert V. Bullough, Jr. is Professor of Educational Studies at the University of Utah.

Lawrence A. Cremin, who died in 1990, was a professor of education at Teachers College, Columbia University.

Arthur W. Foshay is Professor Emeritus of Education in the Department of Curriculum and Teaching, Teachers College, Columbia University.

Martin Haberman is Professor of Education in the Department of Curriculum and Instruction at the University of Wisconsin, Milwaukee.

David T. Hansen is an Assistant Professor of Education in the Department of Curriculum and Instruction at the University of Illinois, Chicago.

Paul R. Klohr is Professor Emeritus of Education at Ohio State University.

David R. Krathwohl is the Hannah Hammond Professor Emeritus of Education at Syracuse University.

Craig Kridel is Curator of the Museum of Education and Professor of Education at the University of South Carolina.

Victor B. Lawhead is Dean Emeritus of Undergraduate Programs and Professor of Higher Education at Ball State University.

Bradley J. Macdonald is an Assistant Professor of Political Science at Colorado State University.

William H. Schubert is Professor of Education in the Department of Curriculum and Instruction at the University of Illinois, Chicago.

Paul Shaker is Dean of the College of Education at Moorhead State University.

Francine Silverblank is Professor of Education at Dowling College, Oakdale, New York.

Robert M. W. Travers is Professor Emeritus of Education at Western Michigan University.

Ralph W. Tyler, who died in 1994, was president of System Development Foundation.

William Van Til is the L.D. Coffman Professor Emeritus of Education at Indiana State University.

Kenneth Winetrout is the M.C. Ells Professor Emeritus of Education at American International College.

Arthur Wirth is Professor Emeritus of Education at Washington University.

INDEX

Shulman, L., 47
Shumaker, A., 207
Silverblank, F., 233-234,
    245-250
Smith, B.O., 186
Smith, E.R., 32
Smith, P.G., 92
Social Frontier, 74, 90, 210,
    219
Social Reconstructionism,
    208, 210, 2121, 213
Sosniak, L.A., 42
Spokek, B., 192, 193
Stanley, W.O., 186
Stratemeyer, F.B., 147-
    150, 163-172, 202
student work
    responding to, 125, 170
Stufflebeam, D., 44
Stivers, R., 78
Taba, H., 36, 55-69
Tanner, D., 90
teaching
    as testimony, 3, 9-11
    approach to, 47, 85,
    128, 133, 142, 164, 174,
    186, 202, 227, 238, 265
Tead, O., 221
Thayer, V.T., 91, 154, 159
Thelen, H., 36
Thompson, E.P., 254
Thorndike, E.L., 20, 55-58,
    88-90, 95-100,
Travers, R., 55-56, 95-100
Tyler, R.W., 12, 15-44, 46,
    53
Vallance, E., 108
Vandiver, F.E., 3

Van Til, W., 91, 195-196,
    198, 217-232
Wagner, R., 81
Whitehead, A.N., 201
Wilshire, B., 8, 9, 264-265
Winetrout, K., 55-56, 71-79
Wirth, A., 12, 55, 56, 81-94
Wittgenstein, L., 133, 134
Wordsworth, W., 133, 134
Works, G., 27
Wundt, W., 15, 20
Zirbes, L., 72, 101-102, 104,
    139-145, 258

SOURCE BOOKS ON EDUCATION

SCHOOL PLAY
A Source Book
by James H. Block
and Nancy R. King

SEXUALITY EDUCATION
A Resource Book
by Carol Cassell
and Pamela M. Wilson

ADULT LITERACY
A Source Book and Guide
by Joyce French

INSTRUMENTATION
IN EDUCATION
An Anthology
by Lloyd Bishop
and Paula E. Lester

CATHOLIC SCHOOL EDUCATION
IN THE UNITED STATES
Development and Current Concerns
by Mary A. Grant
and Thomas C. Hunt

REFORMING TEACHER
EDUCATION
Issues and New Directions
edited by Joseph A. Braun, Jr.

MATERIALS AND STRATEGIES
FOR THE EDUCATION
OF TRAINABLE MENTALLY
RETARDED LEARNERS
by James P. White

CRITICAL ISSUES IN FOREIGN
LANGUAGE INSTRUCTION
edited by Ellen S. Silber

MULTICULTURALISM IN ACADEME
A Source Book
by Libby V. Morris
and Sammy Parker

TEACHING THINKING SKILLS
Theory and Practice
by Joyce N. French
and Carol Rhoder

TEACHING SOCIAL STUDIES
TO THE YOUNG CHILD
A Research and Resource Guide
by Blythe S. Farb Hinitz

TELECOMMUNICATIONS
A Handbook for Educators
by Reza Azarmsa

RELIGIOUS HIGHER EDUCATION
IN THE UNITED STATES
A Source Book
edited by Thomas C. Hunt
and James C. Carper

SECONDARY SCHOOLS
AND COOPERATIVE LEARNING
Theories, Models, and Strategies
edited by Jon E. Pederson
and Annette D. Digby

SCHOOL PRINCIPALS AND CHANGE
by Michael D. Richardson,
Paula M. Short,
and Robert L. Prickett

TEACHING SCIENCE TO
CHILDREN
Second Edition
by Mary D. Iatridis with a
contribution by Miriam Maracek

EDUCATIONAL TESTING
Issues and Applications
by Kathy E. Green

EARLY INTERVENTION
*Cross-Cultural Experiences
with a Mediational Approach*
by Pnina S. Klein

KITS, GAMES AND MANIPULATIVES
FOR THE ELEMENTARY SCHOOL
CLASSROOM
A Source Book
by Andrea Hoffman
and Ann Glannon

PROJECT HEAD START
*Models and Strategies for the
Twenty-First Century*
by Valora Washington
and Ura Jean Oyemade Bailey

EDUCATING YOUNG
ADOLESCENTS
Life in the Middle
edited by Michael J. Wavering

READING AND LEARNING
DISABILITIES
Research and Practice
by Joyce N. French,
Nancy J. Ellsworth,
and Marie Z. Amoruso

PLAY IN PRACTICE
*A Systems Approach to Making
Good Play Happen*
edited by Karen VanderVen,
Paul Niemiec,
and Roberta Schomburg

PARENTS AND SCHOOLS
A Source Book
by Angela Carrasquillo
and Clement B. G. London

BLACK CHILDREN AND
AMERICAN INSTITUTIONS
*An Ecological Review and
Resource Guide*
by Valora Washington
and Velma LaPoint

MULTICULTURAL EDUCATION
A Source Book
by Patricia G. Ramsey,
Edwina B. Vold,
and Leslie R. Williams

TEACHING ENGLISH
AS A SECOND LANGUAGE
A Resource Guide
by Angela L. Carrasquillo

TEACHERS AND MENTORS
*Profiles of Distinguished Twentieth-
Century Professors of Education*
edited by Craig Kridel,
Robert V. Bullough, Jr.,
and Paul Shaker

THE EDUCATION OF WOMEN
IN THE UNITED STATES
*A Guide to Theory, Teaching,
and Research*
by Averil Evans McClelland

THE FOREIGN LANGUAGE
CLASSROOM
Bridging Theory and Practice
edited by
Margaret A. Haggstrom,
Leslie Z. Morgan,
and Joseph A. Wieczorek

42.25